W9-BRY-465

Ports of Call

ROBERT CARSE

Ports of Call

EAST CHICAGO PUBLIC LIBRARY
EAST CHICAGO, INDIANA

NEW YORK   *Charles Scribner's Sons*

ML '67 | 8 9 0 6

156
0046

Copyright © 1967 ROBERT CARSE

THIS BOOK PUBLISHED SIMULTANEOUSLY IN
THE UNITED STATES OF AMERICA AND IN CANADA—
COPYRIGHT UNDER THE BERNE CONVENTION

ALL RIGHTS RESERVED. NO PART OF THIS BOOK
MAY BE REPRODUCED IN ANY FORM WITHOUT
THE PERMISSION OF CHARLES SCRIBNER'S SONS.

A-10.67 [U.J]

PRINTED IN THE UNITED STATES OF AMERICA
LIBRARY OF CONGRESS CATALOG CARD NUMBER 67–21336

973

This is for

Bob Keene

Acknowledgment

GRATITUDE is expressed here for the great assistance given me during the extensive research on this book by Mrs. Gardner L. Dickerson, librarian of the Shelter Island, New York, Free Library, and to John Lamont, Esq., president of the Shelter Island Library Association; also to the various Suffolk County libraries which so generously supplied me with many of the books I sought.

Mrs. Lilla M. Hawes, director of the Georgia Historical Society, Savannah, Georgia, who has previously aided me, is again to be thanked.

Joseph G. E. Hopkins, Esq., deserves praise for his patience and his knowledge of American history, both of which I drew upon quite heavily while at work on the book.

A special note of appreciation is given to Stanley Bard, Esq., and the other members of the Hotel Chelsea staff who in the seven years Mrs. Carse and I lived in that charming hostelry proved themselves true friends of the arts, and extended every support possible to this writer.

R. C.

Contents

Ports of Call

CHAPTER 1

⇆ *Castine*

SAMUEL DE CHAMPLAIN MADE CAREFUL NOTES in his journal even while the pinnace rolled heavily in the evil cross-chop of the great bay. He was the royal geographer, commissioned specially by Henry IV to explore this coast. Frenchmen had fished the Grand Banks off Nova Scotia for a hundred years, since 1504, and St. Malo merchants took a solid profit from the fur trade with the shore tribes. Now Champlain, wiry, tough, a veteran, was determined to enter into the region that was vaguely called Norumbega.

Fog caught him and his crew often when they were close to the rocks below the high, rough headlands, or among the many islands. Tides as severe as any they had known at home along the Breton coast swung the pinnace from her course, and once they holed her on a rock. Currents that the pair of Indians who served as guides were unable to explain added to the hazard of the pas- *3* sage. But his men were good sailors, and unafraid, and Champlain sent the bluff-bowed boat on up the Penobscot, against current and tide.

It was September, with the nights already chill, and the enormous forest that stretched endlessly from the river banks was touched by frost, magnificent in brilliant contrasts of color. He understood that Norumbega was probably an Indian name for a mythical place, and meant no more than the Breton fishermen's term of *La Maine* for all of the coast. Still, he kept going inland as far as the juncture of the little Kenduskeag River with the Penobscot before he decided that he should turn back.

He was at least fifty miles from the sea, and much more than that from his base at the French settlement of St. Croix on the northern coast. There was also a waterfall here that blocked navigation upstream. He inspected the waterfall from a canoe, then gave orders for the pinnace to be anchored. Despite the danger, he and his crew of twelve Frenchmen and the two friendly Indians would stay for a few days.

The Penobscot River, he wrote later in his journal, was beautiful. It was "some two hundred paces in width" past the waterfall. "I landed to see the country; and going hunting, found the part I visited most pleasant and agreeable. One would think the oaks there had been planted designedly. I saw few firs, but on one side of the river were some pines, while on the other were all oaks, together with underwood which extends far inland."

Champlain and the members of his party were resolute men. They had noticed several empty wigwams on the way upstream. The local tribe was along the river; the explorers might meet the warriors at any time.

But Champlain was quite willing to meet the Penobscot warriors. It would be greatly to his purpose and that of his supe-

Some of these Indians of a northeastern American tribe wear white men's hats and suspenders. But the birchbark canoe they are finishing is as graceful as any ever built by their ancestors.

rior, Sieur de Monts, to become friends with them. He studied the forest while he waited.

Timber like this could be readily floated downriver. It was badly needed for the repair and construction of French ships. Some of these pines were six feet in diameter at the butt and reached a height of 240 feet, straight to the sky. There were red oaks and burr oaks, and hemlocks, and balsam firs, and white spruces, and white oaks, and poplars, ironwoods, beeches, and many more that Champlain and his companions could not identify. 5

PORTS OF CALL

No forest as immense existed any longer in Europe. The French were almost undoubtedly the first white men to have stood here. Champlain, in his square-toed, heavy boots, his tight corduroy breeches, steel breastplate and tilted, plumed hat appeared clumsy, comical. The matchlock musket in his hand seemed to be an oversized toy.

A hush made of a myriad of very small sounds, the rustling of the leaves, the river sibilance, the fall of pine needles, the soft-plopping descent of cones, muted bird cries and the scurrying of squirrels, held the forest. Sunlight did not penetrate to the ground. The Frenchmen stood on a damp, soft mat of leaves, needles and brown, toppled ferns. Fungus growths were on the trunks of trees;

The southern tribes, lacking suitable bark, built dugout canoes which they fashioned from tree trunks. They burned the hulls into shape with hot stones or brands from a fire, scraped away the charred wood.

huge toadstools lifted ivory-yellow in the shadows. It had been this way for centuries, unchanged except by the seasons or the violence of storms, the blows of lightning.

When a hawk's cry, thrice-repeated, broke the hush, the Frenchmen were reminded that game was all around them. From their experience in Nova Scotia, they knew that here were black spruce-partridges, duck hawks, porcupine, raccoon and beaver, and the bigger animals, bear, caribou, deer and elk, and the gray, vicious wolf. Going back towards the river bank, the party saw a sharp-eared lynx in the underbrush, and several of the men were tempted to shoot. Champlain forbade that, and took the party aboard the pinnace to prepare for the arrival of the Penobscot warriors, certain that they would come here.

The Indians came in small groups, until on September sixteenth there were thirty of them. They landed from their canoes on the sandy spit of land where the Kenduskeag flowed into the Penobscot. These, Champlain's guides told him, were the Abenakis, which meant "dawn-landers" in their language. They stayed quietly on the shore, built a driftwood fire, fished below the waterfall. But they almost constantly watched the pinnace and her people, and Champlain remained aboard. The chiefs of the tribe were still missing, and this gave him an opportunity to examine the construction of the canoes drawn up on the beach.

The craft were dugouts fashioned from single logs. They were about eighteen feet overall, with an extreme beam of three feet. Bow and stern had an approximate six-inch rise, with little tumble-home, and the broadest beam at the gunwale. These the Abenakis used in the tide-yanked waters of the bay while they hunted seal, porpoise and whale.

But now, here on the river bank, the warriors began to shout, sing, clap and dance. Bashabeh, a very important chief, led upstream a flotilla of six canoes filled with warriors. Another chief named Cabahis followed him, and brought a party of twenty more. They landed and were saluted by their tribesmen, seated themselves cross-legged in a wide circle. It was time for Champlain to go ashore.

He took two of his own men and the pair of guides. His orders to the rest of the company were to haul short on the anchor cable and stand by with their weapons in their hands. There had been earlier acts of treachery among the Micmacs of Nova Scotia.

Champlain found here unflawed friendliness. Bashabeh warmly greeted him; the chief told him and his companions to be seated. The redstone pipe of peace was ceremoniously passed and smoked. A gift of venison and ducks and geese was given to Champlain. He stood erect then, and spoke to the warriors, his words slowly translated.

He thanked the tribe. He said that he was proud to be among them, and greeted as their friend. When he motioned, his men distributed the sackful of gifts brought ashore from the pinnace.

The warriors wore eagle feathers in their hair. Bashabeh, Cabahis and some of the senior warriors held splendid capes of black-squirrel pelts over their shoulders. Bear-claw necklaces were strung on copper wire. Copper bracelets gleamed on their powerful biceps. The totems of their clans, worked in brightly dyed porcupine quills, were on their buckskin shirts that were trimmed with thrums six inches long. Their belts and their moccasins were decorated in intricate designs, and Bashabeh's belt was of very

This scene of a Montagnais tribal encampment near Quebec on the St. Lawrence River was caught in 1788 with amazing accuracy. The boys in breechclouts, the warriors wearing feathers, and the squaws' long smocks are true to Indian life at the time. So are the handsome canoes, the birchbark wigwams, the half-wolf dog, and the iron cooking pot, bartered for beaver pelts. THE NATIONAL GALLERY OF CANADA, OTTAWA

precious, blue-black quohaug wampum. But all of them were made deliriously happy by the French gifts.

They fingered the hatchet blades, and exclaimed at the sharpness of the edges. The eagle feathers were pushed aside for   *9* cheap red-woolen caps. Champlain handed out rosaries, knives, small mirrors, shiny strings of beads and pewter buttons.

The warriors exulted. Their *shamans,* the medicine men, produced rattles and conch-shell horns. Dancing started. The warriors sang, clutching the gifts.

It went on during the rest of the day, and through the night. Champlain returned to the pinnace to sleep. He had done very well. He had secured for his king a source of almost incredible wealth.

One of those black-squirrel capes, when sold to the highest bidder of the furriers' guild in Paris, would bring a hundred times its barter price on the Penobscot. The pelts of the beaver, the fox, the marten and otter and the other small animals would also bring fine prices.

The supply was limitless. Champlain had been told by the warriors that Norumbega was not myth. It was a region that reached back to great rivers and lakes deep in the heart of a vast land of continuous forest. Norumbega offered France riches such as she had never owned.

Champlain sailed down the Penobscot on September eighteenth, took Cabahis with him in the pinnace partway to the sea. Then he cruised along the western shore of the bay, past the high, steep faces of the Camden Hills, and towards Muscongus. But he was short of provisions, and on September twenty-eighth he headed north for St. Croix and winter quarters with the rest of the Sieur de Monts company.

The report Champlain made of his voyage brought about the establishment of a French trading post at the mouth of the Penobscot. It was built in 1613–14 by a French officer named Claude de la Tour on a narrow, small peninsula that thrust out into the eastern side of the bay in the shape of a boot.

10

CASTINE

Vessels of fair size could enter the harbor in front of the log-wall "strong house" de la Tour put up with the help of the Abe-nakis. He possessed the ability to carry on the friendly relationship created by Champlain. He bartered with great skill, and bought cheap, sent many cargoes of prime pelts to France for sale at tremendous profit.

The French called the place Pentagoet, were very happy with its success. But then a hard-bitten Scottish adventurer, Sir David Kirke, one of a powerful family of merchants who made their home at Dieppe in Normandy, came up the bay aboard an armed vessel. This was in 1628, and he told de la Tour that the French were through, were to leave Pentagoet at once.

De la Tour refused to move. Sir David spoke to his gunners and his helmsman, gave the order to open fire. It was the first of a long series of bombardments of the peninsula, and quite effective. The gunners raked the post with their culverin broadsides as the ship was tacked and Sir David's musketeers kept the Frenchmen away from the loopholes and any effective return fire.

With surrender, the French were allowed to go unharmed and take along their personal possessions. Sir David Kirke's people occupied the place until 1629, and changed the name to Mac-habitticus. They rebuilt it and traded with the Indians for furs. But Sir David had other matters on his mind, among them monopoly control of the Nova Scotian cod fishery. The Plymouth Colony received the grant to it in 1630, and it passed into the hands of Puritans.

The Puritans, though, were only able to hold it for five years. A group of Plymouth settlers formed into a syndicate by the governor of the colony, William Bradford, and with Myles Standish as a member, hoped to get rid of a large amount of *11* debt through trade in furs. They called themselves "The Under-takers" and hired for their Penobscot agent a young man named Edward Ashley.

Ashley had come out from England in 1628 as the representative of Bristol merchants. He carried with him merchandise to be sold to the Indians, and decided to be thorough in his indoctrination into Abenaki ways. For sixteen months, Bradford later reported, Ashley lived among "ye Indeans as a savage, & wente naked amongst them, and used their manners (in wch time he got their language)." He was also accused of being a "very profane young man," and of "uncleannes with Indean women." But Bradford further referred to him as "a crafty pate," and was perfectly willing to hire him.

With his truck house in shape, Ashley began active trade with the Indians. Most of it was in contraband goods. His excuse was that French traders had already sold the eastern tribes arms, powder and shot. He imported more of the same items, and added rapier blades. He wrote to Plymouth, asking for further goods, and winter supplies, but he held back his payments to the Under-takers.

They caught up with him in the spring of 1631, and he was discovered in what Bradford described as "a trape," trading "powder & shote with ye Indeans." Ashley was deported, tried in England and released under bond. A man named Thomas Willet replaced him in charge of the Penobscot operation, conducted it completely in the interests of the Plymouth Colony.

Willet was absent from the post in June, 1632, when a party of Frenchmen came ashore off a small ship and made a visit. One of them could use a broad Scottish accent, and he carried on a conversation with the three or four servants at the truck house. 12 He learned that Willet had taken the soldiers of the garrison along as guard for the transportation of some goods. While the man, known afterwards as "the false Scott," kept the servants in talk, his shipmates sidled over to the gun rack.

The servants were then urged, a musket and a pistol pointed at them, to haul the contents of the shelves down to the ship. Beaver pelts worth £400 were taken, and coats, rugs, blankets, other items from the Pilgrim stock. When the transfer was finished, the servants were asked to tell Willet that "some of the Isle of Rey gentlemen have been here."

The mockery contained in the message was not hard to catch. Five years before, at the Isle of Rey, a French force had decisively defeated the Duke of Buckingham. It was clearly remembered by the servants, and they made sure that when Willet returned he was informed in detail about what had happened.

The French waited three years, then made a call which meant the end of Puritan trade on the Penobscot. The governor of Acadia, Isaac de Razillai, sent a well-armed force to take possession of the post. It was led by Sieur d'Aulnay de Charnisay, who spoke enough English to convince Willet that resistance would be very mistaken. D'Aulnay was polite throughout the seizure, even indulged in a show of humor with Willet. He dismissed the English garrison, according to Bradford's account, "with a great deale of complements, and many fine words," and let them have "their shalop and some victuals to bring them home."

There were several changes in ownership during the next few years. Then, in 1688, following the Treaty of Breda, all of the province of Acadia was ceded to the French, with the Penobscot post specifically named. The French officially took over Pentagoet on August 5, 1670, landing from the *Saint-Sebastien,* which had brought them from their naval base at Port Royal. The force was commanded by Hubert d'Andigné, Chevalier de Grandfontaine, *13*

Champlain's North America.

who was the governor of Acadia, and accompanied by his lieutenant, Pierre de Joibert de Marson.

The Pentagoet post was of extreme importance. Although Grandfontaine could only furnish it with a small garrison, he fully understood its strategic value. The unoccupied Penobscot region was between it and the English fort at Pemaquid, to the southward. It served as a key from the north, while from the south it was the key to Acadia.

14

CASTINE

Among the officers assigned to the post was an eighteen-year-old ensign who was to stay there a long time and leave behind him a great deal of romantic legend founded in fact. He was Baron Jean-Vincent d'Abbadie de St. Castin, born in 1652 on his family's large estate near Oléron, in the district of Béarn in the Lower Pyrenees. He enlisted in traditional Basque style at the age of thirteen in the Carignan Salières regiment. When he was fifteen, the regiment was sent to Canada, and he held the rank of ensign in the Chambly company.

St. Castin was assigned to duty at Pentagoet because Grandfontaine recognized his extraordinary ability, had special tasks for him. The young ensign put into commission and emplaced a battery of cannon for a fort on the St. John River. Then he was sent overland from Pentagoet to Quebec, to establish a communications route across-country. He went by way of the headwaters of the Penobscot, and to the Allagash, and the St. John River. The journey had a tremendous effect upon his life. It brought him to a bond of lasting affection for the Abenaki tribe.

Certain of their warriors made the journey with him. He learned to march in their fashion. He discarded the wooden-heeled boots, the glaring white-silk uniform, even the tricorne hat. It was much better without them along the trails that were often no more than eighteen inches wide, and in the birchbark canoes whose bottoms could be punctured by a misplaced movement of a foot. He wore instead moccasins and buckskin breeches. But he kept his sword, his pistols and his musket. He was not yet master of this wilderness, and he regarded it with intense caution.

He was back at Pentagoet and on regular garrison duty when a man named John Rhoades came ashore from a small coasting vessel. St. Castin did not suspect him, and Sieur de Chambly, the commandant of the post, was very hospitable to the stranger. There were, in the summer of 1674, very few visitors to Penobscot Bay. The French had also put the post in good defensive condition, did not fear anything except large-scale English attack.

The log-walled truck house D'Aulnay had used was replaced by a strongly built fort. It was set on the slope back from the beach and the jut of land that was known as Dyce Head. There were four sixteen-foot bastions, and inside them a guard-house, another house for quarters, a two-story magazine of stone construction with a well beneath it, and a small chapel put up by the Capuchins which contained an eighteen-pound bell.

The fort mounted ten iron guns. Two larger pieces, eight-pounders, were given elevation on a platform outside the fort and covered the zone of fire to seaward. A cattle shed was also outside the fort, and a garden guarded from the cattle by a split-rail fence. More than fifty fruit trees grew in carefully cultivated rows in the garden. The garrison was thirty men, and the rest of the inhabitants of Pentagoet a half-dozen civilian men who handled the Indian trade, an Abenaki squaw who lived with one of the civilians and a Capuchin monk.

John Rhoades stayed at the post for four days, and greatly relieved the monotony. It was another case of misrepresentation, like that of the false Scot. This visitor was an Englishman, a spy for Dutch pirates. He disguised his nationality, and hid his purpose, though. Then he went away aboard a coaster. He returned soon afterward, on August tenth, and piloted close alongshore a vessel called *Flying Horse*. She carried Flemish colors at the gaff, came from the West Indies. Her captain was a man named Jurriaen Aeronouts, who had Curacao as his home port and commanded a crew of 110 men.

The recent guest took *Flying Horse* skillfully enough through 16 the passages between the islands in the bay, held her off the beach at Pentagoet against the tide rip as her crew landed. The pirates reached the beach in pulling boats, then made a direct, frontal charge. They raced through the fruit trees and past the startled cows and sheep straight towards the main gate of the fort.

Sieur Chambly, St. Castin and the rest of the garrison kept them off for an hour. But the pirates were men with training as hunters in the mountains of Hispaniola, and excellent musket shots. Chambly was wounded in the shoulder, and St. Castin was hit. The garrison surrendered, and the gate of the fort swung wide.

The place was thoroughly pillaged. The pirates even dismounted the guns, hauled them down to the water's edge, put them aboard their boats and rowed the craft just about awash out to the ship. When everything of value was gone, the pirates carried Sieur Chambly to the beach; he was being taken to Boston for ransom, Captain Aeronouts said, and the ransom was a thousand beaver skins.

But a sergeant of the garrison detachment was told the price to be paid for Chambly. While the pirates had been busy with the last of their pillage, St. Castin managed to get away from the fort. He slid over the rear, landward wall, loped into the forest and joined his friends, the Abenakis.

It was only after *Flying Horse* had headed for sea, cleared Nautilus Island and stood close-hauled into the bay that St. Castin came back. His wound, bandaged by Abenaki squaws, did not trouble him too much. He was able to talk sensibly with the sergeant, and read the letter Chambly had left behind, which contained the details of the ransom demand.

St. Castin took the overland route to Quebec when his wound allowed him. Frontenac, as governor of Canada, arranged to pay the ransom. He sent St. Castin back to Pentagoet, and *17*

QUEBEC

A. Le Fort
B. les Recollets
C. La plate forme
D. Les Jesuittes
E. La Cathedralle
F. Le Seminaire
G. l'Hospel Dieu
H. L'évéché
I. La Redoute
K. Le magasin apoudre

for twenty-seven years afterwards the Basque was in command of the post. But, more and more, he spent his time in the forest. The Abenakis were his real friends, almost his brothers, and from among them he chose one as his mentor and confidant.

This was Madockawando, a famous chief, and a principal *shaman* of the tribe. Frontenac, when St. Castin was with Madock-

18

awando in Quebec, showed the Abenaki definite respect. Madock-awando said that the English were outright enemies of the coastal tribes. He believed that the "Bostonnais" should be attacked before it was too late and the Abenakis and the other people of the Penobscot region were killed by rum, disease and treachery.

When St. Castin questioned him and rejected the idea, the chief spoke again about what had happened to the tribes along the coast to the west who were under English rule. Treaty after treaty had been broken. The English wanted the sea, the land, the forest, and gave only one thing in return—death. Madocka-wando, a calm and reflective man, was ready for ruthless war.

It began in 1675 with the outbreak of King Philip's rebellion to the southward. St. Castin did not take an active part at first, but the harbor at Pentagoet was used as a base by some of the seagoing Abenakis. The warriors knew how to fight at sea, and understood amphibious attack.

They were fine sailors who hunted the whale out of sight of land, ranged the coast for seal and porpoise. Some of them had used a rough buckskin squaresail to move their dugouts on a following wind. They could handle muskets and light cannon, had learned that from the French, and they had an excellent leader. He was an Abenaki chief whose name, out of hatred, the English made Rogue Mugg.

Rogue Mugg took a force of braves in September, 1675, to Saco in a fleet of pulling boats of English design. They burned and killed before the settlers finally made them retreat. Then, in November, they raided New Dartmouth. A new shallop had just been launched by George Hiskett and Thomas Tucker. The Abenakis seized her at the wharf where her rigging was being finished. They took her to sea and used her for months as a raider.

PORTS OF CALL

Then, offshore, she met His Majesty's sloop-of-war *Mary,* which carried much heavier armament. But the Abenaki crew fought hard with muskets, pistols and cutlasses before those who survived were taken prisoner or dived overside and swam to freedom. Rogue Mugg managed to escape, and kept on as the Indian commander.

He increased his fleet of small craft, made a series of raids during the terrible year of 1676 when nearly all of the English settlements and the Indian wigwam villages were burned. His force landed at Jewel's Island in Casco Bay in September, killed the entire garrison and afterwards attacked the Sagadahoc colony.

Rogue Mugg held by the end of that year a thirty-ton ketch, a shallop that could carry eighty men, and another smaller shallop. He commanded, in addition, scores of whaleboats, wherries, canoes and skiffs. They were very useful in his night raids, and he included them in the plan he designed to attack Boston.

He would first seize the so-called fishing islands, Matinicus, Monhegan and the Isles of Shoals. They formed the English lifeline along the coast of Maine and supported most of the colonial population. The settlers were completely dependent on supplies from outside, could not exist without shipping.

Rogue Mugg had captured a local settler, a man named Francis Card, and while he kept him aboard frankly explained his future operations. With the key islands secured, he would soon starve the other settlements into surrender. Then the attack upon Massachusetts Bay would be made. Mugg could muster as many as a thousand braves. He planned to send them in at night to occupy the various islands, using small craft. His force reassembled, he would begin the assault upon Boston itself.

 It was Card's great good fortune to be released by Mugg.

CASTINE

The Abenaki chief, while he had deep hatred of Englishmen, retained a degree of mercy. Card wrote later about his conversation with Mugg. The Abenaki proposed to "take vessels and go to all the fishing islands and soe drive the country before him in the spring." Mugg's ultimate objective, of course, was to "burn Boston."

Rogue Mugg was never able to put the plan into effect. The odds against him were too severe. He lacked trained men who could steer offshore courses at night, handle sail and heavy guns. He lacked powder and shot also when his immediate supplies were exhausted, and only the French at Port Royal could supply him and renew the canvas and rigging and spars that were damaged in action. St. Castin could offer the Indians small arms and some powder, and that was all.

Still, Rogue Mugg kept his craft at sea and continued the attacks. No mercy was being shown by the English. The bounty for an Indian scalp, paid on Monhegan Island either in cash or trade goods, was five pounds. Captured braves whose lives were spared were sold into slavery on the West Indian sugar plantations. Mohawk braves were brought by the hundreds from the Genesee Valley and systematically destroyed the Abenaki villages along the Penobscot, murdered the women and children.

The survivor of an Abenaki sea attack reported in Salem on July 16, 1677, that thirteen ketches, owned locally, and their crews had been captured to the eastward. A petition was rapidly drawn by a group of leading citizens and offered to the General Court. It demanded that measures be taken at once against the raiders. Money was raised, and a strong ketch was outfitted, equipped with cannon and given a crew of forty men. Public proclamation insisted upon a day of fasting when Captain Manning took over command of the ketch. Prayers for his success were given at a lengthy church meeting attended by all of the town's citizens.

Captain Manning managed to find and take back some of the captured vessels. He returned to Salem with them and nineteen men from their crews a few weeks later, and the town rejoiced. The crew of Manning's ketch reported that they had heard in Maine that Rogue Mugg had been killed on May sixteenth during an assault upon Black Point.

The Indians still fought at sea, though, and remained a menace to colonial shipping all along the Maine coast. The peace was not signed until April 12, 1678, and after frightful cost. The New England colonies admitted a loss of 600 men, ten percent of their fighting force. No crops had been harvested for two years; thirteen settlements had been destroyed by fire.

But the tribes were forever shattered. Death in combat, or from wounds, hunger, exposure and a new white man's epidemic had taken 3,000 of their people. The villages were gone, burned by the marauding Mohawk bands; the fish weirs were wrecked and all of the craft except some canoes made useless. Catholic missionaries converted a number of the survivors, led them inland.

Baron de St. Castin stayed on at Pentagoet, and in the forest near the peninsula Madockawando rallied several Abenaki clans and set up a village. St. Castin was determined to keep the post; it had become his home. The crew of a Dutch man-of-war had raided it in his absence in 1676, seized everything of value. He restored that and built a long, rambling house, part of logs and part of stone.

He was a wealthy man, through inheritance from his family and what he made in trade here during the years of peace. He sent to France for fine, slender chairs and tables, and silverware, delicate porcelain. Tapestries were draped over the clay-chinked walls, and crystal chandeliers hung from the logs in the ceiling of the immense main room.

Then in 1682 a Salem fisherman named John Carter rode an armed shallop into the cove on the shoreward side of the peninsula. He landed on the last of the rising tide, came up from the beach with men who carried weapons. This place belonged to him, he told St. Castin, because he had been given the fishing rights offshore. He waved a pistol at St. Castin, and his men had already begun to sample the brandy.

St. Castin chose not to fight. He left, and went over the narrow neck of land to the forest and joined the Abenakis. The shallop did not keep her anchorage long in the cove. The tidal pull was rough there, and Carter wanted to get to the fishing grounds and exert his rights. But when St. Castin returned home, he found a desolate shambles. The belongings that had been imported after enormous trouble and expense were either stolen or wantonly smashed, destroyed.

It was quite logical that St. Castin should marry Madockawando's daughter. She took the French name of Mathilde, and the ceremony was performed in the fall of 1684 by a missionary priest. The marriage was held in a small mission chapel on an island in the Penobscot above Pentagoet. But St. Castin and Mathilde did not live at the post for any length of time.

St. Castin preferred to stay in the forest with his wife's people. His son, Anselm, and his daughter, Anastasia, were born there. St. Castin was certain that the English would return to the post. It was their unshakable ambition to take Pentagoet, the entire bay and the coast to the northward beyond Port Royal.

The royal governor of what had become the Dominion of New England, Sir Edmund Andros, carried out the threat in the   *23* spring of 1688 and anchored off the post in the frigate *Rose.* He sent a lieutenant ashore to bear his evacuation order to St. Castin. But St. Castin was in the forest; he lacked the garrison and the weapons to defend the place against the English.

Andros landed when he had the lieutenant's report. He went through the house and indicated exactly what he wanted removed. All that he left was a small altar, some pictures, a few ornaments. Then the complete stock of trade goods was put aboard the frigate. Andros left a message. St. Castin could have his property back if the Frenchman surrendered himself at the fort at Pemaquid and swore to be a loyal British subject.

That sacking of Pentagoet and the taunt which went with it fused the anger St. Castin felt into frightful rage. He organized and led the Abenaki raids on the English settlements. Pemaquid was captured in 1689, and the next year the attacks were carried as far south as the Piscataqua River, the southern boundary of Maine.

Warriors from broken clans appeared at Pentagoet to join the raiders. Wigwams were built on the beach. Canoes were pulled up gunwale to gunwale past high-water mark. There were 400 braves, among them Micmacs and Malecites from the north, and Abenakis who belonged to Kennebec clans. They rampaged along the frontier, burning, pillaging and taking scalps, and St. Castin went with them, red-daubed in war paint, his desire to kill almost insatiable.

But Madockawando was opposed to continuous slaughter, and St. Castin soon came to regret it. The war slowed, nearly stopped, and then picked up pace with a new border incident. The last action in which St. Castin took part was another raid on the Pemaquid fort. He had never entirely lost his hatred of Andros, and what Pemaquid meant as a symbol.

24   The large force of Indians took the place after two days of

Baron de St. Castin, a very early Maine man,
here is represented by a carver of ship figureheads.
The medieval armor and the sword did not belong to him.

fighting. The English commander, Pascho Chubb, surrendered after he had received a promise that there would be no Indian torture. St. Castin acted as interpreter and intercessor in the affair, and the garrison was saved from the stake.

The war came to an end in September, 1697, with the Treaty of Ryswick. Two commissioners from Massachusetts arrived October fourteenth at Pentagoet and dealt with six sachems of various tribes. But Madockawando was dead, and greatly mourned by the Indians. They acted stubbornly during the conference; the results were inconclusive. The tribes agreed to release their prisoners, while they refused to banish the Jesuit missionaries as the commissioners strongly requested.

St. Castin began to lose his interest in Pentagoet after Madockawando's death and the signing of the peace. He decided that he should go back to France, and in the fall of 1701 he left the post. His hope was that he would not have to stay overseas too long. He had requested a grant of land, and made a formal petition to the government at Quebec. He wrote that "it is proper to concede it to him, having a design to establish a fishery in Molue, and to remove the savages there."

His language, and the thought conveyed, were quite revelatory. He spoke of his wife's people as savages, perhaps unconsciously. Still, he was a Frenchman, writing to Frenchmen. It was through his red-skinned relations that he had learned of the startling diminution of wildlife in the interior. The tribes went further inland each year to supply the demands of the fur trade. So St. Castin saw his future, and that of Maine, in the fisheries, and was willing to relinquish Pentagoet.

But, when he arrived in France, he was arraigned on the charge of having illegally traded with the English. This appeared to him as somewhat ironic. He vigorously protested, made a pro-

26

longed effort to disentangle for his accusers the complex web of New World politics.

St. Castin never left France. He was unable to recover the great family fortune that was supposed to pay him £5,000 a year. There was considerable evidence that the lieutenant-general of Oléron had enjoyed the income for twenty years. St. Castin wrote Mathilde and his son, Anselm, warning Anselm of what had happened. Then the sturdy, leather-faced nobleman, who had left home at the age of fifteen, recognized that his life had reached full circle, and by 1708 he was dead.

Anselm remained in possession of Pentagoet. He needed a vast amount of patience, because it was a favorite objective for wandering and unscrupulous Englishmen. Several of them plundered the place in 1703, and the next year Colonel Benjamin Church, famous for having trapped and killed King Philip, landed at the head of an expedition and closely inspected the fort, the truck store and the entire settlement.

Anselm was fully aware that he held a difficult role. He was the chief sachem of the Abenaki tribe, and also a second lieutenant in the French Navy, with a commission from the king, pay and a splendid uniform. His usual clothing was buckskins, not the uniform, and he tried hard to keep the peace.

While out of a sense of loyalty he gave aid to the seagoing Indians who followed Rogue Mugg's theory of warfare, he was willing to help the English. He agreed to make a difficult overland journey from the coast to Quebec, carrying English dispatches to the French governor, Vaudreuil. He was accompanied by an English officer named Levingstone, and along the way an Abenaki warrior attempted to kill Levingstone with a hatchet. Anselm stopped the attempt, and the journey to Quebec was completed.

PORTS OF CALL

But Anselm was found in 1721 among a war party of Abenakis about to make a raid on Arrowsic Island. He was armed, smeared with war paint. The English settlers sent him to Boston, where he was kept in jail for seven months and examined by a committee. Then he was released, and got back to Maine in time to stop a large-scale Abenaki raid.

He went to Béarn the next year in an effort to obtain his father's property. French law defeated him, and he returned in 1728, and took up life again at Pentagoet. But the St. Castin family's tenure was almost finished there. Anselm, a middle-aged man, took his wife, his son and daughter to live in Acadia.

The fort, the trading post, the cattle sheds, the wigwams on the beach were abandoned. The Maine snows and gales wrecked them, tumbled them into ruin. Only the carefully planted rows of fruit trees remained when the English garrison took over the peninsula.

Those were in blossom on June 17, 1779, as units of His British Majesty's Seventy-fourth and Eighty-second Regiments came ashore from the transports. The 700 troops formed a task force under the command of Brigadier General Francis McLean, a veteran officer. He acted on orders from Sir Henry Clinton, who was the British commander in North America and wanted the depredations of American privateers stopped. Fast and well-armed ships with Continental Congress letters of marque, and some without, had been sailing from the bay ever since the start of the war and picked off British vessels on the approaches to Halifax.

General McLean's redcoats, first using the axe, then the spade, cleared the crest of the ridge in back of the site of the old French post. French rule over Canada had been finished since 1760, and all traces of the St. Castin dwellings and the log-wall fort, even of Abenaki wigwams for use in the fishing season, were gone. The British regulars built a square fort with bastions at each corner, a blockhouse, barracks and officers' quarters inside, and a wide, deep moat outside. It was called Fort George, in honor of George III, and artillery pieces were set in place, trenches dug on the slopes below against the probability of American assault.

The woods were full of Tories on their way from their former homes to asylum in Canada. They flocked into the fort by the dozens, and brought stories of an American task force forming in Boston to take back the place. The British had changed its name again, and it now bore the Abenaki appellation of Majabigwaduce, which was commonly shortened to Bagaduce. But, by any name, the New England patriots could not allow the British to hold it.

An expeditionary force was organized by the Massachusetts State Board of War, with additional men and ships from Connecticut and New Hampshire. It was composed of 1,000 troops, nineteen armed vessels and twenty-four transports. They arrived in Penobscot Bay intact, took the tide and on July twenty-fifth anchored within cannon range of the peninsula.

The commodore of the American fleet was a New Haven man, Dudley Saltonstall, with a record as an experienced sea fighter. He was overbearing and obstinate, listened to nobody, was barely polite with Brigadier General Solomon Lovell, who was in command of the land forces. Paul Revere, holding the rank of lieutenant colonel in the Massachusetts artillery, had charge of the expedition's ordnance, but was given no opportunity to use it.

The British discovered the American fleet during the afternoon of July twenty-fourth, and deployed their three vessels be-   *29* low the entrance to Bagaduce harbor. They were commanded by Captain Henry Mowatt of the Royal Navy, and he handled them very well. Still, several senior American officers who attempted to talk with Saltonstall aboard his flagship, the new frigate *Warren,* pointed out how the British force might be flanked and the peninsula seized. A landing operation delivered from the transports could put several hundred men ashore once the Royal Navy ships were driven from the entrance to the harbor.

Saltonstall replied, "You seem to be damned knowing about the matter! I am not going to risk my shipping in that hole!"

The result was weak, sporadic bombardment of the British vessels and the shore fortifications. Then, during the foggy afternoon of July twenty-eighth, a force of 200 Marines and 200 infantry were put ashore from boats and made a series of attacks on the British, entrenched, warned and ready. An American captain named Hinckley hauled himself up the side of a huge granite boulder, waved his sword and exhorted his men.

A British musket volley finished him. Then a young boy named Trask, a fifer, got behind the rock, and played a tune for the troops crouched uncertainly on the beach. They went up to the assault, and were beaten back by the shrewd fire of the British regulars. The action was over in twenty minutes. The British claimed afterward that a hundred Americans had been killed; General Lovell said that the Continentals lost no more than thirty-four.

But there was no further land action, and dissent and accusation and recrimination continued among the American officers in the fleet. Then, from seaward, on August thirteenth, topsails showed above the islands. It was a British fleet of seven vessels, sent from New York and under the command of Sir George Collier.

CASTINE

The Americans were trapped. There was only one way of escape, and that was up the Penobscot. It meant the scuttling and the burning of their vessels, and spelled shameful retreat. One by one, the American ships hauled anchor, spread sail and headed into the darkly winding Penobscot towards a beach where the destruction could be effectively made.

Leaderless and demoralized groups of soldiers, marines and seamen wandered through the woods for weeks, trying to find their way to the settlements. Most of the units had not seen active service before, came from various "trained bands" of raw militia. They wore a mixture of military and civilian clothing, sealskin or raccoon caps, uniform coats, buckskin breeches and leggings. There were only a few marines who started the march in full regalia, black, shiny shakos, green coats, white cross-belts and white breeches. The trained band officers showed their rank by an epaulette, or by a brass gorget worn on a neck chain.

They carried good weapons, though, and shot plenty of game along the way. Some of them had Kentucky long rifles made by Miles, with his name engraved on the lock plate. There was beside that the lettered inscription, *C.P.* This meant Continental Property, and was disregarded by the trained band members. If they got home again, it would be with the guns, as a part of the pay they would never see. The rest were armed with Falley muskets, or the long-barrelled Charlevilles of French manufacture.

The march to the settlements ended as a huge sort of hunting party. The seriously wounded had been left behind on the Penobscot to be captured and tended by the British. The walking wounded were helped along the trails by their comrades and given rudimentary first-aid treatment. Parties emerged from the forest at different times and places, as the strength or wish of its members demanded. The group with which Paul Revere marched

31

came forth at Augusta, and he took ship as soon as he could for Boston.

The British made a very great deal of the Bagaduce victory. They kept a garrison there until after news had reached it in 1781 of Cornwallis's surrender at Yorktown. That was brought to them by an American woman, Mrs. Joseph Colby, who lived on Deer Isle, twenty-five miles away from the fort. She was rowed to it at night by her two sons despite the severe fall weather. She had been given a handbill which described the battle, and she wanted to show it to some of the British officers.

Local people went to Bagaduce to trade and to get married, no matter what their politics were, and Mrs. Colby was known by the duty officer. When she got out of the boat at the town wharf, she clung tightly to the handbill. The officer, a polite man, asked her, "Well, madam, what news this morning?"

Mrs. Colby told him, "Not much, only there is a rumor that my Lord Cornwallis has surrendered."

She gave him the handbill after that, and when he had read it, he asked to borrow it for an hour. Then an orderly was sent for her, and she was questioned by the ranking officers of the garrison. They were quite blunt at the end of the interrogation; one of them said about the handbill, "We fear the news is too true."

The British left the peninsula when peace was signed, and the garrison went aboard a transport for Halifax. The town slowly grew, and spread towards the harbor below what was still called Fort George. Fishing and not furs, as St. Castin had foreseen, kept the place alive. But there was also a general carrying trade with other port towns around the bay, and a good business in the sale of fish and timber to the West Indies, with return cargoes in sugar, molasses, dyewoods and indigo.

32

Castine took its final name from the baron. It flourished despite raids and wars. Fine houses and churches were built. The Congregational Church was a graceful example. It had a Bulfinch steeple and Revere bell. The British occupied the town twice.

The Perkins family was able to build a spacious house as early as 1765, and in 1790 the Congregational meeting-house was built. It was graced with a Bulfinch belfry, arched windows, a pilastered façade and a Paul Revere bell. The bell tolled long on February 22, 1800, the day of national mourning for the death of General Washington. There were a good many men in the town who had served in the Continental forces, and they were fiercely proud of that.

33

But they showed little patriotic fervor in 1812 for what they called "Mr. Madison's War." A fort that bore the president's name was built to protect the town against British attack, and there were militia drills, and appeals for privateer crews. Although they were cautious how they spent their money, and heartily disliked being known as Tories, a number of the town's shipowners were extremely prosperous, and built beautiful homes.

These had massive doorways with exquisite leaded fanlights and sidelights. The broad central halls led to splendid staircases. Furniture, rugs and wallpaper came from England. The leading citizens lived in considerable luxury, and were, without use of the word, aristocrats.

The citizens had chosen to name the place Castine after St. Castin, and it was a shire town, where trials were held. But when the British put troops ashore on September 1, 1814, the defense was not very spirited. Royal Navy ships proceeded up the river and took Bangor, and both towns were held until the end of the war.

Most of the big, finely appointed houses in Castine were taken as billets for the British officers. They were bored by the lack of activity, which meant a limited chance for advancement, and the duration of the Maine winters brought some of their number to furious gambling and drinking, and, finally, amateur theatricals in a barn.

One young lieutenant, billeted in the newly built Whiting house, was past the point of these amusements. He stood for hours at a downstairs window, scratching at a pane with his diamond ring. Outside, the wind whipped and screeched, and snow lifted in great, blinding flurries, raked white-crested waves across the bay.

34   But His British Majesty's customs officials down at the town

wharves were busy. There were each day at Castine several vessels whose home ports were Portsmouth, Boston, Marblehead and Salem. They carried goods that because of the state of war were contraband, and they were bound for Canada. When they came back, headed into American waters, they would be smuggling British goods.

During the war, American shipmasters paid to the royal customs at Castine the very considerable sum of £13,000 in duties. The young British lieutenant, in the depths of his boredom, decorated the window at the Whiting house with a rather intricate design. It was prompted by homesick patriotism. It showed a British flag and, beneath that, upside down, an American flag. Below the American flag, he had scratched into the glass: "Yankee Doodle upset."

A kind of somnolent quiet pervaded Castine after the British troops withdrew at the end of the war. The embargo and then the occupation had ruined her shipping trade. The height of her activity as a port of call had been during the years of contraband traffic with Canada, and the profit from that had not gone to the local merchants or shipowners.

It seemed as though Castine already belonged to the past. She sent some locally built, pine-hulled ketches to the Banks after cod, and off-season the crews worked the waters of the bay for halibut, mackerel, salmon and shad. Some small two-mast schooners entered the coastwise trade, and "sailed off" in the winter on the prevailing northwesterlies for the Caribbean, came home in the spring when the wind hauled around southwest.

But Castine had been important from the beginning as a trade center and military post. Samuel de Champlain's vision of the future for this region had been dominated by the wealth to be made in furs. Even in the time of Baron de St. Castin that *35* had severely dwindled, and he was very aware of the fact. Now, with the fur trade almost completely finished in Canada, and confined to the Rocky Mountain country in the United States, the port lacked economic purpose.

The Abenakis were gone from the Penobscot, leaving the names of Madockawando and Rogue Mugg, but a hopeless people, lost. The forest where they had lived for centuries was being steadily stripped by the white men. That was the source of Maine's new wealth—timber.

Bangor, twenty-four miles up the Penobscot, and Camden, across the bay, and Rockland and Portland were the thriving ports. The lovely white houses sat gaunt and quite silent in the summer sun along the slope above Castine's harbor. The boys who fished for cunners off the town wharves or repaired lobster pots with the southerly breeze warm and fragrant from seaward upon them dreamed of other ports, not this one. They would come home here when they were finished with the sea, sure. But not before.

They went to Bangor, to ship out in the lumber schooners, or further on along the coast to join a whaler. Some of them went to work in the early Boston steamers, and the freighters that ran foreign. A good many never got back, although they always claimed to be Maine men, and were quick to say they came from Castine.

Coat-of-Arms of Baron de St. Castin

CHAPTER 2

Portsmouth

THE RIVER RAN SO FAST into the sea here that it was rarely blocked with ice, and promised year-round navigation. The Indian name for it was Piscataqua. That was kept by the settlers. They came ashore first in 1631, landed on the sandy beach of the broad, deep harbor. There was no trouble landing. The harbor was above the river mouth, safe from the open Atlantic surf.

David Thompson led the small, one-ship expedition. He was the agent for Captain John Mason, who held through the Council of New England a land grant. It was a loosely defined, enormous stretch of territory that King James I had given a group of court favorites who had organized themselves into the Laconia Company, or Merchant Adventurers Beyond the Seas.

Their purpose was to take an almost immediate profit from both the fur trade and the offshore fisheries. Mason, who had served for six years as governor of Newfoundland, knew about the money to be made from fishing. He believed that a post established at the mouth of the Piscataqua could attract a good part of the Canadian traffic in pelts by way of Lake Champlain and the upper reaches of the river. It would also give the fishermen a base to repair their vessels and spread out the catches to be salted and dried.

The settlers, strong and wiry people of English yeomen stock, brought the cargo ashore out of the ship at what came to be known as Odiorne's Point. The boatloads contained beaver spears, knives, hatchets, iron kettles and bolts of cheap woolen and cotton cloth that would be used as truck goods with the Indians. Then, for the fishermen, there were sailcloth, rope, pitch, tar, and fishlines, hooks and nets. For the settlers themselves were more iron kettles, and guns, and powder, lead in bars, blacksmith tools, and seeds, a very few books—most of those Bibles, the rest almanacs.

Canada was held by the English, and Samuel de Champlain was a prisoner in London. This was the time for expansion and colonization. So the Laconia Company had been formed with the easily gained consent of the king, whose sense of geography allowed the grant to extend north and south from the Merrimack River to the Kennebec, and from the Atlantic as far west as the Great Lakes.

Captain Mason's principal partner in the enterprise was Sir Ferdinando Gorges, a West of England gentleman from an old and distinguished family. Sir Ferdinando had been an officer in the Lowland wars, where he had fought with outstanding valor. When he returned to England, he was assigned command of Plymouth Fort as a recognition of royal esteem. He married in quick but very legal succession several wives, and spent all of their

38

money, and all of his own, on a variety of New World ventures. The Piscataqua settlement was another that sorely disappointed him and his partners.

The French took over Canada again, and within two years the idea for a colony financed and directed from England was finished. Thompson, the Laconia Company agent, packed his belongings, went aboard ship with the other colonists and moved to an island in Massachusetts Bay. They had girdled and burned down trees in the Indian style, built log huts with thatch roofs, done some barter for furs, fished a bit and made potash for fertilizer in the fields they started to clear.

They disliked leaving the pleasant site which they called Strawberry Banke because of the small, delectable kind that grew wild there. Below, the Atlantic rollers thrashed, flung spume high and swept gleaming in recoil. Off to the southeastward lay the low and rocky Isles of Shoals, and it was good fishing grounds around them. Inland, along the river, every creek was full of eels, and every mudflat thick-sown with clams at low tide. The salt marshes held ducks, geese, snipe and plover. Where the enormous forest trees marched the river banks, the Indians had burned away the underbrush so as to get at the deer. A man could tumble a fine seven-prong buck into the river with a shot from a matchlock, paddle alongside before the carcass sank.

But the history of most of the northern settlements had been that of dreadful famine during the winter months. The huts were dirt-floored, the chimneys made of sticks and clay. Animal bladders served as window covering, and the doors were fashioned from rough planks. Wolves roamed close at night, sniffed the hut doors, and left their tracks, bigger than any dog's, in the snow. Massachusetts Bay was better than this, even with all the Puritan ranting and the talk about witches.

PORTS OF CALL

Captain Mason was gathering support in England for another venture on the Piscataqua. He pointed out once more to potential backers the wealth found in the Grand Banks fisheries, and the huge profit the French took each year from the fur trade. Mason received both attention and backers. But meanwhile, close to the site of the former colony, a rugged pair of brothers had created what was soon to become a very bitterly disputed precedent.

They were English yeomen, Edward and William Hilton. They had the tremendous, deep-seated love of land that was so

Portsmouth in the years before the Revolution was one of the most prosperous ports of call on the coast. Many of the merchants built their mansions, like the Chase house, at Strawberry Banke, near the river.

strangely lacking among the French pioneers. It pleased them greatly to make a substantial gain in barter with the Pennacook and Pocumtuc warriors who came downriver in the spring with pelts, and they sold salt and whatever supplies the fishermen needed when a vessel put in from sea. Their major interest, though, was land. They were farmers at heart, and here to stay.

Without any deed of purchase from the Laconia Company or clearance of any sort, they settled at Dover Point. The Hiltons were the first of thousands of New Hampshire squatters.

The stretch of land on the south bank of the river came to be known as Portsmouth. It was made up of two communities, one at the original site of Strawberry Banke, and the other at Little Harbor. There was by 1632 a permanent and steadily growing settlement which owned a herd of twenty-four cows, twenty-one horses and colts, ninety-two sheep, twenty-seven goats and a considerable collection of other animals.

Two ministers arrived at Portsmouth in 1638, then with amazing daring went inland and founded Exeter and Hampton. But those were the only two villages to be built away from the coast for eighty years. Portsmouth and all the surrounding communities had begun to make their living from the sea. There were, as early as 1635, thirteen large shallops kept busy in the coastwise trade. With its location between Boston and the settlements on the Gulf of Maine, this was already an important port.

Men who disliked the undeviatingly narrow and often sadistically cruel laws imposed by the Puritans in Boston came north to Portsmouth. They brought their women and their children with them, were willing to work at almost any task. What they sought was freedom from persecution, and the awful forms of punishment practiced in nearly every English colony on the coast.

It was common practice to hang a man for theft. But, first, he was marched from his place of confinement, usually the set- *41* tlement fort, and whipped across the bare back with a lash that had fish hooks attached. This was continued until the gallows rope was set around his neck. Other, lesser transgressors were towed at the stern of a boat instead of being ducked. They were put in the stocks or the pillory, laid tight-stretched within heavy iron bolts, whipped at the whipping post.

The usual pay given the settler who handled the whip was threepence a victim. The magistrates made sure that he was thorough. The whip he ordinarily used was equipped with a cap of small hemp line, or whipcord. The awful tearing of the flesh which the condemned received from the hook-attached line was not inflicted. The victim was tied heels and neck, though, to the whipping post. This was known as "kissing the post," and was the source of jokes. The smallest punishment given in any of the colonies was degradation in rank.

Many of the newly arrived people had come out from England under indenture, were to all practical purposes slaves until they could buy their freedom from their masters. Sometimes as much as seven years was needed. A single act of violence could send a man back into indenture, his head shaven as a mark of it, his clothing and food the worst, his quarters the meanest, and often in a barn, a shed or lean-to. But in each settlement were former felons. These were a hard-bitten and desperate lot. They were joined by the forcibly recruited who had been ejected from debtors' prison and the London slums.

Fights with fists, clubs or knives were almost daily occurrences. Abusive language was passed between men of all ranks. Bailiffs were chased out of the town taverns when there was excessive drinking of "sack, strong waters and other drinks of like kynde of Canary and Malligo and Allicant Tent Bastard Muskadell." Other refreshments were hot buttered rum, beer, cider, aquavitae, "tamarindo" and arrack. The last had an Oriental origin, and was made from palm wine, but it could also have rice or molasses as a base.

Fornication was just as popular in the New England colonies as it was in Virginia, or in England. It was dealt with in New England, though, as an ecclesiastical offense. The guilty were forced to wear white sheets, and stand up in church and make confession in the presence of the congregation.

The people who emigrated to the Portsmouth region hoped to enter a better, less restricted life. They expressed their feeling in 1635 when an order was passed by the general court that a Negro brought from Guinea as a slave should be freed and sent home. Massachusetts assumed title, though, in 1641 to Portsmouth, Dover, Hampton and Exeter. The Puritans vigorously enforced their laws. The drinking of healths was prohibited in 1649 as "heathenish," and then the wearing of long hair by men was banned.

It was inevitable that when witches were found, Portsmouth should have visitations. A complaint was made in court in 1656 by Susannah Trimmings against Goodwife Walford. She testified that she was struck "as with a clap of fire on the back." Then, according to Mrs. Trimmings, the witch disappeared towards the waterside in the shape of a cat. Oliver Trimmings was next to testify in corroboration of his wife's statement. He reported that when she came home, she said that her lower parts were numb and without feeling. "I pinched her, and she felt not."

This encounter was on March thirtieth, and on April eleventh, another Portsmouth couple experienced similar difficulty. They saw a yellow cat in their garden. John Puddington got down his gun after his wife had been visited by Mrs. Evans, a neighbor, who was suspected of witchcraft. He tried to shoot the cat, but the weapon refused to fire. Mrs. Puddington then saw more cats—the yellow one "vanished away on the plain ground." She was unable to tell her husband or the court which way the other cats disappeared.

The witch scare subsided without serious incident, and the more thoughtful citizens of Portsmouth considered themselves lucky. Still, in 1662, the selectmen voted for a "cage" to be built to hold people who slept on the Sabbath, or who used tobacco on that day. The hope of individual freedom had become very small.

A man could make one of two choices. He could take his family and move forth into the wilderness and, if they survived the winters and the Indian raids, within a few years they would have a homestead. Or he could stay in the Portsmouth area, his family safe, and go out as a fisherman, and between seasons work in a shipyard, maybe sail on a few long voyages to the West Indies and England. If luck held for him, he might buy shares in a Grand Banks shallop, get to own her and end up respected, prosperous, with other men working for him.

A good part of the male population of Portsmouth chose to go to sea or take a living from it. It promised them much more than they could gain ashore. The colony, because of the confusion over proprietary rights, was the only one on the Atlantic seaboard where the ownership of land was in serious doubt. A homesteader could never be sure of the full possession of the acres he had cleared and tilled despite tremendous hazard.

So, as a consequence, there were comparatively few freemen in the region, and as late as 1679 only 207 eligible voters. But in 1664 a shipbuilder, Richard Jackson, could afford to put up in Portsmouth a fine home that was the envy of the Massachusetts Bay merchants. And across the river at Kittery Point, a young man named William Pepperell was making a real fortune.

PORTSMOUTH

Pepperell came to the coast first as an apprentice aboard an English fishing schooner. When he finished his time, he went ashore in Maine, moved south to Star Island in the Isles of Shoals. He caught and cured his own fish, and made a speciality of what was known as "dun fish" and brought in the European market three times the price paid for ordinary dried cod. Then he began to deal with John Bray, an English shipwright who during the 1660s had established a very successful boatyard at Kittery Point.

Pepperell sailed over often from Star Island with a load of fish ready for shipment, and in 1682 he moved to the mainland for good. He married Bray's daughter, Margery, took a share of the boatyard trade, but engaged in many ventures on his own. His keen business sense soon made him one of the wealthiest men in the colonies.

He understood very clearly the commercial possibilities offered by the Piscataqua where it entered the sea. The channel was straight, and free of shoals, with a depth of six fathoms or more, and a quarter of a mile wide. The long tidewater basin that lay upstream was well protected by the shoreline from the effects of the Atlantic gales. The first settlers called the basin Great Pond, but its circumference, all on deep water, reached for nearly a hundred miles. Portsmouth lay on the southerly side, and Kittery on the opposite bank of the river. Here, the enormous forest crowding close, was the place to build ships, load them, send them forth to sea and get rich.

Yards were constructed at a number of places around Great Pond, and on the Kittery side, and along the creeks that led into the river. Pipe Stave Landing, near the head of Great Pond, took its name from the kind of cargo that was loaded there. Most of the early cargoes, though, were cod brought in from the banks for transshipment to England, the West Indies and Europe. The majority of the vessels built were also designed for the fishing trade; there was considerably more money in fish than in furs.

The largest fishing vessels were 200-tonners, and the yards held space to handle them. Massive timbers were laid in rows eight to ten feet apart, parallel with the waterside, when a yard was started. They reached inshore the length of the proposed vessel, and each log was thirty to forty feet long, and firmly embedded in the soil. These were called the "bed logs," on which a ship rested while being built, and their tops were carefully smoothed by the yard carpenters.

The permanent yards were built with stone-filled log cribs at the water's edge. Their purpose was to shield the slips that led inward from the water and held the launching ways. Great care was taken to make sure that the ways sloped down to the shore at the correct angle to send the new ship out into the deepest water. Sawmills that used power from the Piscataqua or one of the creeks served most of the local yards. A good deal of saw work was also done by hand, and for that purpose a pit was dug, and sawyers took turns standing in it, faces and eyes protected from the yellowish drift of dust by cloths hung from their hat brims.

A big lean-to structure at the head of the yard gave shelter to the workers during bad weather. The loft above it was the drafting room. Small shops were used by the men who made ships' wheels, figureheads and sternboards. There were in addition a joiner's shop, a blacksmith shop, an oakum shed and an office for the owner or his manager. Sails, cordage, pitch, tar and varnish were at first imported, mainly from the Baltic. Then sailmakers opened lofts in Portsmouth, and ropewalks were built, and men who specialized as block-makers took orders from various yards.

The yard workmen, almost from the beginning, as soon as 46 experienced shipwrights arrived from England, were highly skilled.

PORTSMOUTH

A carpenter needed only a few more tools than the broadaxe, the saw, adze and pod auger. The shipsmith, with his apprentices, who were called "strikers," worked his own iron and forged on his anvil each spike, bolt, mast cap and chain link for a ship. Painters mixed their own varnish and shellac from the gum, mixed and blended the paints they used. Riggers, while forced to handle clumsy and heavy purchases, securely set up standing and running rigging, and caulkers became famous for their deft touch with a hammer.

Men worked long hours, from sunup to sundown. They turned to during the summer months at five o'clock, and did not knock off until seven in the evening. The average wage was around a dollar a day, in present currency, but it of course held much more buying power at that time. Many of the workers preferred to take their wages in the form of barter, or buy a share in a vessel that they had helped build.

Rum, always a great aid to New England shipbuilding, was another form of collateral payment. It was estimated that yard workers consumed a gallon of rum for every ship's ton built. The resounding call, "Grog-oh!" shouted by the foreman often stopped the rapping of hammers, the whine of saws and the screech of blocks, particularly on a February day with a northeaster that brought snow.

The forest right at hand supplied all of the timber needed. It had been found early that white oak was the best for oars. Buttonwood was used for windlasses, and blocks. Elm was fashioned into keels, and hornbeam and ironwood into handspikes. Hackmatack served for knees, locust for treenails—which were commonly pronounced "trunnels." Maple was worked by the joiners for cabin finish. The toughest wood of the lot, white oak, went into the stem and stern pieces, and the frames.

47

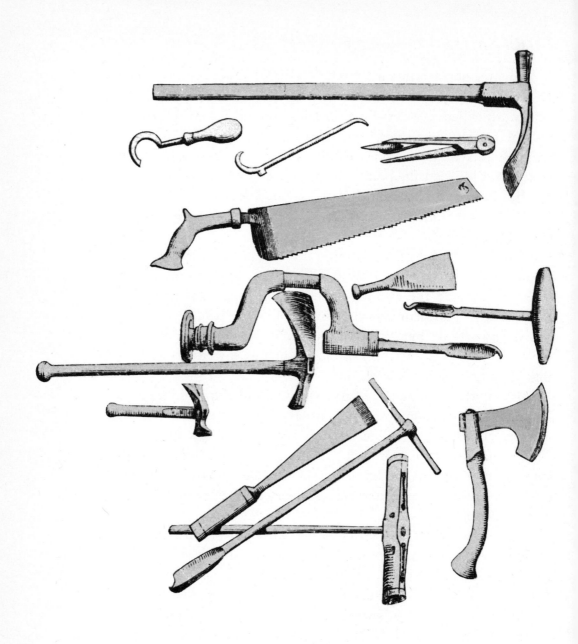

These are some of the tools used in the early Portsmouth shipyards. Most of them are in use today wherever wooden craft are built.

PORTSMOUTH

Spruce was for spars, and joists, and some of the knees. Flooring and planking came from yellow and white pine. The masts and the heavier spars were chosen from the white pines, the mightiest trees in the entire forest expanse along the Atlantic coast. Samuel de Champlain had admired them when he stood beside the Penobscot and waited for the arrival of the Abenaki warriors.

Many of the early craft built in the Piscataqua yards were of the 200-ton class, carried fifty men in their crews. They were fore-and-aft-rigged, and called "fore-and-afters"; the term "schooner" was not yet in popular use. Then, in the latter half of the seventeenth century, when the shore fisheries were fully established, smaller boats were sent to sea. These were shallops, and carried four men. The master handled the steering; and there was a midshipman, and a foremastman, and a shoreman. The shoreman served as cook and tended to the fish onshore. He washed, salted and turned them on the flakes—the log platforms set up along the beaches for the purpose.

It was common practice in the big boats for each man to pay twenty shillings towards the provisions for a voyage. The vessel, in the ancient fashion, was worked on shares. Those were divided into thirds, with one-third going to the vessel, another for the men's rations, the salt, lines, hooks and gear needed for the taking and curing of fish. The average outfitting cost was around £800, and the remaining third of what was made on a voyage was divided among the members of the crew. It came out at about £26 a man, and an average of three voyages a year were made. Pretty much the same payoff system was kept in the smaller craft, although aboard those a man had more chance of increasing his shares, and of eventual purchase.

The typical shallop was twenty-three feet along her keel.   *49*

She was built with a long and low cuddy, which contained a fireplace and bunks. The fireplaces often smoked and in rough weather were a hazard to the vessels, and were not used. The bunks were called "cabins," but were really narrow plank troughs, filled with hay or spruce boughs. The cuddy overhead was so low that not even the small-statured men of that time could stand upright when below. Hand-lining for cod in the winter months, the cockpit and the cuddy awash, and with no hot food, was a rough trade.

Still, the two-masted craft were cherished in the Piscataqua region, and all along the northern coast. The shallop foresail was loose-footed, and the long main boom tarred against the weather. Yellow was a favorite hull color, and some boats also had a "color" strake as trim. Masts were painted yellow, and the mast tops black.

The pinnace was another popular type in the Piscataqua region. Some of these, although open-decked, were as much as forty-five feet long. They were fitted with lateen-rig sails, and the bigger boats carried three masts. But they were essentially pulling boats, meant to be moved by oarsmen. It was in this way, with great success, that Francis Drake had used them in his raids against the Spanish on the Isthmus of Panama.

Among the pulling-boat class, the wherry was well liked for river and lake use. These were given square bows and sterns, and a very shallow draft, seldom were more than eighteen feet overall. The Piscataqua boatyards found quite a demand for them; the colonists had never been entirely happy with the Indian dugout "cannow," often suffered a ducking when in the cranky craft.

The lean-hulled and marvelously seaworthy whaleboat had come into colonial service early on the Greenland coast. Then fishermen from Nova Scotia introduced the type on the Grand Banks, and several were brought to the mainland. Builders took them for their models and somewhat sharpened the lines, but the Piscataqua designers kept the overall length at twenty-four feet. They were keenly aware of the superb qualities of the original boat.

Special crews of eight and ten men were organized in Portsmouth to handle the whaleboats put in the coastwise service. This was for mail, and express cargo; it was vital to the people in the widely separated little settlements in Maine. The men recruited as crew members were an exceptionally hardy lot. They were as much Indian fighters as sailors. Most of them went to sea wearing buckskin, and armed with their own muskets, cutlasses, pistols and tomahawks.

The cargo they carried often included tools badly needed by some settler who had lost everything in a recent Indian raid, and who had the courage to start all over again. There were spectacles, repaired in Boston, or bought new on order, an occasional ear trumpet, a musket lock, pewter dishes, a copper kettle, a Bible or two, an almanac to replace one whose pages had become tattered past use.

Sometimes there was a little tea, and a case of spices, a very carefully wrapped piece of lace for a settler's wife who still possessed the energy to treasure her looks. Rum was in every cargo. It was an essential part of life for the people who endured seven months of winter, and on any dawn might hear the war whoop as the cabin door was smashed from the hinges.

The men of a whaleboat crew took regular turns at the sixteen-foot oars. Jib and mainsail were set whenever there was favorable wind. If it was necessary, a crew camped onshore, and stationed a guard after darkness. But as much as possible the men tried to move from one settlement to another during daylight. People along the way used many stratagems to delay them. *51*

PORTS OF CALL

For the gaunt, tight-eyed settlers, the whaleboat men represented civilization, and a world that was so distant as to resemble dream. But the crew spoke of the cargo that was needed further on up the coast. They shook hands again, patted the children and the dogs, went aboard. Goodbye cries followed them until they were out of sight around the next point of land.

Samuel Vetch took the same courses into the Gulf of Maine when he settled in Boston and soon after 1700 started a single-handed trading business. Vetch was tough, a Highland officer who was one of the very few survivors of what had been known as the Darien Expedition. That had been the effort of the wealthiest merchants in Scotland to establish a settlement on the Isthmus of Panama. Fever and repeated Indian and Spanish attacks brought tragic defeat. But the Scots were allowed to march out to the ships with their flags, and with the bagpipers playing. Vetch, penniless, managed to get to New York, and married the daughter of Robert Livingston, a fellow Scot and a very rich man.

But Vetch wanted to work alone. He took a small shallop out of Boston after he and his wife were established there. He loaded the craft with truck goods for trade with the Indians, then put into Portsmouth on his way east.

He held long talks with the veteran whaleboat crews, jotted down pilotage directions they gave him, made charts that would be of great assistance later in the Maine tidal rips and currents. He gathered, too, the most recent information on the movements of the French-directed bands of Iroquois that roamed the coast and sporadically raided the English settlements.

They aroused no particular fear in Vetch after his service in the malaria jungles of Darien. Still, he was careful as he made good his courses, returned west with packs of prime beaver pelts that filled the shallop's hold to the hatch coaming. He had traded successfully with the Abenakis and all of the coastal tribes to the eastward. He had navigated the Saco, and the Androscoggin, the Kennebec and the Penobscot, and then sailed past Mount Desert Island to the St. Croix.

He came to profoundly dislike the French. They were in his mind miserable traders and equally bad colonizers. Shipload after shipload of young French girls, their average age thirteen, had been transported to Canada as wives for the men already there. The men married them, under the threat of losing the right to hunt and carry on trade with the Indians. But French trade goods cost twice as much as English, and the tribes had stripped the forests as far west as the Great Lakes of the bigger, most valuable fur-bearing animals.

The French attempt to hold Canada, as Vetch saw it, was certain to fail. They tried to check the English advance by sending their privateers against the fishing fleet and the vessels homeward-

bound into New England ports from the West Indies, England and Europe. Ashore, they sent their terrible Algonquin allies to attack the settlements, burn, pillage, scalp, even slit the throats of cattle and chop down fruit trees.

Vetch had a plan to take care of that. He went back to Portsmouth, then to Boston, and explained it. Port Royal, in Acadia, he said, was the key to control of the coast. The French privateers outfitted there, and the nation that held the place could move up the St. Lawrence and take Quebec, then Montreal, seize possession of all of New France.

The merchants, the shipowners and traders agreed. Portsmouth had carried on a flourishing trade in ships' masts since 1665, and her shipyards built a number of vessels for sale in the home country. The Piscataqua ports by 1671 exported 500 tons of fish and several thousand pelts, and imported 2,000 tons of salt, along with 300 casks of wine and brandy. Richard Cutts, the wealthiest man in the Portsmouth region, when he died in 1680 left his dwelling house, bakehouse, brewhouse, barn, log warehouse, and garden, orchard and wharves to his wife, and other property to his daughter. Over across the river, at Pepperell Cove, the family enterprise was so large that it was known as "the William Pepperells business."

The splendid mansion built by the former fisherman stood in its own broad lawn, with gardens and a deer park beyond that. Then there were the stores, the warehouses, the shipyard. The fishing trade was the most lucrative part of the firm's business; over one hundred vessels were kept on the banks. Other Pepperell vessels ran to the West Indies with dried cod, timber and hogsheads, and on around the famous commercial route to England, Spain and Portugal for dry goods, salt, iron, cordage, wines and

54 fruit.

PORTSMOUTH

William Pepperell's six daughters shared his trading ability. They carried on ventures of their own, in furs and fish which were exchanged overseas for the dresses, laces, combs and shawls which were the latest rage in London. But, conspicuous among the buildings at Pepperell Cove was the high, thick-walled blockhouse. Men were always on duty there, armed and ready to give the alert in case of a French-Indian attack.

The French had inspired a raid on Oyster River in 1684 that took the lives of almost a hundred people. During the Dover raid in 1689, its leading citizen and a famous Indian fighter, Major Richard Walton, was scalped and met a terrible death. The entire coast, including Massachusetts Bay, was vulnerable. There was a single answer: The French hold on Canada must be broken, and it should be struck first at Port Royal.

The blockhouse shown here is almost a fort. Cannon and a big brick chimney were rare. Frontier folks ordinarily fought alone. Their senior men were the officers. The women reloaded muskets, tended the wounded. When necessary, they fired the muskets, too.

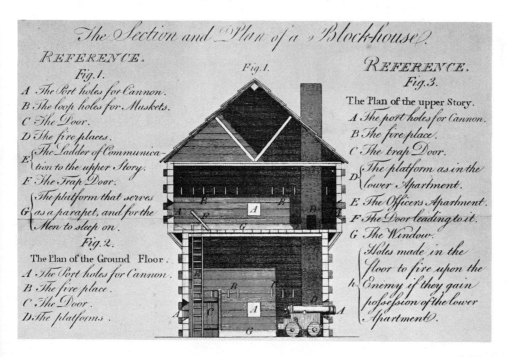

The Section and Plan of a Blockhouse

REFERENCE.
Fig. 1.
A · The Port holes for Cannon.
B · The loop holes for Muskets.
C · The Door.
D · The fire places.
E · The Ladder of Communication to the upper Story.
F · The Trap Door.
G · The platform that serves as a parapet, and for the Men to sleep on.
Fig. 2.
The Plan of the Ground Floor.
A · The Port holes for Cannon.
B · The fire place.
C · The Door.
D · The platforms.

Fig. 1.

REFERENCE.
Fig. 3.
The Plan of the upper Story.
A · The port holes for Cannon.
B · The fire place.
C · The trap Door.
D · The platform as in the lower Apartment.
E · The Officers Apartment.
F · The Door leading to it.
G · The Window.
h · Holes made in the floor to fire upon the Enemy if they gain possession of the lower Apartment.

PORTS OF CALL

The New England authorities sent Vetch to London in 1708 to represent them. Queen Anne granted him an audience at court, and gave great attention to what he had to tell her. She was very aware that since 1635, because of the prodigal waste of the royal forests, England had been unable to supply masts for ships of any size. A considerable amount of the timber used at present came from the Baltic, and went into what the shipwrights called "made" masts.

Samuel Pepys, the secretary to the Admiralty, had entered in his diary on December 3, 1666, an event which had not been forgotten. He wrote: "There is also the very good newes comes of four New England ships come home safe to Falmouth with masts for the King; which is a blessing mighty unexpected, and without which, if for nothing else, we must have failed the next year. But God be praised for thus much good fortune, and send up the continuance of his favor in other things! So to bed.—"

Portsmouth was the port from which those ships had sailed, carrying the king's masts. It lay at the southerly corner of the vast white-pine belt that stretched north to Nova Scotia and reached back into the country west of the Connecticut and Hudson Rivers. Enough unflawed timber was contained there, the royal surveyors estimated, to supply the needs of the Navy for more than a hundred years.

Portsmouth was unlike any other port in the North American colonies. Without it and the naval stores it supplied, England would be in most serious, even irremediable danger. France could take advantage of her at will, easily destroy her clumsy, slow-sailing fleet.

Vetch had seen the haulage of a newly cut mast from the Piscataqua forest in wintertime. He described it to the queen and her courtiers. The mast, one solid, single piece of absolutely straight white pine, was just a few inches more than 120 feet long. It was nearly three feet through the butt, and the axemen and then the teamsters were extremely careful in the "baulking." That meant the way in which the tree was felled, but also the complicated operation that came afterward when it was dragged from the woods to the waterside.

The government paid a bounty of £1 a ton for hewn timber, and the larger masts weighed from 400 to 600 tons. So the men were well paid, and skillful. A slight error either in the felling or the handling could ruin a tree for use as a mast, and cost the local contractor a considerable sum of money. The best time to fell a mast tree was when the snow was deep, and a bed could be made to soften the fall. The snow was also valuable to smooth out the road over which the mast was hauled.

Gullies and hollows were filled. Boughs weighted with snow-covered boulders protected the mast from being gouged. It was levered after tremendous labor onto a flat-bottomed sled of thick plank construction. Then the spans of oxen were chained to the load and the baulking began. Thirty-two spans of oxen were generally hitched up ahead of the sled, and another four yokes used halfway along the load to help swing it, and to act as a brake.

When the waterside was reached, the mast became part of a raft, and was floated down to Portsmouth harbor with spring. There it was loaded aboard one of the specially designed mast ships bound for England or one of the royal dockyards in the West Indies. Many of the mast ships were built in Piscataqua yards, and with exceptionally large side ports to accommodate the stowage of their bulky cargo. They could load from fifty to one hundred of the biggest masts, and take cargo in the holds, and, in addition, other ship pieces—yards, bowsprits, spars and oar rafters.

The departure of a mast ship from Portsmouth turned out *57*

The first time American colonial forces served together was in 1758 at the siege of Louisbourg, on Cape Breton Island, Nova Scotia. Ships of the French fleet were burned or captured, an amphibious landing made, the fortress taken after bombardment. The volunteers came home victorious, and bearing the name of Yankees, given them by their British comrades-in-arms.

the whole town. She flew the royal ensign, often sailed with an escort and carried troops and mail. Marine drummers marched the main deck, flourished their sticks as the fifes shrilled. The captain made good use of his speaking trumpet, and down at Fort William and Mary at the entrance of the river a salute was fired. Portsmouth felt very proud of itself, and just as important as Boston.

Queen Anne granted all of Vetch's requests for the Port Royal expedition. She promised to make him governor of the place if 58 he took it from the French. He went happily home in the next ship, but then had to wait until September, 1709, for the force to be organized. Sir Charles Hobby was commander-in-chief, with Vetch as chief pilot and second in command.

Colonial militia mustered from the various northern provinces were formed into four battalions and made a regiment of about 1,500 men. They sailed from Boston in twenty-four small transports, escorted by five Royal Navy frigates, a bomb ketch, a tender and several coasters. The convoy stayed together and reached Port Royal harbor on September twenty-fourth, anchored in plain sight of the French garrison.

Vetch was given command of two battalions, and they were put ashore at the northern side of the fort the next day by whale-boat men. Colonel Francis Nicholson landed with the other two battalions and occupied the southern flank. The force held on despite severe French fire, and crawled forward to within 400 yards of the ramparts. Then, before the Royal Navy broadside pieces could be brought to bear, Subercase, the French commander, surrendered.

Vetch took over as governor right after the evacuation of the French troops. His garrison force was 200 Royal Marines and 250 colonial militiamen who had volunteered for the duty. The name of the place was changed to Annapolis Royal, and all along the coast and inland, at Quebec, the effect of the English victory was felt.

The Iroquois raids lessened for a time, and Portsmouth prospered. She drew more and more upon the interior regions for her timber needs, though; the forest land around the Piscataqua soon after 1720 was almost completely depleted. The huge, chain-lashed rafts still came down the river in the spring, and the ox teams strained grunting and sweaty to bring out the mast pieces over the snow-covered trails. The royal surveyors, who picked the "king's trees" and marked them with the three blows of the hatchet that resembled the famous broad arrow of crown possession, already ranged the slopes of the White Mountains.

Portsmouth began to direct more of her trade to the West Indian market, satisfied by timber products of smaller size. The sugar planters were pleased to get joists, beams, deal boards, shingles and clapboards for their homes, and staves, hoops and headings for their sugar, molasses and rum casks. Several of the Piscataqua merchants grew wealthy in the West Indian trade, and new families joined the little group that was soon to be called Tory aristocracy.

John Langdon, a local farmer's son, went to work for one of these. He started in February, 1760, as a junior clerk in the counting-room of Daniel Rindge. The Rindge family had done very well in Portsmouth, taken their share of the profits to be made from shipping. The account books that young Langdon studied showed that between 1747–48 more than 120 vessels entered from foreign ports, and seventy-five cleared for long voyages. There were also some 200 Portsmouth vessels in coastwise trade. The volume of business had since greatly increased, and, with it, shipbuilding.

Portsmouth in 1760 had a population of 4,500 people, and the other Piscataqua towns considerably less, and yet they held an excellent shipbuilding record. Among the colonies, only Massachusetts produced more tonnage than New Hampshire. It had become common practice for a Portsmouth shipmaster to sell his vessel, cargo and all, in a British port, return home passenger, with a fine profit.

John Langdon entered into the spirit of the port and began to speculate just as soon as he could get together the money. He was twenty-one years old when he received a letter from Captain

PORTSMOUTH

George King, the master of a Rindge family ship that had just recently arrived in the West Indies. The captain, quite a loose speller, addressed the letter to "Mr. John Langdon, Marchant, Piscataqua, N: England." The letter read:

"Martinico, Decr. 26, 1762

Mr. Langdon

Sir:

I have sold your adventure as follows: Boards for £8 per M, Boats for £12, Hoops for £8 per M, and all four Cash. Sir: you hear by Mr. Rindge's Letters What Brought me hear. But had I None [known] What a Dam'd old Eel pott I wass Gowing to sea in, they that had parasuaded mea must have had a Deal of palavour.

Sir, thear [is] Nothing New only the pease Which I suppose you have heard of Befour this.

Sir, Your Humble Servant

G. King

The profit he made from the voyage of the "old Eel pott" helped decide John Langdon that he should leave the counting-room and go to sea. He sailed in several of the Rindge ships, as supercargo, then mate, then master. His elder brother, Woodbury, who remained in Portsmouth, offered him canny advice and shared in a number of ventures with him, and they both grew wealthy.

It was the time of Portsmouth's greatest success as a port. Her merchants, most of them portly and staid men, dressed in plain-colored coats, with ruffles at the wrists, and knee britches, silver buckles on their low-heeled shoes. From their counting-house *61* windows, they looked out upon the river where as many as thirty ships loaded for England or the West Indies. A system of lookouts and boatmen brought word from the Narrows that a ship was homeward-bound, about to begin her run upstream for her wharf. The youngest clerk was sent to inform the families of the crew, then everybody went down to the wharf.

But the work at the other wharves did not stop long. There were too many cargoes to be handled. Lumber, and casks of pickled beef and salt pork, and oxen, horses, mules, sheep, pigs and geese were being put aboard. Most of the livestock came downstream in gundalows from the inland farms along the tributaries of the Piscataqua. These were a unique type of craft developed locally for shallow-draft river work.

The origin was in the early flat-bottomed and square-ended scow. She was propelled by poles, and headway was slow and hard against the current. Then a rudder and a tiller were added, and a removable mast that took a squaresail. The bow was re-designed into a spoon shape, and the stern rounded. The vessel was decked fore and aft, and equipped with leeboards.

Her cargo capacity was around thirty-five tons, and loaded she drew four and a half feet of water; light, she drew only sixteen inches. The sail was bent onto a stump mast that rotated, and could be lowered to pass under a bridge. The squaresail became a lateen rig, which could be more easily handled. Gundalow crews took advantage of every fitful gust of wind between the high, irregular hills, and made it a rule to reach Portsmouth on one tide, take the next back upstream.

Craft smaller than the gundalows brought in the fish, the lobsters, oysters and clams to the narrow wharves. They were loaded into baskets or panniers there and carried to the market on Spring Hill. The market square was the center of gossip, and

The struggle upstream was often cruel and slow for the keelboat men who in the early 1800s worked the Mohawk River. The sail-rigged boat is about to pass through an opening in the center of a fish dam built by the Iroquois. Stones were taken from the river bed to form the dam, a common type of construction used by a number of inland tribes.

the town crier passed back and forth with a big bell and his long list of announcements.

Queen's Chapel was built in 1632 for the large number of Episcopalians in the town, and the Earl of Halifax Inn took care of the less spiritual needs of the citizens. The Assembly Hall was used for town meetings, dances and occasional theatricals. Most of the new homes were built of wood, and those owned by the wealthy were superbly designed, with long, high halls, and great staircases. But Captain Archibald Macpheadris, who had made a fortune from shipping and married the daughter of the royal lieutenant governor, decided that his home should be built of brick.

It was erected in 1716, and became famous for the murals that decorated the main staircase. They depicted two Indian chiefs who were presented to Queen Anne in 1710 during a visit to England. Having spent a good deal of money on his house, Captain Macpheadris proposed to protect his investment. He arranged for the installation of a lightning rod under the supervision of Benjamin Franklin.

Although he was of local birth and a Harvard graduate, John Wentworth, when he returned from England to Portsmouth in 1766, tried to surround himself with almost regal splendor. He was twenty-nine, handsome and a bachelor, had been appointed governor of New Hampshire by the king, and surveyor-general of His Majesty's woods in North America. Oxford University had given him an honorary degree while he was in England, and on his way home he stayed with the Byrds and with the Randolphs in Virginia.

He brought a number of Yorkshire footmen with him for the staff of the house he occupied on Pleasant Street and filled with expensive English furniture, ordered from Boston. When he rode out, it was in a carriage that bore his coat-of-arms, and he was accompanied by eight servants. Some of the Yorkshiremen soon discovered what New Hampshire could hold for them as individuals, and disappeared, leaving their livery.

The frontier was still close to Portsmouth. Men who met at the Custom House or in Market Square or over a mug of flip at the Earl of Halifax talked of the Stamp Act, and with great displeasure. Some of them had lost members of their families in Indian raids that had occurred only a few years earlier. Others 64 had worn the green buckskins, the beribboned Glengarry caps and wampum sashes of Rogers' Rangers. They had served against the French, been at Fort Number Four and Ticonderoga.

The times were out of joint, they said, with a governor like Wentworth. The Sons of Liberty were right. The colonies deserved their freedom from England. That was long past due.

But the history of Portsmouth in the Revolution was mainly drama which happened elsewhere. Wentworth, the last of the royal governors, went meekly enough after a band of patriots trained a small brass field-piece on the front door of his Pleasant Street house. Crews were recruited with fife, drum and free rum for privateers, some of which returned bearing large amounts of loot. Sixteen companies of New Hampshire militia replaced Connecticut troops in the encirclement of Boston after the battle of Bunker Hill.

John Langdon, a prominent figure in the Continental Congress, brought government orders for shipbuilding to the Piscataqua. The *America* was built there, and the *Ranger*. When John Paul Jones took *Ranger* to sea on November 2, 1777, he carried word of Burgoyne's surrender, and he flew at the mizzen peak the first starred-and-striped flag.

The port was never bombarded, or the town besieged. It prospered due to the privateering and the ship contracts that Langdon had secured. General Washington paid a formal visit at the end of the war and was most enthusiastically received. The next big event was the celebration in June, 1788, of the ratification of the federal Constitution. The *New Hampshire Gazette* glowingly described it in the June twenty-sixth issue.

The news of the ratification came on Sunday, but the town's expression of joy was restrained until one o'clock, Monday morning. Then, the Lord's Day past, the church bells began to peal, and several citizens paraded the streets "with musick."   *65*

PORTS OF CALL

John Langdon, newly elected president of the State of New Hampshire, was on his way from Concord. Portsmouth prepared for him with parade formations of Colonel Wentworth's Corps of Independent Horse, Captain Woodward's Company of Artillery and Colonel Hill's Company of Foot. There was a great turnout of carriages, and men on horseback. When Langdon arrived within a mile of town, the artillery company honored him by firing a federal salute.

Thursday was appointed the official day of celebration. Navy ships anchored in the river. The people from the inland settlements and the fishing communities on the coast and the Isles of Shoals moved into Portsmouth for the day, took their places on the Parade with the townsfolk. The ceremony was to be long-remembered by those who saw it.

It began with the passage around the greensward of the Parade by a band of musicians riding in an open coach pulled by six decorated horses. Husbandmen marched next, and after them came a plough drawn by nine yoke of oxen. Then there were reapers, threshers, mowers, hay-makers, all with their implements; and blacksmiths and nailers, with their forges, anvils and sledges at work.

Shipwrights strode proudly, carrying their tools. They were cheered along with the rope-makers, the caulkers, riggers, joiners, mast-makers and block-makers. Behind them were the mathematical instrument-makers, who bore an azimuth compass. A sturdy pair of horses pulled a wagon on which was mounted a nearly completed boat, the builders hard at work to finish her. There were carvers, and painters, and glaziers, and coopers, and cullers of fish. Pilots marched carrying spy-glasses and charts, and ship-masters held their quadrants.

66   The ship *Union*, "compleatly rigged, armed & mann'd, under

easy sail," was mounted on a carriage with colors flying, and drawn by nine horses. A tenth horse, emblematic of Virginia, and fully harnessed, was led along behind the *Union* float, ready to join the rest.

All of the trades, callings and professions of New Hampshire were represented. The bakers marched smartly, preceded by a flag that displayed the bakers' arms. Cordwainers had decorated their lasts. Tinmen held as their exhibit nine pillars, and a star on a pedestal. Card-makers marched with cards held aloft.

The printers had as an advance formation a pair of boys who held open quires of printed paper. Various type cases and printing apparatus followed. But, all during the march, while perched high on a decorated carriage, compositors worked steadily at the new Dearborn printing press. They struck off copies of songs in celebration of the day. These were distributed to the crowd, and drew somewhat from the applause that should have been given the march-past of the clergy, the sheriff, the judges of the common law and admiralty courts, Langdon and the members of the legislature, and the officers of the militia in dress uniform.

The procession went on, through all of the principal streets of the town, the band playing, the crowd singing the federal song, "It Comes! It Comes!" Then, while the band still played, a cold collation was served on Union Hill. Several toasts were given, and with each three cheers were raised, and salutes fired by the artillery.

During the evening, each window in the State House was illuminated by nine candles. A large company of "ladies and gentlemen" gathered in a semi-circle in front of the State House and listened to a concert played by the long-laboring band, from the prominent height of the balcony.

The *New Hampshire Gazette* closed its account: "Language is too poor to describe the universal joy that glowed in every counte- *67* nance. —Tis enough to say that the brilliancy and festivity of the evening, were only equalled by the decorum and hilarity of the day."

It was to be known later as Portsmouth's most memorable day. The town continued to prosper for some few years. Her shipbuilding, her fishing and overseas trade-interests formed a happy combination for her people. She served also as an outlet for the products sent down by the rapidly increasing farm population in the interior. Immigrants who purposely sought the wilderness life had gone up the Piscataqua into the far reaches of the White Mountains and founded new communities. They were of hardy stock, English, Irish, Scots and some few runaway sailors from European ships, and they made the boulder-strewn farms pay.

Timber was still an occasional item of export. The Portsmouth merchants were quick to tell a stranger that the masts for Nelson's great line-of-battle ship, the 100-gun *Victory*, came from the forests above the Piscataqua. But they recognized that they were boasting about the past.

Boston merchants had begun to concentrate trade in their hands, and to control the economy of nearly all of the New England ports. The Essex River yards and the others around Massachusetts Bay turned out vessels just as fine as any built along the Piscataqua. The younger Portsmouth shipowners moved over to Boston, or allied themselves as partners with the merchants there.

Portsmouth, after the disastrous effects of the Jefferson embargo and the War of 1812, was no longer a principal port of call. Her sea trade had dwindled to fishing craft and coasters, and a few brigs, a snow and some schooners that ran foreign when they could pick up a cargo.

The Piscataqua yards built only for the local trade, and more 68 gundalows than brigs or schooners. Inland, almost to the White

PORTSMOUTH

Mountains, the great stands of timber had been gone for generations. Maine firewood schooners put into Portsmouth on their
way to Boston and discharged deckloads by the cord.

Portsmouth was concerned with Boston, too. Her people
turned more and more towards the small, closely built city. Boston
held the future. It was not to be found here, where just a short
time ago all of the promises had seemed so bright.

CHAPTER 3

 *Boston*

WHEN HE STOOD IN THE DOORWAY of his hut on the western slope of what was soon to be known as Beacon Hill, the ex-Reverend William Blackstone looked straight across at the Puritan settlement. The name for it was Charlestown, he recalled, and the site had been very badly chosen. The water over there was brackish, and the settlement could only be defended with difficulty against Indian attack.

The former Church of England clergyman was a recluse, who had voluntarily come here five years before, in 1625, to the wild, narrow peninsula that jutted out into the tremendous bay. He had his books, and he farmed a little, planted an orchard in front of the hut, used his musket for game, and occasionally traded with the Indians for furs to keep him warm and buckskin for new 70 britches and moccasins.

BOSTON

He greatly disliked the idea of giving up his solitude. He had never seen, either at home in England or along the coast of this vast continent, so much natural beauty. His orchard of fruit trees was planted on the gently sloping open land that would become Boston Common. The bay lay beyond it, and among the many islands, unexplored by white men, and nameless, whales disported, and seals, and auks; bears came down to tide mark to scoop up fish. Behind his hut here, the rest of the peninsula was covered in tall stands of native timber, a part of the absolute wilderness on the mainland.

The peninsula was almost an island. A long, narrow neck like the handle of a ladle joined it to the mainland. It was a mile wide at its widest, and three miles long; at high tide, the sea nearly submerged the neck, and in wintertime rough chunks of ice cluttered it. Over to the west was a mud flat, which was to take the name of Back Bay. A deep cove was on the north, and that was to be dammed up and become a mill pond. A small river on the east cut off the northerly end and made an island of it. There was a deep cove, later called Town Cove, and on the south another deep cove, both fine anchorages.

The Reverend Blackstone felt a twinge of conscience. He was impressed by the true religious fervor of his Puritan neighbors despite the form it took. He had heard their psalms, and the prayers for the dead. There would be many more to mourn, he realized, unless the settlers were decently housed and protected. He went down to the cove where he kept the canoe he had taken in barter from the local tribe, the Massachusetts. Then he paddled across the harbor at slack water and invited the Puritans to share the peninsula with him.

The Puritans were led by a vigorous and hard-dealing man named John Winthrop. There were eight hundred of them, many already sickly, and afraid of the approaching winter. During it, *71* two hundred of them died. They had landed in September, too late to plant crops. Their shelters were log and bark lean-to huts. Starvation, exposure and pneumonia filled the graves dug through the snow and the frost-locked ground.

The Reverend Blackstone's admiration grew. These were a hardy lot who survived. Then, in February, the long-overdue supply ship *Lyon* entered the bay, and the colonists rejoiced. They had decided to name the settlement Boston, throwing aside Trimountaine, the name Blackstone had given it because of the three hills along the spine of the peninsula. Their gratitude persisted, though, and the Puritans asked Blackstone to join them.

Blackstone was Cambridge-bred, and deeply polite. He thanked the Puritans. Then he told them, "I came from England because I did not like the Lord Bishops, but I cannot join with you because I would not be under the Lord Brethren."

But his solitude was gone forever. The Puritans, with spring, began to build small, one-and-a-half-story houses of crudely hewn beams, planks and puncheons. The chimneys were fashioned of clay and sticks. The windows were covered with oiled paper or animal bladders. Most beds were spruce boughs that covered a plank platform two feet off the floor. The attic, reached by a ladder, was for the children or the few indentured people who remained in the colony. Food was coarse, and always in limited supply—dried or salted cod, venison when the hunters could get it, clams and mussels and, day after day, Indian corn.

A housewife was lucky if she still owned a chest of drawers or a chair brought out from England. The big iron kettles were used for all kinds of purposes. Cooking utensils, forks, spoons and plates were made of wood. A pewter dish was as rare as a Bible. Clothing was patched, and passed on by sizes to the children, and worn until patches were put on patches.

BOSTON

Blackstone knew Indians who lived with considerably more ease than these people. Still, the Puritan wives, as they planted their gardens under the warm spring sun, laid out rows where flowers would grow. Dooryards were fenced, each house separate from its neighbor. A street emerged, and a common grazing ground for cattle. There was talk about a fort, and a meeting-house, the need for a pillory, stocks, a whipping post. The hills had been named—Beacon, and Copp's, and Fort.

The Puritan men took off their somber gray coats and waistcoats when they went into the forest after timber, or hunting game. But they kept their narrow-brimmed, black felt hats. Guards in casques, corselets and impossibly clumsy boots clumped along, carrying musketoons or half-pikes. The women and even the young girls while they worked in the gardens took care to stay prim in their severely plain dresses and snoods. If a boy chased a laggard rabbit from the corn rows, he was stiffly punished. Husbands and wives were forbidden to kiss in public.

Reverend Blackstone was aware that he no longer belonged here. He was reminded that at the first meeting of the General Court of the Massachusetts Bay Colony there had been only eight members present. These, in addition to the two chief magistrates, were the six assistants. They voted, though, in direct violation of the charter terms, that the governor and deputy governor be elected from the assistants, by the assistants. It meant that the original Board of Assistants, not one-half of the legal number, arrogated to themselves complete legislative, executive and judicial power.

Here were people, Blackstone knew, who would prove to be ruthless in the consummation of their ambition. They dressed, worked, worshipped and lived as they wished, and any restraint they accepted was of their own making. Blackstone got together   *73* his few belongings, then he disappeared from Boston and went to Narragansett County in Pawtucket.

The colony rapidly expanded. Governor Winthrop ordered built the next year the thirty-ton sloop *Blessing of the Bay*. She was made of local locust, and launched on July 4, 1631, at Malden, over on the Mystic River. Trade between the settlements around the bay kept her busy, and another Puritan vessel *Rebecca* cleared Cape Cod, put into Narragansett, where the crew bartered successfully with the Indians for a load of corn.

Shipbuilding had begun at Medford, on the Mystic River, in 1629, right after the first Puritans were ashore. There were shipwrights and master carpenters and highly qualified artisans among them, and in 1630 more of their kind came from England. They made the term "Medford-built" famous in the colonies and then in England, where a number of the ships were sold.

Freight rates between England and Massachusetts Bay were set at £3 a ton. Passengers paid £5 each for their passage. But to ship a horse from England, because of the care demanded and the space taken, cost twice as much as the passenger fare. The Puritan leaders calculated that with one round voyage—if the commission of the English agent were left out—a ship could pay for herself. The agents were rapidly eliminated.

Most of the colonial fleet remained small, single-decked vessels, smacks, shallops, pinnaces and the lateen-rigged ketches preferred by fishermen. Coasters weighed twelve tons, average, but the ketches went to twenty and thirty tons, and some were fifty feet overall. Those set topsails, and the biggest vessels broke out double topsails.

Then Benjamin Gillam at his yard near Copp's Hill built a 300-tonner, *Welcome*, at the order of a merchant named Valentine Hill. Construction costs were still less than £3.5 a ton. There were yards all over the bay, at Newbury, and Ipswich, Salem and

Gloucester, as well as the thriving group along the Mystic River. Costs in the English yards were twice as much, and the work inferior because of corruption and graft created by royal patronage contracts. New England was already in competition against home trade.

Within four years after the founding of the colony, the original settlers had been joined by 4,000 other English emigrants sent out by the Puritan leaders. Twenty settlements spread around the bay until the peninsula town was the center of a Puritan com-

monwealth. Fishing was still the major concern; most of the fur trade was in the hands of the French and the Dutch. A lot of the young men among the new arrivals soon found themselves aching-backed, and enormously weary, bent over the midships rail of a ketch while they hauled cod from the chill and foggy wastes of the Grand Banks.

It cost approximately £420 to send one of the bigger fishing vessels from Boston to the Banks with a crew of forty men. An average return for a catch was £2,100, and the merchant who outfitted her got a third, or about £700, as his share. The ship-owner took another third, but if he had borrowed money to build the vessel he paid the immense interest rate of forty percent. The members of the crew divided the remaining third of the profit among them, and usually made three offshore voyages a year. They averaged better than £5 a month for their work at sea, considerably more than they could get for shore labor.

The risks along the lightless, practically uncharted coasts and out upon the banks in the winter gales were almost incredible, though. The men also paid for their own gear, which came from England and was not cheap. They paid £6 for twelve-dozen woven cotton lines, and £2 for twenty-four-dozen iron fish hooks. The lines reached down to a maximum depth of seventy-five fathoms, and were weighted with an accumulation of eight pounds of lead sinkers, and the bait cut from mackerel, clams and mussels.

The Boston fishermen and the others who put out from Massachusetts Bay, particularly the Marblehead crews, were proud of their soft, flop-brimmed hats, their scabbard knives worn at the hip, their high and wooden-pegged leather seaboots, and the big leather aprons they wore in approved West of England style and called "barvels." Their women knit for them against the bitter cold of the northeasters soft woolen scarves, and undervests, and mittens, which most of the time were stuffed inside the barvels.

Men who worked ashore as part of the fishing trade were relieved of militia duty. They tended, built and repaired the stages where the catches were spread to dry. Shipwrights and carpenters who worked on the construction of fishing vessels were given the same exemption from militia duty, and men in each community were officially appointed as "fish viewers" to report the size and movement of prospective harvests alongshore.

Several kinds of cod were prepared for market. Dunfish were considered to be the best, and were "made" by burying the largest cod in the ground, then drying them in the open air on the

Codfish kept Massachusetts from extreme poverty and started the first fortunes in the colony, created overseas trade. Men who handled the catch were well paid, and relieved of militia duty, did not share the Grand Banks dangers with the boat crews. They worked hard, though, at splitting, drying, smoking and salting the fish.

shore stages. Their ripe taste pleased the palates of European Catholics, and the variety was popular in France, Spain, Portugal, the Canary Islands and the Azores.

The local market took care of the middle-sized codfish, which was a staple in any New England household. It was salted, smoked, dried and usually kept in a hogshead in a corner of the main room. The contents of the hogshead was supposed to last through a winter, and a trencher of codfish stew dipped right out of the fireplace kettle and eaten along with a piece of maize hoe cake satisfied even the most extreme hunger.

The remaining type of cod, small, or partly spoiled, was rendered into train oil, and got a good price in England and on the Continent. But with the growth of the slave population in the West Indies, and the transporcation of thousands of political prisoners from England, a new use was found for what was called "corfish." It was sold to the island planters as food for their field hands, and at a price which still brought the Boston merchants a substantial profit.

The West Indies had become a major market for all of the Massachusetts Bay towns. But they used Boston as a port of clearance, often sold or consigned entire cargoes there, put them in the hands of the merchants who specialized in dealing overseas. Boston dominated the commerce of the Atlantic coast from Maine to New Amsterdam. She was in open, defiant competition with the most powerful of the London merchants, who had reason to fear and crush her.

Only five years after the founding of the colony, the Commission of Foreign Plantations was formed to control it. The proposal was made in London in 1634 that New England should be divided into a number of provinces under proprietors, with a
governor-general over the whole, appointed by the Crown. Mean-

while, the Bay Charter was to be returned home for investigation by due process of law.

The Puritans decided at once that they should resist. They made plans to fortify Boston harbor, with solid stone breastworks built on what Winthrop liked to call Castle Island. It was steep-shouldered, and lay on the northern side of the peninsula, inside short cannon range of the main channel. Then, at Salem, fiery and arrogant John Endecott, the commander of the militia band there, decided to show his profound dislike of the king, the king's counsellors, and all their ways.

Endecott took the royal standard from the hands of Richard Davenport, the ensign-bearer, while the band was at drill. It held a red St. George cross upon a white field, and Endecott shouted that the cross was a talisman of popery. He pushed aside from his thought the fact that this same ensign had been carried at Crécy, and Agincourt, and the Armada.

He drew his sword and defaced the flag, cut from it part of the St. George device, which, he said, made it no longer objectionable. The men of the trained band were both shocked and thrilled by Endecott's action. None of them seriously protested what he had done. They approved, instead, an ensign which bore a red and white rose as a device. Several of the more cool-minded members of the General Court wished to discipline Endecott, and let their efforts end in censure. The new rose-device flag was adopted for use in the colony while, as a compromise gesture, the St. George cross ensign was flown at Castle William and displayed by the military.

For the first time, the people in power in England understood that they were confronted with a form of deliberate rebellion by the residents of the Bay Colony. The process of separation from the mother country had begun, would never be stopped

79

until the Revolution, and Lexington. The Bay Colony settlers were willing to accept all of the advantages of the Crown's protection, but they were not going to yield obedience in return.

It took two years for the English courts to void the Massachusetts Charter. Then old Sir Ferdinando Gorges was appointed governor-general and his business partner, Captain John Mason, made vice admiral. They were supposed to go out and regulate colonial affairs, take care of the fisheries, shipping and general trade. But Mason died, and Sir Ferdinando did not receive enough support from King Charles's Privy Council to assume the task alone.

Sir Ferdinando died in 1647, and two years later John Winthrop followed him. But, in 1652, King Charles was beheaded, and Puritans ruled England. The Bay Colony enjoyed almost complete freedom; it reached forth and made Maine part of the Commonwealth of Massachusetts. With the Restoration, the General Court was reminded by the king that some payment was due Sir Ferdinando's family. He had at the last accounting owned enormous tracts of Maine timberland. The General Court met in session and a vote was taken. Sir Ferdinando's grandson was awarded £1,250 as total reparation.

The Bay Colony felt herself too strong to care what the home authorities might think about the severely limited amount of the payment. Massachusetts was already very close to being independent from England. Her merchants, her shipowners and shipmasters, her shopkeepers and her farmers and artisans and fishermen and sailors, even the indentured folk, experienced a heady intoxication that was wholly unknown to them. Within the space of a generation, in some cases within the space of a few years, a man could move from one class to the other, and end up wealthy, a member of the colonial landed gentry.

Coastwise trade, particularly with Virginia, was greatly expanded. The Virginia tobacco planters had brought in thousands of slaves, and they bought the poor grades of codfish as a subsistence ration. The same market developed in the West Indies as tobacco and then sugar planting started there. A Dutch ship as early as 1635 discharged a West Indian cargo of tobacco and 140 tons of salt in Boston. It proved very instructive to the Puritans. A Salem ship came home on February 26, 1638, after a seven-months voyage, carrying cotton, tobacco and Negro slaves from New Providence Island, and salt from the Tortugas.

Richard Vines investigated the West Indian market and reported to Governor Winthrop in 1647 about the English-owned islands. "Men are so intent upon planting sugar that they had rather buy foode at very deare rates than produce it by labour, so infinite is the profitt of sugar workes after once accomplished."

The difficulty of obtaining furs emphasized the importance of the West Indies market, but Boston ships cleared regularly for England and Holland. They were loaded in cargoes of wheat and rye, and what furs were available, came home with linen, woolens, shoes, stockings and dry goods.

Newfoundland proved to be another good market. Ships homeward-bound for Boston with bulk cargoes of Canary or Madeira wine took both freight and passengers there. Many of the people headed for the settler's life in Newfoundland were willing to sail as workaways to save passage money. There were soon complaints, though, that "one third part of the companie are onely but proper to serve a stage, carry a barrow and turne poor john." The governor of Newfoundland was much happier over the exchange of Massachusetts corn and cattle for his colony's fish and train oil.

But the Bay Colony fishermen had taken away most of the

Grand Banks trade. The Boston merchants kept their fleet in northern waters, so that the crews could regularly make three voyages a year. They also arranged for a "magazine ship" to relieve the fishermen of the complication of sending money home. The magazine ship appeared at an established rendezvous in a Maine cove at the end of each voyage. Rum was sold, and snuff, and tobacco, and various items of clothing or gear the fishermen lacked. Maypole dancing with troupes of Indian squaws in the warmth of beach fires was encouraged. Profit of one hundred percent from a magazine-ship rendezvous was common.

The amazing increase in Bay Colony prosperity had not gone unmarked by the London merchants. They made strong representations at court regarding it. The Privy Council was told in 1661 that New England was "the key to the [West] Indies without which Jamaica, Barbadoes and ye Charibby Islands are not able to subsist, there being many thousands tunns of provisions as beefe, pork, pease, biskett, butter, fish, carried to Spain, Portugall and the Indies every year."

The English merchants were acutely conscious that they could no longer successfully compete in the Atlantic trade. Their colonial cousins had taken it from them, with faster-sailing ships, and with better merchandise sold at smaller prices. Sir Joshua Child, the leading English authority on shipping, wrote in his *New Discourse of Trade* in 1660:

New England is the most prejudicial plantation to this Kingdom. . . . New England produces generally the same we have here viz. corn, and cattle, some quantity of fish they likewise do kill but that is taken and saved altogether by their own inhabitants which prejudices our Newfoundland trade, where, as has been said, very few are, our ought according to prejudice, to be employed in those fisheries but the inhabitants of Old England. The other commodities we have from them, are some few great masts, furs, and train-oil, of which the yearly value amounts to very little, the much greater value of returns from thence being made in sugar, cotton, wool, tobacco, and such like commodities, which they first receive from some other of his Majesty's Plantations, in barter for dry cod-fish, salt mackerel, beef, pork, bread, beer, flower [*sic*], pease, etc., which they supply Barbadoes, Jamaica, etc. with, to the diminution of those commodities from this Kingdom. . . .

Sir Joshua possessed very clear vision. He could see the future as it was taking shape at Massachusetts Bay, and what he saw profoundly worried him. He informed His Majesty:

Of all the American plantations, his Majesty has none so apt for the building of shipping as New England nor more comparably so qualified for the breeding of seamen, not only by reason of the natural industry of the people but principally by reason of their cod and mackerel fisheries; and in my opinion there is nothing more prejudicial and in prospect more dangerous to any mother Kingdom than the increase of shipping in her colonies, plantations, or provinces. . . .

Of ten men that issue from us to New England and Ireland what we send to or receive from them does not employ one man in England. . . . I must confess that though we lose by their unlimited trade with our foreign plantations yet we are very great gainers by their direct trade to and from Old England. Our yearly exportations of English manufactures, malt and other goods from hence thither amounting in my opinion to ten times the value of what is imported from thence.

PORTS OF CALL

The key figures in the Boston trade were the merchants who served both as importers and exporters. Many of them had started as retail shopkeepers, and still kept active interest in that field. They engaged in wholesale business, too, using their shops as outlets for goods they imported, and sending the goods on to the frontier settlement stores and the trading posts where barter was still the common form of exchange. Another of their functions was to act as broker or distributor for local exports to other colonial and foreign markets.

The merchants' control of the trade came from their having the capital or commanding the credit necessary to carry accounts for months, and years. Some of the Boston group were soon able to call themselves wealthy, and many of them kept the fact secret, although pride gradually corroded caution and they built fine houses that they filled with English furniture. They wore clothing made for them by fashionable London tailors, and bag wigs, and carried swords. Their Puritan faith was confined to attendance at church on the Sabbath; with the Restoration, they were not ashamed to admit their Royalist leanings.

Other, lesser merchants owned a single store and a couple of coasting vessels that they kept in service "Down East," in the Maine frontier trade, or in picking up cargo in the spring at the little river settlements inland where farmers came with their winter's production of axe helves, ox bows, buckets, brooms, wooden dishes and saddlery. But they were really middlemen for the wealthy merchants, sold the goods they handled to them or accepted their scale of prices.

Nearly all of the big Boston merchants maintained or were part owners of shipyards, warehouses and wharves, as well as the ships that carried their goods. They represented in the Massachusetts Bay area the largest source of labor employment. A number held investments in ironworks, sawmills, fulling mills, breweries and distilleries. Their vessels brought north general West Indian cargoes in exchange for New England products, and among those imports was sugar from their own plantations.

More than any other class or group, the merchants were the internationalists of the colonial era. Travel except by ship was difficult, slow and dangerous. Merchants transacted a great part of their business by correspondence, but also kept social contacts in other colonies, and in England and the West Indies. Young men about to enter a family firm were sent out on voyages that

The lady with the fancy bonnet and the very short legs is out for a ride in a miserable conveyance called a Yarmouth coach. Both the coachman and the horse are sad-looking, and no doubt the coachman would like to be aboard the ship in the background. The vehicle, designed in England, was made bigger in North America, but that did not take the bumps out of a colonial road.

might last a year, but introduced them to a trade network that reached from Charleston to Cadiz, and from St. Petersburg to London. There were some intermarriages as a consequence, and a few of the businesses descended from one generation to the next.

Boston merchants of the seventeenth century developed a habit of meeting each other almost every business day. They used the comfortable and popular Green Dragon Inn, or the arcade of the Town House, or a counting-room from which the clerks discreetly withdrew. Contracts were made then, and local and overseas commercial conditions discussed, and the latest batch of news.

Following the Elizabethan tradition of "ventures," the Boston merchants entered into long-range investments, but at high rates of interest. Eight and ten percent were common, often considerably more, and as much as twenty percent was charged. It was remembered that during the early, desperate days of the Plymouth Colony when Miles Standish had gone to London to borrow keenly needed funds, he had been forced to pay fifty percent to make a £150 loan. Later loans had carried interest rates of forty percent.

The Boston merchants were quite content to handle "book" accounts for their customers. These were settled by cash payment usually once a year or, if the cash were not available, there might be a transfer of goods, or a mortgage, a letter of credit or some English government bonds. The interest paid for the extension of a debt made the delay in settlement worthwhile.

Ship insurance was settled usually by a group of policy holders who were well known to each other. A merchant who wanted to speculate that a certain vessel would make port with her cargo intact signed the policy which stated the total sum required. Then, below his name, he noted the amount for which he would be responsible. When the full amount of the policy was subscribed, and after the vessel arrived safely in port, the premium was divided among the underwriters, pro rata, according to the amount they had underwritten. But if the ship was lost, the broker collected the various amounts from the underwriters for the man who was insured.

During the early 1700s, it became the custom in Boston and the other Bay Colony ports to enter a stipulation into the ship insurance policies. This stated that the assurers were willing to bear the "adventures of peril," including those of the "Seas, Men of War, Fires, Enemies, Pirates, Rivers, Thieves, Jettesons, Letters of Mart and Counter Mart, Surprisals, Taking at Sea, Arrests, Restraints and Detainments of Kings, Princes, or Peoples of what Nation, Condition, or Quality forever, and Barratry of the Masters and Mariners." Legal sanction was given to this document by stating further it should "be of as much force and effect as the Surest Writing of Policy of Assurance heretofore made in Lombard Street or elsewhere in London."

The underwriters assumed their risk for a premium that varied from ten to eighteen percent. The "Lombard Street" stipulation had little if any effect on the Boston insurance market. What counted was the condition of the ship, and where she was bound.

A very substantial part of all early Boston trade was carried on by the clerks who worked for the big merchant firms. They started young, some of them at the age of twelve, or fourteen, and if they were smart and industrious they were often sent to sea in a company ship after a couple of years of counting-room training. And it was the ships that offered the chance for real success. They led to advancement as supercargo, and mate, and *87*

A MERCHANTS COUNTING HOUSE.

master. Then, before a man was thirty, he might leave the sea and become a full partner in the firm with the profits made during his various voyages.

The clerks worked a twelve-hour day, six days a week. Some of them were apprentices, and shared quarters in the garrets of the counting-houses built along Water Street opposite the wharves. They swept out the inner offices that belonged to the senior partners, and then the big, main counting-room with its rows of high stools and high, narrow desks, the chief clerk's desk next to the fireplace. Brass doorknobs and handles were shined; the front steps were swabbed and, with the appearance of sidewalks after 1700, the stretch at the front door. Fires were laid and started, quills sharpened, and shot-glasses and inkwells filled. Then the huge account books and the correspondence books were ranged from desk to desk, and the real day's work began.

Breakfast for the clerks was a dish of tea and a piece of johnny cake. The midday meal was a little more ample, and supper was usually codfish stew. It was a hard and a lean life, with wages no more than five or six shillings a week, and no time off without pay being docked by the ever-watchful chief clerk, and no excuses accepted for errors made in the four copies kept of each document.

The clerks waited patiently for the chance to be given an errand that would take them out of the counting-room and along the wharves, possibly aboard a ship just arrived in port. But they recognized the importance of the knowledge they picked up right here at their desks. They were familiar with the financial resources, the day-by-day dealings and the personal characteristics of the principal English merchants engaged in the colonial trade. Among them were Henry Ashurst, an early friend of the Bay Colony people, and John Pocock, one of the merchants who had helped the Pilgrims, and William Stratton, and Robert Knight, and Joshua Woolnough. Then there were Joshua Foote & Company, and Edward Shrimpton, whose brother was a Boston merchant, and William Peake, and a lot more.

The Boston men who corresponded with the English merchants as absolute equals were Stephen Winthrop, the governor's son, and John Leverett, and Henry Shrimpton, and David Yale. John Hancock owned considerably more than that farm alongside the Common, and Thomas Boylston was supposed to be gathering the greatest fortune in the colony.

A deal like that made in Barbados, where barter, paper and cash were all used, was memorized by the brighter clerks. An outstanding debt a Boston merchant owed was wiped out with the delivery of a single cargo. Half of the shipload was refuse fish. One-quarter was what was marked on the ledgers as "merchantable fish." Another quarter was train oil, and beef, and pork, mackerel and sturgeon, sold at local Bridgetown prices. There was still a sum to be paid to meet the full amount of the debt, but it was settled in cash and beaver pelts.

The Boston clerks kept themselves informed daily about the price of beaver. It was legal tender in several of the colonies, and yet the value severely fluctuated.

Currency of many kinds, some of it extremely spurious, was in circulation in all Boston trading. Portuguese reis and crusados were used, and Spanish reales, pistoles, dollars and pieces of eight. English "good and lawful" money was mostly in silver, and from coastwise deals came Dutch guilders, French livres and what was known simply as "Barbary gold" and had been quite recently a part of pirate loot.

There was very little gold to be used, though. Most of the silver was badly worn, and had been sweated, washed and clipped, the value drastically reduced. Counterfeit coins were commonly passed, and the merchants, in their function as bankers, were stuck with a lot of it. So in 1652 the Bay Colony started a mint and produced her own money. John Hull was the mintmaster. He was supplied with silver plate, and bullion, and coins imported for the purpose, and turned out pine-tree shillings, sixpences, threepences and twopences whose value was unquestioned.

Boston, the largest town in the North American colonies in 1690, had a population of 7,000 people. The early houses with their clapboard and shingle fronts and overhanging second stories with small, many-paned windows were being replaced by larger, much better built structures. Some of these were of three-story construction, with broad chimneys at each end, wider, higher windows and fanlights over the doorways. A few were built of brick that had come out as ballast from England, or had been fired in local kilns. The houses were grouped closely together, although the more pretentious occupied space that gave them front dooryards, side and back gardens, and stables.

Among the big, new houses were those that belonged to French Huguenot families like the Fanueils and the Bowdoins, and to Scots like the Shaws and the Cunninghams, Irish like the Tracys and Magees, and Germans like the Crowninshields, who had changed the spelling of their name.

The beacon which had been built almost at the beginning of the town's history stood tall and gibbet-shaped on the hill named for it and was still the chief aid to navigation for mariners. Copp's Hill held the windmill whose long, cumbrous sails flapped creaking in the harbor breeze and could be heard all the way across the Common. The third hill was called Fort Hill yet, despite the fact that the fortifications of any importance had been established much closer to the harbor.

Cornhill, Hanover, King and Ship Streets were given mainly to small retail shops. A young clerk from one of the merchant firms sent to deliver records at the Custom House often made a slight detour to peer in and examine the stock. It would be in a shop like this where he would start on his own when he had enough money to make the investment.

A number of the shops belonged to competitors among the large firms, and, standing here for a few minutes, the prices and the merchandise could be compared. There were general shops, stocked with a variety of goods. Those sold carpeting, and window glass, and pewter ware, and Russia leather chairs, boots and shoes, and fowling pieces and pistols and fishing gear. The specialty shops were much higher-priced.

They dealt in silks and fine cottons and satins, silk notions and threads, silver and silk buttons, along with fancy handkerchiefs and combs, rings, necklaces and stomachers. Men were attracted by crimson britches, wigs, enamelled French snuff boxes, Bristol crown glass decanters and Waterford long-stemmed clay pipes.

Down along Ship Street, ironwork and suits of sails, hooks, lines, nails were sold, and coarse woolen stroud cloth for seamen's coats, and duffel cloth, and Osnaburg stuff, and goose shot, and powder in kegs, tomahawks, knives and kettles meant for the Indian trade. There were men who specialized in making silverware, and cabinets, and chaises, and saddles, and harness.

Each shop had its own heavy wooden sign hanging out in front that told what was offered there. The apothecary's doorbell rang all day long while from behind his high counter lined with jars he sold balsams of life, female medicines, vomits and purges, and smelling salts and salves. He carried in stock also "anodyne necklaces" for the easy breeding of children's teeth, and "teeth drawers," and "blood stones," and several kinds of

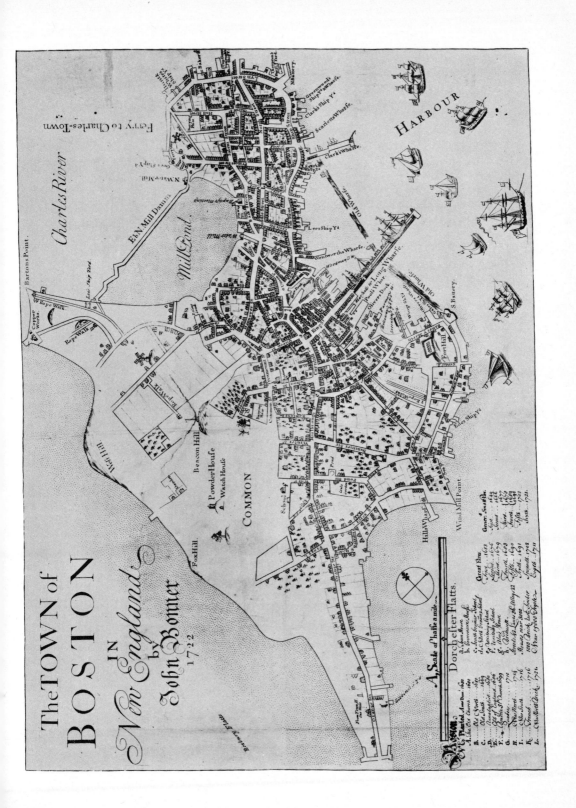

medical apparatus. Customers' demands made him keep on hand supplies of saltpeter, soap, spices and white sugar candy.

There were seven bookshops in town before the great fire of 1711, and one of them, run by John Usher, had a branch in Portsmouth. They imported and sold books, published books and pamphlets, bound books, did job printing of all sorts, including blank forms for bonds, certificates and charter parties. The governor employed them to print the official colonial announcements. They issued the first public newssheets, and these in a few years became regular newspapers.

Taverns, dramshops and alehouses were found in several parts of Boston. It was not hard for a young clerk to get a drink. Boys of twelve years of age were allowed to buy whatever they wanted. Popular drinks in cold weather were flip and hot buttered rum. Flip was made in different ways, but a common variety was a mixture of rum, pumpkin beer and brown sugar, into which a red-hot poker had been plunged. Lighter, summertime drinks were British ale or beer, and citron water, or cider, and a long list of local cordials, usually mixed with water.

The Green Dragon and The Mermaid were among the best of the town's taverns. They were in many respects men's clubs, and served as centers for political gatherings, and assemblies of merchants and militia officers. Their whale-oil lamps were a welcome sight on snow-whipped nights. Whist, and a game called "ombre" and billiards were played until dawn. Skittles and shuffleboard and bowling in specially-built alleys drew the skillful and those who wished to gamble and were bored by cards. Boston, as the years passed, had become less and less Puritan-minded.

But, in 1660 a woman named Mary Dyer was hanged on the Common because she was a Quaker. Three other women, Mary Jones, Mary Parsons and Ann Hibbins, were hanged as

94

witches. The Reverend Nathaniel Ward, speaking for all good Puritans, declared, "All Familists, Anabaptists, and other Enthusiasts shall have free liberty to keepe away from us."

The people of the Bay Colony had refused to accept in 1651 the imposition of the king's much-discussed Navigation Acts. They did not do this on political grounds, though. They claimed they were moved by "the higher law"—which was purely religious, and put them above King Charles II, the Lords Commissioners and any opposition.

Pirates were hanged and their bodies left to rot in chains on islands in the harbor, despite the law which stated that all such punishment should take place in England.

Smuggling had become a common practice in Massachusetts Bay since the passage of the Navigation Acts.* Those restricted the importation of American, Asian or African cargoes. They in addition barred foreigners from English trade, and demanded that all foreign goods shipped to America must clear from English ports. A further act forbade one colony from trading with another. Between 1675 and 1715, customs offices were opened in forty-nine different ports. The staff included more than ninety surveyors general, surveyors, riding surveyors, collectors, comptrollers, searchers, preventive officers, landwaiters, tidewaiters, clerks, accountants and boatmen.

The Bay Colony people flouted the establishment in broad daylight. The masters of inward-bound ships put their cargoes ashore on Cape Ann. Then "wood boats" were loaded with the cargo, a thin layer of kindling pieces stacked on top. But a number of Boston merchants would not indulge in any form of subterfuge. They ordered their ships to come straight to their usual

---

*They were passed between 1650 and 1767.

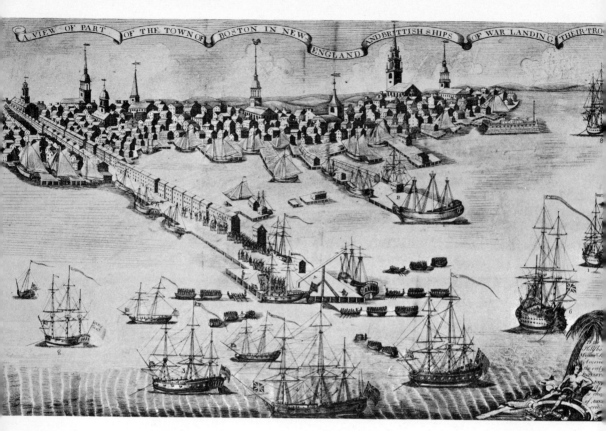

British troops begin the occupation of Boston. They landed at Long Wharf, in the foreground. Cannon were run out aboard the ships of the fleet. The troops were infantry and artillery. The route of march was up King Street. The British paraded, with their band playing. Bostonians furiously resented the display. It led to hatred, and then to the Revolution.

wharves and discharge. While the surveyor general was fully informed of the ship movements, he took no action. There were sixty-three wharves in Boston, and fourteen more in Charlestown. It was impossible to muster enough king's men to guard them.

The three principal wharves, India and Griffin's and Long, were busy all year round. Long Wharf, built in 1710, stretched more than 2,000 feet out into deep water, the shore end at King Street. Solid rows of warehouses occupied it and the others, the space there shared by ropewalks and sail lofts. Cranes that moved

96

heavy cargo were set on the stringpieces, the lifting power from capstans that were turned by men or teams of horses.

Drays, wains, carts and wagons were hub to hub among the clutter of cargo. Ships just back from long overseas voyages tied up alongside rough-hulled Maine schooners loaded with fish and furs. Coasters from Virginia and the Carolinas discharged tobacco, cotton and turpentine. Shallops whose home ports were Nantucket and the small Cape Cod towns hauled out casks of whale oil by hand, and there were hundreds of hogsheads of West Indian sugar, and rum, and Madeira and Canary wines.

Out in the bay, boys in skiffs herded cows from one island grazing ground to the next. The cattle swam with a line rove around the leader's horns, and prodded by poles. Gundalows were loaded with piles of firewood, sea-coal, hay and oats. Lobstermen pulled their pots off the island ledges, and eel pots were hauled and emptied. The Charlestown ferry ran clanging her bell.

The boys stared curiously at the rusted chains of the gibbets on Nix's Mate and Bird Island where pirates had been hanged. The sun caught hard on the tall white tower of the lighthouse, built, too, in 1710, and set far out at the harbor entrance and equipped with a cannon whose sound could be heard at least a mile away in fog. That was the first lighthouse in North America, and Boston was the greatest port.

But with all of the wealth that came from her deep, well-protected harbors and her length of coastline, the Massachusetts Bay Colony did not hold any natural advantage over other sections north and south of her. Cape Breton Island and Newfoundland were nearer the home markets in England. The Maine anchorages were better, and the harbors deeper, more sheltered. The Chesapeake Bay area offered enormous amounts of agricultural products. Like the Delaware, it was almost an inland sea, and seldom obstructed by snow or fog.

PORTS OF CALL

Massachusetts lacked a river which could be compared with the St. Lawrence, the Hudson, the Delaware. Those opened to ocean shipping the riches of a vast hinterland. They made possible the trade which flourished in New York, and Philadelphia, and Baltimore.

A Bay Colony man never forgot that handicap. He was extremely conscious that Boston had become a great port despite

Yankee captains relaxed ashore. These are shown in Surinam. They disliked tropical heat. Rum and conversation helped. Some got drunk and drowsy, though. Among them

it. He held a peculiar and very profound sense of superiority.
Boston merchants and Boston sailors were the smartest anywhere.
He had been told so from his earliest youth.

A Boston-born shipmaster carried with him the unshakable
belief that he was a law unto himself. It was an outgrowth of the
doctrine that had insisted upon the killing of Quakers, and
women who were supposed to be witches, and the hanging of

were prominent men. Esek Hopkins was later famous. He commanded the Continental
Navy.

pirates, although the law said that should be performed only in England. It related to the flouting of the Navigation Acts, and practically every other attempt at regulation by the Crown.

The hours-long Sabbath sermons, hectoring and threatening, filled with baleful logic and dire predictions about those found unworthy, had left their mark. There was a strange admixture of greed, great daring and mystical confusion in the minds of the men who took the Boston ships to sea during the seventeenth and eighteenth centuries. They expressed in concentrated form the motives of the merchants at home, who maintained a single credo: Profit was to be considered above anything else.

If a ship failed to come home without making money for her owners, the master was held responsible. The blame was entirely his. It did not matter that many of the mates were indifferent navigators, and charts rare, and bad. Boston ships were being sent before 1700 to Alexandretta in the eastern Mediterranean past the Barbary corsair squadrons, and to the Guinea coast, and to Madagascar and the Indian Ocean.

A master transacted all of a ship's business. He negotiated for and bought or sold or transshipped her various consignments of cargo, confronted with language problems, the effects of suddenly declared wars, fluctuant currencies, illness, desertion and insubordination among his crew.

Wrecks and the total loss of vessels on unlighted or uncharted coasts were common. The erection of Boston Light in the island-strewn bay was of decided help. But it was only after 1716 that the construction of others along the North Atlantic coast was begun. They were mostly built of brick, and from fifty to 120 feet high, and still the lights were poor, often unreliable.

The Boston Light was supplied with a glazed cage, roofed with copper and supported on a brick arch. It was necessary to *100* furnish the lamps with oil two or three times a night, and even though they were snuffed every hour the glass was never entirely free from soot. During snow squalls or fog, the beacon was practically useless, and with the wind wrong the warning cannon could not be heard.

The result was that under the extraordinary stresses of command, the Boston shipmasters became known in the world ports as grasping, remote and ruthless. Money meant everything to them, their competitors said, and given enough of it they would take a ship and her cargo anywhere.

Back home, though, shipmasters in the period before the Revolution held a very high place. They ranked just below the clergy and the magistracy. Many of them, while still in their early thirties, retired from the sea, bought shares as partners in merchant firms. They built splendidly designed and spacious brick houses, bought the finest of furniture, ordered carriages from London and commissioned Smibert, Copley and Blackburn to paint portraits of their families.

With continuing prosperity, they built country seats at Milton Hill and at Cambridge. They entertained there on a lavish scale. There were enormous house parties, and pageants, and feasts, and routs and drive-outs to rural inns for dinner. English rods were used for trout fishing, and English fowling pieces for partridge and duck. Some men, still in love with the sea, took pleasure cruises into the Gulf of Maine during the summer months.

When they joined with John Hancock in what was afterward called the "Boston Tea Party," it was in answer to a challenge from the British government. English tea had been dumped on an already glutted local market. The problem was once more pounds, shillings and pence. The men dressed as Mohawks who raided the tea ships at Griffin's Wharf were among the wealthiest in the town. They took action against George III only be-

The Paul Revere engraving of the Boston Massacre on March 5, 1770, that was remembered at Lexington.

cause he threatened the maritime trade, and that was what made them prosperous.

But, with Lexington, and Concord, then Bunker Hill, their attitude changed. They were no longer self-centered, thinking of their own affairs and class interests. Some few of them remained Tories, and waited for British victory. The rest, out on the Concord road, and on the slopes of the hill above Charlestown, were reminded of their early heritage, and how their people had come here.

They lost the sense of class, and cleared from their thought the knowledge of what belonged to them, and very certainly now would be taken by the British. They and the men in linsey-wool-sey and cowhide boots fought for the same reason. They were New Englanders, and had just become Americans.

There were ten Massachusetts shipmasters among the twenty-two New Englanders appointed to command in the Continental Navy. Several of them were Boston men, and they served with distinction. Congress was grateful for their effort in helping to create the new organization.

Boston throve again as a port after the war. But there was a stubborn retention of some of the old ways. The forward-looking merchants of the Bay area welcomed in 1840 the pro-posals of Samuel Cunard to make Boston a terminus port for his trans-Atlantic steamers. A monopoly agreement was reached, and New York completely excluded. Champagne banquets for Cunard were given by the Boston merchants, and when ice closed the harbor and held up one of his ships, they hired a pair of tugs to clear a passage and get her out to sea.

Then Donald McKay settled in East Boston and began to build his superb clipper ships. The same men who had been overjoyed by the award of the Cunard steamer monopoly to the port began to invest heavily in McKay's enterprise. When it was pointed out to them that the interests sorely clashed, and that steamers threatened to drive the clippers from the sea, the tradition-conscious merchants said that might well be true. But coal cost a lot of money, and while sailcloth wasn't cheap, there was surely no charge for use of the wind.

103

CHAPTER 4

 *Salem*

FOR A BOY BORN IN SALEM in the 1740s, the sea was dominant. The town was located on a thin neck of land, the forest stretching enormous back beyond that. Boston was just a few miles away to the south, and still remote. A boy had a better chance of getting to Barbados or Funchal in a Salem-owned ship before he reached Boston.

The town took great care to send its boys to sea young. They began their active training when they were ten, and many of them were aboard ship and outward-bound by the time they were fourteen. A belief in the ability of youthful shipmasters was shared in all of the Bay Colony ports. Salem, though, had several vessels under the command of men too young to vote.

There was a road around the bay, but it was impassable most of the year. The islands out in the bay, close offshore, were densely covered yet with stands of pine. Salem, despite the fact that she had been settled in 1626, was set within wilderness.

Wolf pits were dug right past Salem Neck fence. Bounties of £2,10 shillings were paid for killing a wolf. The selectmen insisted that the beast's head be shown to them before payment was made. They also gave bounties for squirrels and rattlesnakes, and wanted no nonsense.

Boys or men who went into the forest alone were severely warned. No longer ago than September, 1725, twenty bears had been killed within two miles of Boston. There was an annual wolf rout—a drive in which all of the Salem men and boys engaged. A large circle was formed in the forest near the village, and slowly closed, and every wolf caught within it slaughtered. One day a year, not only in Salem but in almost every village along Massachusetts Bay, there was a wide-open hunt for anything living and wild. Prizes were given to the hunters who did the most killing.

Salem boys were skillful hunters. They knew the sign of wolf, and bear, and elk, and otter, panther and beaver. They hunted turkeys through the forest underbrush, carrying battered old blunderbusses their fathers had discarded. Pigeons were hunted from blinds, using live decoys. The boys knew how to "prate"—imitate the calls—and bring the birds within easy range.

Salem's living came from the sea. Her people prospered there, and the boys were taught to fish, row, sail as soon as they had the strength and understanding. The forest to them was always a barrier they had no desire to penetrate or explore.

The work of the port occupied them. Salem during the first half of the eighteenth century increased her trade until in the Bay Colony she was second only to Boston. There were no good harbors between Boston and Salem, to the southward, and none

Captain John Carnes is wearing the quite plain uniform of the Continental Navy, and no wig. The only sign of his rank is the long-glass held in his left hand in the traditional portrait manner.

except Gloucester, far out on Cape Ann, between Salem and the mouth of the Merrimack River to the northward.

It was much easier to unload the cargoes of the Marblehead and Gloucester fishing fleets at Salem for export to Boston. And Salem was nearer to the lumber and fur trade of the eastward settlements. There were merchants in the port who had clearly seen what was happening to the coastal forests as far north as the Piscataqua region. So, without much talk about it, they bought timberland, put up sawmills in the Maine villages of Wells and Kennebunk. When the local supply of timber was exhausted, they would have those sources from the eastward for ship construction, and for barrels and boards to keep the new ships busy in the West Indian trade.

Salem boys came to know exactly the distance across the harbor mouth. That was for them the front door to the world, and lead to adventure, wealth and fame. From Naugus Head in Marblehead, over to Hospital Point in Beverly, was less than two miles. Salem peninsula pushed out and almost cut the inner bay in half. The harbor reached to the south, and widened until it was divided again by what was called the South Fields. There was a narrow channel to the north, and the North River, which ran back to the high land called Gallows Hill.

A ferry was in operation early, from the wharf owned by the Blue Anchor Tavern at the foot of English's Lane. It ran to Marblehead and put the passengers down near Fort Darbie on Naugus Head. The service was started in 1636 by John Stone, who charged a penny fare to local folks, but doubled that for strangers.

The shipyards had begun almost as soon as the town was settled. There had been one where Boston Street crossed the cove, but that had been filled in, and was called Blubber Hollow. *107*

PORTS OF CALL

Along the channel which drained into Mill Pond were a lot of wharves, and Bartholomew Gedney had his shipyard there. Close to that, Jonathan Felt, the anchorsmith, kept a forge. So many shipyards were around the creek off Norman Street that the place got the name of Knockers' Hole because of the noise made by the mallets and the hammers.

The route taken by the nineteen people convicted of witchcraft was along Essex Street. Their trial was in 1692, and all of them were convicted, then hanged. They were marched from the jail on St. Peter's Street to Essex, and up Boston Street to Gallows Hill.

There were better things to remember about the early days. A famous old-time herdsman was named Jonathan Milk. Boys who whispered in class were unfailingly caught by Mr. Edward Norris, even when his back was turned. He taught school for thirty years, and his punishment for an offender was a rap across the knuckles with a ruler that was so sharply delivered it made the rest of the class wince.

The big, dark old houses built first here were right beside the water. They faced the wharves and the counting-houses that belonged to their owners. Those had many gables, and clusters of central chimneys, small windows with heavy leads, and the second story was built out over the one below.

Mr. Richard Derby's house was like that. He was one of the richest merchants in Salem. All of his money was made from shipping, and he owned a fleet of half-a-dozen vessels that he kept at sea as much as possible. Boys who went to work for him in their middle teens received very careful training.

They served as counting-house clerks for several years, and then Derby sent them to sea. It was an opportunity offered to only a few Salem boys, and no outsiders. But the long hours at the ledgers and letter books blunted the ambition of a number of them, and they quit. The rest found their restlessness restrained by looking out the window at the new home Derby built for himself and his family.

It was finished in 1762, and made of brick, the first of its kind in town. It had a gambrel roof, and a pedimented doorway, and four-flue chimneys joined in pairs. Lawns and gardens and fine trees were around it, but the counting-house was close, and Derby Wharf next to that. Standing on the walkway along the broad rooftop, Mr. Derby could watch his ships until their topsails were gone from sight over the horizon.

An apprentice making a voyage to the West Indies in a Derby-owned ship learned a lot, fast. Navigation was no longer a profound mystery to him; it was worked each watch, and his questions were answered. But sail handling, until he fully mastered all of the parts of the standing and running rigging, was much more difficult. He was often thankful that the bosun was there on deck, and that the rough-voiced mate was really a very patient man.

It was arrival at the first island that had the greatest effect upon an apprentice. He had grown accustomed to the sharks, the barracuda and bonito, the trade wind that kept the topsails full, the yellow clots of Gulf Stream weed, the turtles that lay loafing there, black-mottled backs a fathom wide. He could even repress his rapture during the star-pale nights with the wake laced and made resplendent by phosphorous, flying fish in gaudy streaks across the fo'c'sle-head.

Then the ship made her landfall. The anchor went down. Canvas was furled with men from a number of ships critically watching. This was Bridgetown, Barbados.

Bridgetown, after a boyhood spent in Salem, and after weeks   *109* at sea, was an almost shocking experience. The boy went ashore to the tightly built, noisy town where sailors from the ships jostled soldiers from the garrison and every narrow street seemed to be filled with talking, laughing, shouting and gesticulating Negroes.

The boy wandered out from the town along a white coral road where frogs leaped sidewise in the dust and coconut palms laid black, regular bars of shadow. He remembered old stories about this place, heard at home and told by men returned from a voyage. Thousands of indentured people, English, Scots and Irish, had died here in the last century, and with them Indians from the New England tribes caught in battle, and African folks like those he had seen in Bridgetown.

They died because they were not fed enough, and were weak, and slow. So the overseers whipped them without mercy. Barbados, the old Salem sailors said, was a great big jail, and the folks who owned the plantations were the jail-keepers.

The boy went back to his ship while dusk spread swiftly over the orange, the lemon and lime and pomegranate trees in the gardens of the wide-winged coral houses that belonged to the planters. But not even the exotic trees with their heady mingling of odors stopped him. He was not interested either in a shrilly beaten drum inside a tavern door, or a wench who called to him and slipped her chemise low from her shoulder. Right now, he was homesick. He missed Salem.

All of the crews of the Salem ships felt the pull of homesickness and native pride in the troubled period just before the Revolution. Each outward-bound ship, when she came to anchor in a West Indian port, brought more news of what could only end as war. A letter received from Mr. Derby vigorously showed a large part of the home sentiment:

110

SALEM

Salem, May ye 9, 1775.

Capt. Danl. Hathorn of Schooner Patty, West Indies.

I suppose you will be glad to hear from home, but things are in such a confused state I know not what to write you. Boston is now blocked up by at least 30,000 men. We have had no action since ye 19 of April which was very bloody. They, ye Regulars, came out in ye night, silently up Cambridge river, and got almost to Concord before day, so that ye country had a very short time to get out. Had we had one hour longer not a soul of those blood-thirsty creatures would ever have reached Boston. However, they got a dire drubbing so that they have not played ye Yankee tune since. We have lost a number of brave men but we have killed, taken and rendered justice, I believe, at least 8 to 1, and I believe such a spirit never was, everybody striving to excel. We have no Tories, saving what is now shut up in Boston or gone off. There hath not been as yet any stopping of ye trade, so I would have you get a load of molasses as good and cheap and as quick as you can and proceed home. If you have not sold and ye markets are bad where you are, have liberty to proceed any other ways, either to ye Mole, Jamaica, or to make a fresh bottom, or anything else that you may think likely to help ye voyage, but always to keep your money in your hands.

A year later, by June, 1776, the Derby fleet was being outfitted as privateers. The ninety-ton schooner *Sturdy Beggar* was armed with six carriage guns, and her crew increased to twenty-five men. The Massachusetts Council on June thirteenth gave   *111*

The *Grand Turk* served as a home-away-from-home for many Salem apprentices making their first voyage. She was owned by "King" Derby, who sent her to Africa, then to the Dutch East Indies and China for cargo. Built for privateer work, she was fast, brought home a great amount of tea, silks and nankeens.

Peter Lander his commission to command the vessel and "to make Reprisals on the Enemys of the united Colonys of North America agreeable to the Laws and Regulations of this Country."

The twelve-gun *Ranger* followed *Sturdy Beggar,* and took four Jamaican ships that carried 733 hogsheads of sugar. It became both patriotic and profitable for Mr. Derby to send the other vessels to sea as privateers. There were 158 armed vessels equipped at Salem during the Revolution, and of that number Derby owned twenty-five, and held shares in twice as many. He emerged from the war as one of the wealthiest men in New England.

Soon after the war, one of his sons, Elias Hasket Derby, took over the business. He vastly expanded the fleet and, although he had never gone to sea and lacked formal training, he designed the new ships himself. He also started the navigation class for Derby apprentices that was to produce many famous Salem shipmasters.

The class was conducted in the counting-house when the regular day's work was finished. The principal instructor was Captain Jonathan Archer, a veteran master who had retired from the sea. He explained the use of the sextant, and often had recourse to a big, ornately mounted globe of the world while he described lunar distance and the determination of longitude.

The boys learned the constellations, repeated over and over the names of the first-magnitude stars. They told themselves as they went home at night after class that the midnight position of a star altered by an hour every fifteen days. Heads back, staring aloft, they walked in imagination with Columbus, and Galileo, and Magellan.

An old brig named *Rose* that ran in the West Indies trade was used as a training ship for Derby's apprentices. They worked aboard as captain's clerks, and then, as they qualified, were assigned as supercargoes to other vessels. The most eagerly sought assignment was to a ship in the East Indies trade.

Thomas Handasyd Perkins possessed unusual qualities, or he, a Bostoner, would not have been given the supercargo's job aboard the Derby ship *Astrea*. He was twenty-four, but he had already been at sea for years, was a canny and thoroughly experienced trader, could assume a great amount of the work in port and relieve the master, Captain James Magee.

Astrea was a full-rigged ship that had served as a privateer in the Revolution, carried the news of the signing of the peace in April, 1783, to America. When she sailed for the East Indies, she was loaded at Derby Wharf with 32,000 pounds of butter, forty-eight barrels of beef, fifty barrels of salmon, 1,792 gallons of rum and 6,300 pounds of codfish; 336 barrels of flour and fifty of tar, these probably picked up in coastal trade from southern ports; 8,933 pounds of spermaceti candles, very likely from Nantucket; a hundred tons of bar iron from Russia, 56 pipes of wine from Madeira and France and 72 barrels of beer from Philadelphia.

She took, too, nine kegs of snuff from Newburyport, a phaeton, and a lot of harness and saddlery made by Folger Pope and James Bott of Salem. Then, Perkins found as he studied the manifest, there were a lot of small items, and "adventures" that included thousands of pounds of ginseng and more than $30,000 in specie, all packed in boxes and bags.

Astrea cleared from Salem on February 17, 1789, and 140 days later was abeam of Java Head. She entered Batavia on July thirteenth and went to the anchor. Another Derby ship, *Three Sisters,* was already there, had been waiting for two weeks to get permission from the Dutch officials to discharge cargo.

Perkins went aboard *Three Sisters* and talked with her supercargo, Samuel Blanchard. They held several long discussions under the poop awning. The Dutchmen were all very pleasant, Blanchard said, and generous with their square-face gin and cheroots. But since *Three Sisters* had been here, a British ship had landed her cargo and sold it, made a tidy profit. It was time that American ships were allowed the same privileges.

Perkins and Blanchard took great care with their manners

when they went ashore. The young men wore their best nankeen suits, highest stocks and biggest shoe buckles. They hired a carriage at the water-steps and rode in style to call upon the governor. That gentleman and the *Edelheers,* the members of the council, accepted their invitations to dinner. Patience was needed, and several dinner invitations, then permission to discharge cargo was given.

Perkins kept a journal while his ship was at Batavia. He described it as a tremendous center of trade where American ships could find a very profitable market, and where the power of the once great Dutch East India Company was rapidly declining. He wrote:

> Batavia, which is the warehouse of the Dutch East India Company, and the most important by far of all their possessions round the Cape of Good Hope, is about fifty leagues from the entrance of the Straits of Sunda and about twelve leagues from Bantam. It has a fine harbor, which is well defended from the winds by the many small islands which surround it. The latitude of Batavia is 6° south, and about 106° east longitude. It is at this time well guarded by a stone wall, which is well built, and about twelve feet high. These walls are well stored with guns and the necessary appendages, which are always kept in order in case of necessity. The bastions are so laid out, that they would be serviceable as well against an insurrection as an invasion.
>
> The one or the other they would have great reason to fear, had either the Chinese, who were inhumanely cut off here, or the original inhabitants, who have always been under the lash of the present possessors, courage enough to retaliate; but fortunately for the Dutch, they have people to deal with, in the Chinese, who do not appear to have the passions which govern men in general. They appear to have no resentment in their composition.

115

PORTS OF CALL

Perkins had a hard time repressing his own resentment when ashore. It was local law that an oncoming carriage occupied by a foreigner pull over to the side of the road and stop when a Dutch official's carriage approached. This, as a free and extremely independent Bay Colony man, Perkins considered to be ridiculous. His Puritan background also caused him to be critical of cockfights and the betting that accompanied them, and the promiscuous chewing of betel nut by most of the native population. He confined his criticism to his journal, though, and made it brief. The wealth to be made here through trade claimed nearly all of his thought, and he wrote:

There are said to be forty thousand Chinese in Batavia and its vicinity. They are governed by their own officers, but are all restricted to the general outlines of the Dutch policy. Many of them are immensely rich, and enter very largely into trade; have stores in town, and elegant country seats without the gates. They parade about in their carriages with a great degree of state, and seem to feel their consequence. They are the principal mechanics, and the best husbandmen. Their merchants deal for the largest and the most trifling article; for the same man who will sell you to the amount of fifty thousand dollars will bring you a pot of sweetmeats which cost a couple of ducatoons.

Great care, however, is to be used in purchasing from them; for they are in some instances employed as spies upon the conduct of strangers by the Dutch Company; and in others they will deceive you in whatever they sell, if they find you a green hand; so that it is necessary to have one's eye well about one to deal with these people, the character of whom is to me unfathomable.

The Chinese have a free trade to Batavia, where they bring tea, china, japanned wares, nankins, silks, &c., and take, in return, Spanish dollars and ducatoons, though the former are preferred.

Spices, bird's-nests, pepper, tin, sugars, coffee, candy, beeswax, oil, hides, burning-canes, ratans, sandal-wood, and, when there is probability of scarcity in China, rice, which will always pay a good freight, are exported.

Perkins, while he was tremendously impressed by the Chinese, gave a lot of attention to the people he called "Moormen." He meant, of course, the Malays, who were the original inhabitants of Java, and who still, despite Dutch rule, were powerful in their own right. Perkins wrote:

There is at Batavia a great medley of inhabitants. The principal persons in business, after the Hollanders, are the Moormen. Many of them are very rich. They have an ease of address and an air of good breeding which one would not expect to find in their country-men. They are the best shaped of any of the Eastern nations whom I observed while there; their complexion nearly the same as that of the aboriginals of America; their features regular and well-set, with the most piercing eye of any people I ever saw. Their religion is Mohametanism. They carry on a great trade to the different islands in the Indian seas, and by their traffic make great fortunes.

Astrea went from Batavia to China to pick up cargo for home. She was at the Whampoa Anchorage in the Pearl River below Canton when *Three Sisters* arrived. They had both finished the complicated formalities with the Chinese merchants at Canton and were taking tea aboard when on October fifth they were joined by two other American ships. These both flew the Derby house flag and were *Atlantic* and *Light Horse*.

There were before the Derby ships cleared for home fifteen American vessels in the anchorage. Among them was *Columbia,* the

ship which had sailed from Boston in October, 1787, for the northwest coast of America by way of Cape Horn. She had spent a year on the coast, bartering for furs with the Indians. Now she was homeward-bound, and would be the first American vessel to circumnavigate the world.

The trade with the Orient brought a large amount of wealth to Salem. The town's appearance changed a great deal as a result; many new houses were built in the first years of the nineteenth century. The rich merchants and shipowners had decided to move back from the waterfront.

They left the old houses whose hand-rifted clapboards had turned almost black with age. The space around them was all cobblestoned. No trees, no grass or flowers grew there. But, over on Essex and Chestnut Streets, and facing Washington Square, were huge elms. There was space for front and back yards, and gardens, and stables. The area became very popular.

Samuel McIntire, a man born and raised in Salem, built most of the new houses, and designed them. He used Flemish-laid brick instead of the old-style white clapboard. His plans generally allowed three stories, with four rooms to a floor, and a hip roof. The front doors were arched, and embellished by fanlights and side lights. Elliptical porches supported by Ionic columns gave dignity and grace to the house fronts. McIntire had quite completely discarded the Puritan tradition of plain lines and economy of construction.

His interior designs were in the Adams style. He told his clients that the rooms should be decorated in rich-textured wallpaper imported from England. Carpets should cover the entire floor. He used ornamental moulding from the floors to the ceilings, and suggested that the heavy furniture pieces of maple and oak and cherry wood, made in the early colonial years, be put away in back rooms.

PORTS OF CALL

Mahogany pieces that were ornately worked and took a high polish were purchased. They were installed in the new houses with teak and camphorwood and sandalwood pieces that came from the Orient. Chinese screens were set among them, and table covers, bowls and vases.

The Oriental influence was very strong. The wives and daughters of the wealthy merchant families felt it. Their dresses were made of Chinese silks, or fine Indian cottons. They wore shawls of white camel's hair, the borders worked in green, blue or red designs in the shape of a broad palm leaf. When they went to routs or the cotillions at Hamilton Hall, they put on pearl teardrop earrings and red cornelian necklaces. Gold bangles made in Calcutta and Madras were at their wrists; cobweb muslin was in their bodices.

The Orient invaded New England parlors. This fine highboy has a Chinese motif. It is circa 1800, made of maple and pine.

120

SALEM

The male population of the town responded just about as much to the call of the Orient. The Salem seal carried the motto, "To the uttermost gulf of teeming Ind." The Marine Society, formed in 1799, held an annual ceremony that lasted all day and was featured by a parade of the members dressed in Chinese costumes.

A local boy was picked each year for singular honor in the parade. He rode around town in a silk-swathed palanquin borne on the shoulders of men dressed as natives of India. This was much more than a sign of individual respect. It was done to show all of the Salem boys that they were the crews, the mates, the masters and shipowners of the next generation. With them grown to manhood, Salem would continue to prosper.

The parade was led through town by a member of the Marine Society dressed in the bright silk clothing of a Chinese mandarin, and he wore a Chinese mask over his face. The boy chosen to ride in the palanquin wore the robes of a maharajah. There was a large ruby on the front of his turban; a gold-crusted dagger was in his belt; his boots were made of scarlet leather. The main body of the society members marched behind him, each bearing some valuable piece of Oriental ware, silk screens, ivory statuettes, bowls and vases.

When the parade was finished, the palanquin, the robes and all of the Oriental objects were put back on display in the society's building on Essex Street. But the marchers kept on celebrating. They were served a large meal, and a lot of toasts were drunk.

Ships in the East Indies trade lay tiered three-deep at the Salem wharves during the 1800–1810 period. The custom house entered more than 1,000 ships, and the trade for the port was $7 million. The warehouses were full of teas and silks from China, *121* pepper from Sumatra, coffee from Arabia, tallow from Madagascar, hemp from Luzon, cotton from Bombay, palm oil from the west coast of Africa, figs, raisins and almonds from the Mediterranean, wine from Portugal and the Madeiras, salt from Cadiz, ivory and gum copal from Zanzibar, sperm oil from the South Seas, whale oil from the Arctic and Antarctic and hides, wool and rubber from South America.

The average dimensions of the Salem vessels engaged in foreign trade were a hundred feet in length, twenty-eight-foot beam and a tonnage of slightly more than three hundred when loaded. Most of them were built on the North River, near Medford, and purposely kept small. Their shallow draft was designed for work among the uncharted reefs of the Malay archipelago, where the ships picked up the incredibly lucrative pepper cargoes. Salem harbor was shallow, too, and over in Boston there was only twelve feet of water at Long Wharf at low tide.

But many of the new generation of apprentices concerned themselves with the China trade more than anything else. Salem's monopoly of the Sumatran pepper trade was being broken as other shipowners found the supply ports. Deep-draft ships could be bought or chartered, and cargoes delivered at New York instead of Salem or Boston, and for the same profit. Thomas Handasyd Perkins had set the example which should be followed. He had established himself in the tea business at Canton as soon as he had finished his commitment to Mr. Derby.

The English were already well established along the Pearl River, at Whampoa Anchorage, and seven miles above it, at Canton. The Chinese emperor by official decree in 1720 allowed the English and other foreigners trade rights. John P. Cushing of Boston, and Captain William Sturgis were among the first Americans to go into business there. Then, in 1818, Samuel Russell

The calm-faced merchant portrayed by a Chinese artist was Eshing, a Yankee favorite. He was known as "the most candid man in Canton" by the foreigners who around 1800 traded there.

joined the foreign colony, and Phillip Ammidon. The various members of the Low family, from Salem, were next, and all of them made money.

Life for the foreign traders at Canton during the early 1800s was reasonably comfortable. The British-owned East India Company had not yet increased to an enormous amount the opium it smuggled each season into the country aboard its ships, and the entire colony was on good terms with the local viceroy. But the immensely wealthy organization—known commonly in the Orient as John Company—had nothing but disdain for the local Chinese officials.

The Imperial officer in charge of foreign customs collection at Canton was named Hai Kwan Pu. The English thought that was very funny, so they made it into Hoppo. But Hoppo was a Manchu, a court grandee, a member of the Imperial clan, and a relative of the Emperor. Sooner or later, word of John Company's smuggling would reach Peking. That and the slights offered Hai Kwan Pu could cause a great deal of trouble, and end in the dismissal of all foreigners from China.

Young American apprentices assigned to the trading firms in Canton, particularly the Salem contingent, which had been given long training, took extreme care to be polite with the Chinese they met. They dealt almost completely with the thirteen Co-hong merchants permitted by the Emperor to conduct foreign trade. Other than those astute and remote men, the apprentices only came in contact with company clerks, translators and servants. Their life was severely confined except for the summer months, when they were allowed to travel by sampan to the old and frivolous city of Macao, at the mouth of the Pearl River and under the casual rule of the Portuguese.

During their time at Canton, apprentices and their superiors were kept within an area that had a thousand-foot frontage on the river, and a maximum depth of a quarter of a mile. The foreign factories, so-called, were set back about fifty yards from the river bank. The factories were really stout, three-story stone buildings that held showrooms, treasure vaults and living quarters for the staffs. John Company took up twice as much space as any other nation or group of merchants and paid £20,000 a year rental for it. But the company maintained a walled English garden, a billiard room and a library. An invitation to dinner was keenly sought by the Salem apprentices, and broke the awful pall of homesickness.

The Salem youths who were determined to stay in the Canton trade spent their spare time studying Chinese. They learned in exact detail the qualities of the various kinds of tea traded and shipped home. When an American vessel arrived at the Whampoa Anchorage, they went down and boarded her, talked at length with the master, mates and crew. If it were a Salem ship, they received a thick bundle of letters, and had a larger bundle to send home. They stayed aboard overnight, and it was very hard for them to leave, go into the boat that would take them back to Canton.

But the tea trade was making a number of the old Salem families solidly rich. Faster ships were being put into the service for the 15,000-mile drive around Cape Horn. There was talk of a new design that would have concave bows and raked masts, be called a clipper. Some of the far-sighted merchants left and went to New York, and set up in business on South Street. This was to be the center of the clipper trade, and not Salem.

Members of the Low family were among the group that transferred to New York. They built homes on Brooklyn Heights with views out over the Narrows, watched their ships bringing in the prime tea cargoes. The Lows had cousins, brothers, uncles on the China-side. The family was famous.

The apprentices at Two Suy Hong, the American factory at Canton, created a ditty about the Lows. It was sung in ship's chantey style:

> Old Low, old Low's son,
> Never saw so many since the world begun!

But the Lows didn't mind. They were, in fact, pleased. It was already obvious to them that Salem, with her shallow harbor, was doomed as an international port of call. Her trade would move elsewhere, some of it to Boston, but the greater part to New York, and Philadelphia, and Baltimore, where the first of the new clippers were being built.

The Lows and the other transplanted families kept their ties intact, made periodic visits back to Salem. But in the 1840s the town wharves were nearly deserted. A few fishermen and an occasional lumber schooner tied up there, and that was all. The custom house was so quiet, gulls could be heard dropping clams on the pavement outside. The fine homes around Washington Square had begun to look a bit shabby. Salem belonged to the past, and lived upon her memories.

126

CHAPTER 5

Bristol and Newport

THEY HAD LIED TO PHILIP, and broken the treaties, and stolen his land. When he led his people of the Wampanoag tribe and the other Indians of the Narragansett region in revolt in 1675, the colonists furiously fought him. The revolt was crushed. Philip was killed while almost alone, deserted by his tribesmen. His hands were cut from his body. He was quartered, and beheaded. His head was hung from a pike on the gateway wall of Plymouth Fort.

But the Pilgrim wrath was lasting, and terrible. Philip's widow Nanuskooke and his nine-year-old son were kept in Plymouth jail for a month after his death while their fate was decided. Most of the colonists wanted them executed. It was argued that the best thing to do was get the boy out of the way before he was big enough to avenge his father. The question was finally referred to a pair of clergymen, although John Eliot, a major figure in the colony, had asked the General Court for the captives' release.

The two clergymen involved, John Cotton of Plymouth and Samuel Arnold of Marshfield, made public on September 6, 1676, a letter which in murky religious language demanded death for the son. But the members of the General Court thought that banishment to slavery was severe enough, and the sale would bring a bit of profit to the colony.

Nanuskooke and the boy were shipped on March 20, 1677, to Bermuda as slaves. They were never heard of again. Philip's land, 7,000 acres around Narragansett Bay that included his beloved homesite on Mount Hope, was sold in 1679 to the Plymouth Colony for an annual quit-rent of seven beaver skins. The quit-rent was supposed to be paid at Windsor Palace each St. John's Day.

The General Court turned over the land for £1,100 to a Boston syndicate, and on September 1, 1681, the settlement held its first town meeting. The settlement was on the easterly side of a peninsula and close to the head of a deep harbor. Another peninsula, which kept the Indian name of Poppasquash, was across the harbor to the eastward, and protected it from the southwest storms that swept Narragansett Bay. Islands out at the harbor mouth served the same purpose against the Atlantic winter gales.

The settlers of the new town named it Bristol, after the great slaving port in England. The name was chosen in all probability because of nostalgic longing. But it had an astonishingly accurate prophetic quality.

Bristol and the neighboring settlement of Newport, thirteen miles away, were part of what had been known as the Providence
128 Plantations. These were founded between 1636 and 1643 by peo-

ple from Massachusetts who came seeking religious and political freedom. They offered haven to Quakers and religious dissenters of all sorts, established a strong liberal tradition. Newport was built on the lovely island of Aquidneck, a mile from the mainland, and served by an often balky ferry.

Both Bristol and Newport became thriving ports in the latter part of the seventeenth century. They carried on a brisk trade along the coast in timber, rum and furs, dealing with the Connecticut and Long Island towns and with the Dutch in New Amsterdam. There was also a large overseas trade, and in the West Indies a keen demand was found for Bristol reds, the famous local onions, and Narragansett pacers. The smooth-gaited, chunky and powerful horses could withstand the Caribbean climate and were welcomed by the planters and their wives for use on the island trails and in the cane fields.

Newport competed successfully with Boston as a New England port. Her population increased to 7,000 people, and her merchants built fine homes on the profits made at sea. The liberal tradition still endured, and in 1726 the descendants of Pilgrims and Puritans attended the first service in Trinity Episcopal Church. The church spire carried the royal crown as recognition of colonial status, and the parishioners were well dressed, very much at their ease. But the Quaker meeting-house, the oldest in America, dated from 1699, and had a devout and large congregation.

Then, in 1748, with money furnished by a pair of merchants, Abraham Redwood and Henry Collins, the Redwood Library was opened. It was the first public library in America. The Jewish people who had been attracted to the town gave the design of their Touro Synagogue to Peter Harrison, the superb local architect. He built it in 1763, a year after he finished the Brick Mar-   *129* ket. The market building was inspired by London's Old Somerset House, whose architect had been the great seventeenth-century master, Inigo Jones.

The Touro Synagogue had a rather severe exterior. Harrison had contained nearly all of the beauty to the interior. That cool delicacy and grace of line made of it a magnificent house of worship.

Less religious men were proud of the fact that William Mayes, Sr. had been granted as early as 1687 a license to keep a tavern. It was called The White Horse Tavern, and although the

The Touro Synagogue, built in 1763 in Newport, is one of the most beautiful structures of its kind. It was designed by Peter Harrison, who also planned the Redwood Library and Old Brick Market.

Great delicacy and grace of line were achieved in the interior of the synagogue by Harrison's talent.

name was not original Mayes served very good toddies, flips and hot buttered rums. He could put on the table at short order tautog chowder, roast duck, baked eel, and venison, elk and bear meat.

Bristol, while her population was only a little over 1,000, strove hard to keep abreast of Newport. Her merchants and her   *131* shipowners and the people of the town in general ignored almost completely the colony's tradition of liberalism. They violated it with a kind of nonchalant cynicism unusual if not unique in the New England character.

What was known as King Philip's War had cost the Plymouth Colony and the Massachusetts Bay Colony the sum of £100,000 and 600 men, who represented one-tenth of their fighting force. It had not been difficult for the General Court to reach a resolution to sell 500 Indian slaves to the West Indies. Not nearly enough money had been made from the sale of Philip's land.

Right after the war, when the supply was plentiful, the average price for a slave was thirty-two silver shillings or, in barter, twelve bushels of corn, or one hundred pounds of wool. When the paper currency depreciated in value around 1750, and the supply was low, £50 could be received occasionally for a healthy young male. The Indians did not propagate well in captivity, though. They were proud, intractable. Many of the Bristol people admitted that they were afraid of them. It became common practice in Bristol to trade Indians for Negroes brought in by ship from Virginia or the West Indies.

There were in 1774 only sixteen pure-bred Wampanoags left in Bristol. The town, without much conscious knowledge of it, had actively entered the slave trade. She made a very considerable profit from the sale of both Indians and Negroes. When the supply of Indians was exhausted, she kept on, and extended the traffic to Africa.

Her ships, loaded with leg irons and rum in addition to cheap trade goods, sailed out past the islands named Patience, Prudence, Hope and Despair. Their captains carried orders for the Slave Coast.

BRISTOL AND NEWPORT

Most of the ships were fast topsail schooners, built with a shallow draft that allowed them only a six-foot space below the main deck. The cargo was stowed here, and on one voyage the 300-ton ship *Ann* took 184 hogsheads, twenty-six tierces and thirty-three barrels of new rum. It had been distilled in Bristol, and cost ten cents a gallon to make. The total investment, ship and cargo was less than $15,000, and was insured. The crew usually mustered twelve hands, with wages ranging from eight dollars a month for a deck boy to thirty dollars a month for the master. Slave prices, upon delivery in Cuba or South Carolina, greatly varied with the condition of the market, but the profit was never much less than one hundred percent.

The ships went to anchor in the Gulf of Guinea while they gathered their cargoes. That sometimes took weeks. The crews were not permitted ashore. Painting, scraping, soogeying and the renewing of gear were soon finished despite the oppressive, terrible heat. There was nothing left to do except watch the carpenter build the slave deck that gave exactly sixteen inches headroom, and the barricade that was intended to keep murder-minded slaves from the quarterdeck.

Seams opened on a ship's main deck as the tar liquefied. Men doused each other with buckets of sea water, or lay motionless under the awning. But it did little good. The ship still yanked at the anchor cable with the impact of the long, low rollers. The green jungle still stank, and from it rose with the noxious, grayish vapor gnats, mosquitoes and giant flies. The tall and lanky blue-black Kroo men, who had won their freedom by their skill as boatmen, stood stiffly on the beach. They had drawn up the ship's longboat among the mangrove roots, and waited for the captain and the first load of slaves.

They did not speak to each other, and they did not gesture. *133*

PORTS OF CALL

The ship's crew, staring at them in bitter jealousy, were sure that the Kroo men could not feel the sting of the insect bites. All day, and most of the night, the sand-ridden, parching *harmattan* wind blew. The sand covered the decks, entered the mess-kids, and the crew, as they tried to sleep, shook it from their hair and bodies.

Then, brought in the longboat, the slaves started to come aboard. There were flat-nosed and very dark Mandingos, and Fulas with round heads and skins the color of apricots, and people with high cheekbones and sharp, straight features who were called Ashantis, and others who were Bibis, and Mabis, and Fous.

The crew learned the tribal names and characteristics fast. They were curious, because this meant leaving here, and money, and home. They listened while the mate explained about the palaver houses ashore where the trading had taken place, and the barracoons where the slaves were kept. The black folks' own kings often sold them, the mate said. Rum was almighty powerful on this coast.

The same sort of disregard for the past prevailed in Newport as well as Bristol during the Revolution. A force of 5,000 British troops occupied Newport in 1776, and burned, looted and badly mistreated a number of the citizens. There were three regiments of Tory Americans in the Newport garrison, the Prince of Wales Volunteers, the King's American Regiment and the Loyal New Englanders.

But many Rhode Islanders defied the British. They manned the privateers and enlisted in the Continental Navy. Hundreds of them served with Washington's armies throughout the war. The state recruited a regiment of slaves, whose pay was divided between their owners and themselves. A bounty of $180 was also paid the owners, and the slaves were promised their freedom within three years.

BRISTOL AND NEWPORT

Then, at the end of the war, Bristol went back to the slave trade. She was joined by Newport. Profits were high, and the market was wide open, although in 1787 the Assembly banned all participation in foreign traffic. The penalty for violation of the law was £100 per slave, and £1,000 per ship. There was no attempt made at strict enforcement, and the framers of the Constitution, worried by the threats of South Carolina and Georgia to secede, had compromised the slavery issue.

A letter from a young Bristol sailor while aboard the slave brig *Sally* in Havana showed only boredom compounded with a trace of homesickness. Slave-running had become as monotonous to him as hauling a load of Bristol reds and Narragansett pacers. He wrote:

Havaner, Jany. 17, 1804

My dear Parence:

I now take the opertunity to In form you that I am well at present, hopeing that these lines will find you the same. I am a frade it will not hold so long. Capt. Gladding talks of heaving the Brig out a gin to grave her, for wee do not no when we shall git out of this durty Howl. you may not look for us until you see us for God noes when wee shall git out of this place. . . . I have been gorn so much longer than I expected I have nearly got out of Clothing and Clothing is verry dear heaar and verry sces and tell Betsey to tell her Father if hee sells eny more trousis such as mine wus hee will never git to Heaven in the world hereafter. . . .

I roght 2 letters by Capt. Cartwright bound to Newbryport. I expected by Capt. Bradford or Capt. Munrow to have a letter but I have rec. none as yet. I was glad to hear that my Father had moved out of that old rattrap for I was afraid it would Blow down upon them, and tell Unkle Throop I shall beware of the third time for he cheated me once with an old gun out of 9 shillings and one Bitt and the second time he cheated me was with

135

an old bantum Hen that warnt worth ninepence and charged me one and sixpence. If Unkle Sam asks after me ask him if he dont want me to help him pitch of hay agin? Wee all keep up a good hart. In hope to git away some time or other. remember my love to Grand dady and grand mamma Waldron and to all of the Family and so no more at present I remain your loveing Son un till Deth

Richard Waldron

Many of the slaver captains had already become tired of the long waits at Havana. They had enough of that on the Guinea coast while they bartered with the traders. Here the sleepy-eyed but cunning Spanish officials took weeks to make up their minds, then asked for enormous bribes. The Bristol and Newport ships made landfall much more frequently on the mainland coast. They risked seizure by a Revenue Marine cutter, but it was worth it to put a cargo directly ashore somewhere near Charleston.

Captain Charles Clark, master of the Bristol slave brig *Nancy,* landed a load of slaves on a desolate winter beach, then took them on foot into Charleston. This was in January, 1802, and he brought the shivering, stumbling people half-naked through the city without being challenged. The citizens were accustomed to the sight. Some nights, columns of 200 or 300 newly landed slaves were marched from the beaches. Captain Clark understood that since New Year's Day about five hundred had entered. He hoped to get a good price for his lot before the market was glutted.

There were twenty-two firms in Charleston by 1807 that engaged wholly in slave-dealing. They maintained close contact with their business associates in the North and were among the first

136

to make Newport popular as a summer resort. Upon their return home in the fall, their description of Mount Hope Bay, the surf breaking in silver descent on the Aquidneck rocks, and the delights of walks past the old, ivy-covered mill decided other prosperous southerners to attempt the journey.

Newport, no longer the active port she had been before the Revolution, her sea trade taken by Providence, welcomed them. The Charleston merchants passed a great deal of time in the sunlight on the promenade where the southwest breeze stirred the lace on their wives' bonnets, and, below, their children played happily in the surf warmed by the Gulf Stream. The talk was of the weekly Jockey Club races back home, the balls given by the Saint Cecilia Society and dinner parties at the Marine Hotel.

But a brig came up-channel from seaward, bound for Bristol. Her sails were chafed and patched. Hull and decks needed paint. The crew moved slouching, listless when the mate shouted, were slow to haul braces, a sheet or halyard. An odor spread from her in the warmth of the afternoon. It held the reek of stale urine, defecation and wood soaked with the sweat of sick, close-jammed bodies.

The wives of the Charleston merchants stared around, and then quickly lowered their eyes. Their husbands spoke of a seaweed sloop whose crew raked the stuff from the rocks close inshore. But one of the Charleston men lost his temper. He cursed, and said that such a ship was too foul to be ordered home. Once the slaves were out of her, she should have been sold—for what she would bring in that condition—or burned on some Windward Passage beach in Cuba. It was sheer stupidity to return her here, and damned poor business.

There were a number of people in both Newport and Bristol who during the War of 1812 were happy to hear Captain Ben

Early view of Newport

Churchill's story. It was a change from the talk about slavers, and how trade in general was being ruined. Churchill served aboard Bristol's famous privateer *Yankee*. He wrote home to report that *Yankee* had taken five prizes. Then he added, "P.S. I lost one of my legs on this cruise."

The ship's carpenter carved him four magnificent spread eagles as compensation, presented them out to sea. When he reached port, Captain Churchill mounted them on the balustrade of his house on Hope Street. His neighbors were proud of him. He was an honest patriot, and said very little about his loss.

He was the kind that was needed around the bay. The

138 slavers, the other kind, couldn't last, no matter the amount of

money they made. Those men thought that freedom was something meant for them alone. But after the war the law would catch up to them, put an end to their black-birding forever.

The prediction was accurate. The Bristol slavers left the trade when the law tightened in the post-war years. Men who had sailed the Guinea coast in handsome, clipper-lined topsail schooners took what work they could get. There was a bad shipping depression. A number of them went to work in the lumber hookers. They hauled huge loads in the ungainly craft from backwoods ports in Maine and South Carolina. Top pay was thirty dollars a month. But they considered themselves lucky. They were out of jail.

CHAPTER 6

⟿ *New York*

IT WAS SEPTEMBER, 1609, when the Dutchmen came in from sea. Their English captain, Henry Hudson, conned the vessel with the sounding lead in use, then went to the anchorage near the western shore of the bay. Vast meadows stretched there, noisy with water fowl. Some of the larger, bolder birds circled the ship, looking for food. Indians stood among the cattails where a small river entered the bay. Hudson and the other officers saw them clearly through the spy-glass.

Hudson waited for slack water to send the pinnace ashore. There was as yet no white man's report about this country, and he was not sure of the Indians. He wanted to be able to get his boat back quickly to the ship. When he gave the order to shove off, the oar blades made ripples that broke the almost perfect 140 reflection of *Half Moon*, twisted the glittering image of her ornamental work and the motionless droop of the big ensign at the stern.

The boat was back soon, but the men rowing without haste. The Indians were friendly, the officer in command of her reported to Hudson. They offered gifts of squash, beans and corn. A cask of gin was hove on deck from the ship's strong room and put in the boat. Hudson went ashore with it. He should talk with friendly Indians. His order from the Dutch East India Company were to find the sea route to China, the fabulous Northwest Passage.

The Indians here did not know anything about that. They were the Raritans, they made Hudson understand. A great river reached to the northward, but they had never gone far along it. Fierce tribes occupied the territory. Not even the Manhattans, the tribe that lived across the bay on the high-hilled island, were their friends.

Hudson studied the immense bay while his officers and the crew were entertained by the Raritans. Their red-dyed scalp locks bobbing, the warriors danced through the evening to the music of drums and bone rattles. Bird designs were painted on their cheeks with delicate care. But their eyes were glazed, vacant from the initial shock of raw, undiluted gin. Behind them in the shadows, the young squaws stood patiently.

The squaws smelled of bear grease, and they had smeared a red mixture of eagle grease and berries on their faces as rouge, darkened their eye sockets with more grease. But, after months at sea, the blond-bearded Dutchmen were quite happy with them. The piece of land where the first night's festivities were held was marked in Dutch maritime history as *Hoeren Hoek*—Whores' Point.

Hudson sailed up the majestic main river as far as present- *141* day Albany. Then he became convinced that it was not a part of the Northwest Passage. He swung clumsy-sailing *Half Moon* around and headed for the sea, to continue his exploration further along the coast. He did not put a boat ashore on the Manhattans' island, and offered the crew no chance for further social activity among the Raritan squaws. Tremendous wealth would come to the man who found the Northwest Passage, and he sought that with almost compulsive eagerness.

But Hudson mentioned in the report he made when he returned to Holland that the Indians "brought us Bevers skinnes and otter skinnes which we bought for Beades, Knives, and Hatchets." Dutch traders marked the fact, and realized the possibilities of the fur trade in the New World. The year after Hudson's voyage, a Dutch ship was sent out to barter for furs. She entered the same great bay, and anchored off the western shore. Some of her crew had sailed with Hudson, and they hurried to visit the Raritans. The rejoicing lasted all night long.

't Fort nieuw Amsterdam op de Manhatans

NEW YORK

Other Dutch vessels followed. Hendrick Christiansen, in command of *Fortune,* and Adrian Block, master of *Tiger,* became leading traders and explorers. Block dared make the dangerous passage up the East River, and it was named *Hellegat*—Hell Gate. He discovered the Housatonic and Connecticut Rivers in 1613, and Rhode Island, and Block Island, which was named for him. His chart was the first to show Manhattan and Long Island as separate islands.

Lower New York Bay was estimated to contain a hundred square miles of shore line, and to be open to the sea for approximately six miles. The natural channel that was to be called the Narrows was about 3,500 feet wide, and from forty-five to one hundred feet deep. The Upper Bay was practically landlocked, and held 650 miles of navigable water. There were Gowanus Creek and Newtown Creek in what the Dutch called Breucklin, and the Harlem River that separated Manhattan from the mainland, and then Newark Bay, and the Passaic and the Hackensack and Raritan Rivers, and the Kill van Kull, and the Arthur Kill, which was rightly the *Achter Kol,* because it lay to the west of Staten Island and was "behind the bay."

Thirteen Dutch shipowners were actively interested in the New World fur trade. They organized in 1614 the New Netherland Company, with a three-year trading monopoly between forty and forty-five degrees north latitude. The charter was not renewed, but a prominent Amsterdam merchant, William Usselinx, sought another from the States General, and it was granted.

It conferred a trading monopoly and the right to colonize in the New World along the west coast of Africa below the Tropic of Cancer. The organization was called the Dutch West India Company, and the colony New Netherland. The director-general, while chosen by the company, had to be confirmed by the States General, the Dutch ruling body.

PORTS OF CALL

The colonists were divided into two classes, those who received transportation, seeds, cattle and the necessities of life for the first two years, and could own their homesteads; and the *bouwlieden*—indentured husbandmen who were forced to work for a stipulated length of time on the company's *bouweries*—farms—or on the farms that belonged to company officials. Trading with outsiders was prohibited, and the export trade held exclusively by the company.

Pieter Minuit took over as director-general of the colony in September, 1626, and settled a new group of immigrants on Manhattan Island. They built thirty houses, and the name was made New Amsterdam. Minuit saw the Manhattan site as the heart of the colony, looking to the forest for trade instead of the sea. He saw the fur trade as secondary and withdrew all but sixteen men from the fort erected on the bank of the Hudson at Albany.

But, as early as 1617, there were at least two Amsterdam commercial groups which sent ships "to fetch furres, wch is all their trade." The New Netherland colony, with its indefinite boundaries, soon proved itself immensely rich as a source of pelts. Communication between the various parts of the colony was easy. There was a water route from Manhattan Island by way of the Hudson and the Mohawk to the rich fur country of the Iroquois. It was also a short voyage from Manhattan through Long Island Sound to the Montauk region where the finest *wampum* and *peage* were made. These furnished the Dutch with a currency that passed readily among many distant tribes.

The early Dutch called the Indian currency *sewan,* but the more common Algonkian name of *wampum* persisted. It was cleverly fashioned by braves of the Montauk tribe from the purple-shaded neck of the big quahog clam. The Dutch established its worth at five shillings a fathom. The stuff called *peage* was made

144

from the smaller, lighter periwinkle shell, and generally was considered worth half as much as wampum.

The Dutch, expanding their trade, moved up the Connecticut River and the other streams flowing into the Sound. Posts were established, and "free traders" worked back and forth among the Indian summer villages, usually set up at the mouths of rivers. The Dutch went further, into the Narragansett country, which supplied beaver and deerskins. There was to the southward the rich fur-bearing valley of the Delaware, which soon became the object of fierce competition between the Dutch, the English and the Swedes.

The most valuable furs were prime beaver, taken during the winter months when the animal was in heavy coat. The raw side of the pelt was scraped by the Indian trappers, and the roots of long hair dropped out. Several of these prime pelts were sewn together and worn for a short time by the Indians as robes. The skins became soft, impregnated with grease and the fur was smooth and downy. Summer beaver had the tendency to be thick-skinned, and to bear little fur, and was not much good for hats. Dry beaver—pelts that had never been worn—got the smallest prices.

The price in the Amsterdam and London markets around 1630 was twenty shillings a pound for prime beaver, and somewhat higher in Paris. The average cost was three shillings a pound. But the hat-makers were shrewd in their estimates of the pelts offered, and paid various prices for different qualities of fur. It was only in the 1670s that a popular demand for other furs, raccoon, marten, skunk, weasel, otter and fox began.

The Dutch West India Company, through its patroon system, tried to make the colony self-supporting. With huge grants of land in the Hudson River valley, the patroons carried on exten- *145* sive agricultural work. But many of them received more immigrants than they could use profitably in farming. So they entered into illegal hunting beyond the borders of their estates, and started trade with the Indians, forbidden, too, by the regulations of the colony. Then a lot of the artisans and other people in the settlements decided that life would be much better in the wilderness, away from both the patroons and the company.

These illegal traders took the name of *bosch-lopers,* or "woodsrunners." They were a rough and tough and often desperate lot. Dutch law was very strictly observed, and all trade was supposed to be done at the company posts. Fur had become the currency of the colony; the States General counted on it for regular revenue. But the *bosch-lopers* went into the woods wherever they could pick up pelts.

They ranged westward from the Hudson valley to the Delaware, and eastward to the Connecticut. They went up the Mohawk to trade with the Iroquois, and they dealt with the tribes to the north, in French territory. Most of their trading goods, beads, knives, kettles, mattocks, axes and all kinds of ironware were bought at the storehouses of the Dutch West India Company. Their packs of furs were sent eventually to New Amsterdam and became part of the colony's shipments to Holland. They also bought, though, guns and ammunition at the company stores, and sold those to the Iroquois, a very dangerous people even when armed with bows and arrows.

Bosch-lopers sold alcohol to the braves along with the guns, powder and shot. They concocted a number of drinks, which they named "Hans in the Cellar," "Bride's Tears," "Little Mill," "Ship's Sails," "Great and Small Fisheries," and "The Abbot and His Monks." Their favorite remained Barbados rum, which they refused to pollute with water, and called "Kill Devil." Sometimes,

146

after a hard trading session among the Iroquois and several applications of Kill Devil, a *bosch-loper* became a bit careless and let a brave get in back of him. Then he lost his scalp, his weapons and his trade pack.

But the *bosch-lopers* were indefatigable. They were often able to buy many more pelts than the company traders. The veterans visited the Indians in their villages and while the warriors were out hunting. A number of them spoke the various tribal dialects, and kept squaws whom they visited with regularity. An early company report regarding trade along the Delaware River stated that only thirty pelts had been gathered, and in the same period *bosch-lopers* had secured more than 500 skins. Another company report, made in 1624, declared that two illegal traders sold £5,000 worth of furs to an English ship.

Fort Orange, at Albany, continued to be throughout the seventeenth century the greatest fur market in America. An average of one million pounds of prime beaver skins were brought down each year to the post by the Iroquois or the *bosch-lopers*. The men who traded for these pelts were some of the wealthiest on the continent.

Albany furnished many of the beaver skins sent to England, and practically all that were sent to Holland, including those delivered from Holland to Russia. Prices declined during the Restoration period of English rule, but the profits were always enough to bring more traders to invest in the market. The movement of beaver cargoes from the West down the Mohawk to Albany in Iroquois canoes, and then down the Hudson in smacks and sloops and pinks and snows to Manhattan, never stopped.

The Dutch had located their town at the lower end of Manhattan, looking out over the bay. They named their fort William, after William of Orange, and built blockhouses for the garrison, *147* and a wall. The wall was ten feet high, palisaded and sodded, and the two gateways in it strongly arched. There were several churches, and a number of windmills, many gilt weathervanes.

Most of the houses were of yellow brick, and the rest meticulously whitewashed. The roofs were high-peaked, with gable ends, and crow-stepped. The houses along Wall Street, in what became the best neighborhood, were surrounded by gardens, with trees in trim rows and paved walks that were swept each morning.

There were high-backed chairs and strong, handsome tables in the prosperous homes, and big oak cabinets, and tiles brought from Holland around the fireplaces. Fresh white sand was

sprinkled across the floors of the "great rooms" where the families usually gathered at the end of the day. The men, heavy, flush-faced, proud and crafty, sat stolid and watched their wives and daughters and servants still at work. They wore broad, black hats, and dark clothing, square-toed shoes or boots. The long clay pipes they smoked were filled with Virginia tobacco accepted in coast-wise barter trade. They drank "Hollands," pale yellow gin from crockery bottles.

While they liked to see their womenfolk at work until candle-lighting time, they abhorred what they called "hurry-scurry," and thought all household duties should be conducted in absolute quiet. Their favorite poet was a fellow Hollander named Jacob Cats. They admired him for what they described as his "common sense." When they visited the town taverns soon after their suppers were finished, they drank more gin, then ate cheese, sausage and biscuit. The *bosch-lopers* had a term for these townsmen, who were the principal figures in the colony.

They called them *Hogen Mogen,* which was a corruption of *Hoogenmogenheiden,* and meant "High Mightinesses." The backwoods traders used it in contempt more than anything else. Still, on occasion, the New Amsterdam officials and merchants could unbend.

Pinkster, which was Whitsunday, was a great Dutch holiday, and joyously celebrated. Jugs of punch were passed from hand to hand in the narrow town streets. The Negro slaves joined in the singing, dancing and cavorting. The garrison troops paraded on the common outside the walls; trumpets were sounded, drums sharply rapped. Boys played *hoeky*—pranks on each other. There was a lot of splashing around in the fresh-water pound where the boys skated during the winter. Gingerbread, cakes, cider and birch beer were served to the young in vast amounts.

Otherwise life in New Amsterdam was almost oppressively staid and serious. Small boys and girls dressed very much like their parents, and were supposed to act like them. The massive family Bible, with silver clasps and corner-pieces, was read every evening, and often was quoted. Sabbath was a day of absolute piety, when children were not supposed to run, or play, or laugh.

When in the summer of 1664 a squadron of five English frigates entered the harbor and without fight took over New Amsterdam and the colony, there was a considerable change. The first royal governor, Colonel Richard Nicolls, was a gay and convivial man with a passion for horse-racing. He established in 1665 at Little Plain, near Hempstead on Long Island, a track called Salisbury Plain and a course he named New Market in memory of the famous course in England.

Nieuw Amsterdam was huddled in 1640 near the end of Manhattan Island, the settlement close around the fort at the left. The windmill ground corn, the flagstaff crosspieces helped lookouts who watched for ships, and the gallows swung men high. The governor's house was next to the peak-roofed church with the windvane, and the tavern located on the other side of town.

The plain was sixteen miles long, and four wide, and very smooth. For years, the best horses to be found in the colony raced there for a silver cup. Nicolls, in the height of cavalier fashion, came to the event in a crested chariot accompanied by outriders. He wore a flat, wide hat with an ostrich plume at the side, his hair was down over his shoulders and his stockings were sheer silk. The ladies who were his guests managed enormous hairdos, low-cut gowns and countless ruffles, as well as their ivory fans.

There was from time to time a little muttering in the crowd by former Dutch subjects. They said they missed the last director general, Peter Stuyvesant, and good, solid Dutch rule. A Puritan pamphlet circulated in some of the town taverns was quoted. It spoke about the length of cavalier hair as worn by

151

the king's men, and the title of the pamphlet was the "Unlove-liness of Lovelocks." But Colonel Nicolls was a good governor, fair and generous in his treatment of the colonists. He created a new, much more equitable court system before his three-year term was finished and he was recalled to England.

The town accepted the name of New York without much difficulty, and began to prosper as a port. Beaver was still the chief export item, but gradually a triangular trade route devel-oped and she entered into competition with Boston. The Hudson valley farms were sending constantly larger cargoes of flour down-river for shipment. The colony passed in 1678 a very important act that required the sifting, or "bolting," of flour which was to be exported. This work was concentrated in New York to fa-cilitate inspection and to safeguard the uniform quality of the product, also to please the city millers.

Before the passage of the Flour Regulation Act, New York had not been considered a major colony from the mother country's standpoint. It did not offer the immense profits of sugar from the West Indian islands, or the tobacco taken from Virginia, the rice and indigo raised in South Carolina. But New York sold her flour in the sugar islands, and to the southern European nations, and along the Atlantic seaboard. There was only a very small frac-tion of it sent directly to the northern European countries.

The New England colonies, according to the home govern-ment, were "prejudicial" to England's trade. They dealt in fish and, increasingly, in ships. Both of these sorely damaged home trade, and were in stiff competition with it. But New York, with her furs and flour, had become a welcome source of profit.

There were in 1678 only three ships, eight sloops and seven boats using the port. But sixteen years later, when the flour bar-rel had almost completely replaced the beaver pack on the New

York wharves, there were sixty ships, sixty-two sloops and forty boats. Boston was still in the ascendency, but she would not be much longer.

France and England began in 1689 another bitterly protracted war which was to last through various truces and lapses of uncertain peace until 1815 and Napoleon's defeat at Waterloo. This was really a duel for empire between the two nations and, because of her geographical position, her spreading commerce and the enterprise of her merchants and shipowners, New York took a major part in it.

The city was still physically small, and would remain so until after the Revolution, when a lot of new construction was needed. It occupied only the southern tip of Manhattan Island, an area about a mile square. The extreme northern boundary ran roughly from today's Grand Street on the East River to Vestry Street on the Hudson. Beyond the wall (along present Wall Street), on a rough sort of common, the City Council had set up the gallows, and past that, to the northward, were farmlands, woods and marshes.

The water gate was at the foot of Great Queen Street, with wet docks at Whitehall, the Battery, the Beaver Path and Broad Street. The Broad Street canal had by 1690 become garbage-littered and almost stagnant. People who lived near it said it should be filled, and complained to the council. But there were six wards, North, East, South, West, Dock and Out. The council struggled with many problems.

The entire muster of the City Watch at the time was only twenty-eight men. A watchman carried a club and a lanthorn lantern, and wore a distinguishing sash, used a wooden rattle to warn of his passage through the streets. Discontented citizens said the rattle gave notice to thieves and miscreants to get out of the

153

way, achieved no other purpose. The sheriff was severely criticized, and the water bailiff, a greatly overworked man, was supposed to be a confederate of the harbor pirates.

Due to the rapid current in the East River and the menace of ice in the wintertime, all of the larger vessels tied up at wharves or alongside the wet docks. The waterfront was poorly lit after dark, and was a maze of alleys, canals and slips surrounded by tall, blank-walled warehouses built of stone or brick. A man who ventured there alone at night was exceptionally daring.

Well-organized gangs of pirates went along the docks and wharves on foot, or in canoes and skiffs. They stole anything of value that could be lifted, pried loose. Rope was taken by the coil, and sails cut from the gaskets, stripped from ships' booms and yards. Brass was seized, a compass binnacle, a port deadlight, a culverin mounted securely on a bulwark, but the bulwark chopped away beneath it; iron fittings, blocks, cleats, small anchors, galley stove pipes.

Watchmen privately hired by shipowners were often struck on the head by quiet-moving visitors and, if they fought, were sometimes stabbed, or dumped over the side unconscious. Pursuit on the part of the City Watch led invariably to the wide reaches of the bay, but first into the dock maze and past the hazards of manure, hay, wood, brick, stone and oyster barges. A wise watchman gave up the chase and left the area.

Sailor hangouts were in Dock Street and Great Queen Street. The port had become cosmopolitan in the last few years, and as many as eighteen languages were heard in the taverns. But most of the fo'c'sle-hands were of colonial birth, and English-speaking. They wore their roughly cut hair at shoulder length, and a number of the older men, in West Indian buccaneer style, sported a single gold earring.

Their clothing, short, loose smocks and wide-bottomed trousers that went no lower than the shins, were called Osnaburgs, because the coarse cotton material was made in Osnabrück, Germany. They wore wide leather belts, and hung their cutlasses on the left side, called the weapons "hangers." Most of the year they went shoeless. Their winter clothing was stroud cloth, the same rough woolen goods sold in barter to the Indians, and duffel coats, named for the Belgian town where the thick, warm material was manufactured.

They understood, even the youngest of them, that their years of service were limited. With luck, a man might last at sea until he was forty. But storm, fever, the pox, the French privateers and the buccaneers were in the way.

The sailors who gathered in the Great Queen Street taverns ate well after they had been paid off from a voyage. They ordered leg of mutton steeped in wine, and partridge barbecued in bear fat, rusks, scones, candied apples and pears that had been heated with cinnamon and grape wine. It was habit for them to recite a piece of doggerel that Long Island men had passed on to their shipmates:

If fresh meat be wanting to fill up our dish,
We have carrots, and pumpkins, and turnips, and sich,
And if there is mind for a delicate dish,
We haste to the clam banks and there we catch fish.

But as men left to go back to a ship, when they had settled the account and pulled on their stocking caps, their hands went to their weapons. All of the gayety was gone after they stepped from the ellipse of light at the tavern door. Anywhere between here and the ship, they might meet footpads, thieves with long arms and knives who appeared mysteriously from alleys, or an *155* entire gang of harbor pirates who had not found loot tonight and were willing to rob rum-dulled sailors.

Privateering against the French, which had been encouraged in the port for some years, lost favor around 1700 and took the form of forthright piracy. New York got the name of being the most popular pirate rendezvous on the Atlantic coast. Merchants who had formerly sent out vessels only after the captains had been issued letters of marque that gave legal permission to raid French shipping now became fascinated with the profits which could be made from "the account" itself.

Spanish ships caught in the Caribbean while outward-bound brought tremendous sums when the cargo was sold at auction at the Exchange. Bales of damask were offered, and striped and raw silks, bolts of uniform cloth, pieces of velvet by the thousands, and bolts of sheer linen, bales of laces, hundreds of stands of arms, many fowling pieces and pistols whose barrels and grips were inlaid and damascened with silver and gold. When the auction crowd began to lose interest, other forms of loot were displayed, fine wines, Indian spices, candlesticks, religious statues, copes, chalices and miters.

Sailors in the port who had gone on "the account" talked freely about their last voyages. Some of them had been taken prisoner in action at sea. But the Spanish colonial authorities would, if properly approached, accept bribes. A "flag" was often arranged, a ship that flew a truce flag, carried word of prisoners and the sums needed for their transfer. Men came back to New York wearing palm-thatch hats made in the prison at St. Augustine, and blue-striped cotton suits, grass sandals. They said they liked the Florida climate better than this, and missed the easy, torpid life where most of their time was spent staring out the cell

window at the huge white herons and scarlet ibises.

Then the pirate trade expanded from the Caribbean to Madagascar, and the Indian Ocean. It was financed by various New York merchants and government officials. Madagascar was made a pirate base supplied from New York, and the sources of loot were the thousands of native vessels which sailed the Indian Ocean, the Red Sea and the Persian Gulf, often with enormously valuable cargoes or hundreds of Meccan pilgrims, all worth ransom.

Gun powder and shot were sold the pirates, at very high prices, and flour and rum and raw alcohol, and all sorts of naval stores. Pirate crews were openly recruited in New York, and the men, back from a voyage, spent their "Arab gold" with such abandon that it soon became common currency.

The royal governor, Benjamin Fletcher, was proud to have the more successful of the pirate captains as guests at his mansion. He was seen publicly with such notorious Red Sea rovers as Moston, and Coates, and Tew, and Glover, and Hoare. It could be readily suspected that the governor had an interest in some of the pirate ventures.

Colonel Frederick Philipse, who for twenty years was a member of the City Council, made no secret of the fact that he furnished the supplies needed at Madagascar. Tavern gossip also identified Robert Livingston, a manor lord and a colonel of militia, with the trade. The officers assigned to *Richmond,* the Royal Navy station-ship anchored in the bay, were either below or ashore when a pirate vessel entered port.

But in 1697, alarmed by the loss of regular revenue, the home government sent out the Earl of Bellomont to suppress piracy in North America. He reported that piracy was rife along the seaboard from Maine to Maryland. There was general connivance in New York, and Rhode Island, and around Philadelphia. Bellomont, a querulous man, wrote a lengthy, meandering

157

missive. He reported that "they not only wink at, but Imbrace Pirats, men and shippers."

It had become necessary to dispatch the East India Company ships in convoy, with strong escort, and in 1699 an act was passed by Parliament that made piracy a capital offense. This for some time was practically ignored in New York. Then, as arrests were made, and men were transported in irons to England for trial, a certain amount of care was taken.

A man named Giles Shelley served as the chief diplomatic agent for the port. He owned a number of well-kept and handy sloops that patrolled the New York and Jersey coasts. Shelley was informed of the arrival of each pirate ship. Then he went aboard and brought the captain in touch with the political situation and the latest prices asked for immunity.

The usual bribe given the authorities was £700 for a ship and £100 apiece for the members of her crew. This entitled her to full protection while she got rid of her cargo. Moonless nights, favorable tides and the right place to discharge were chosen. New York shops displayed a good part of the loot for sale a few days later, and then the crews came ashore to get rid of their pay in the taverns and pot-houses and with the doxies.

Earl of Bellomont stayed in New York and was elevated to royal governor, although most of his anti-pirate measures were not yet effective. He had entered into a strange deal in 1695 with a Scottish shipmaster named William Kidd, and made representations to the king that Kidd was a good man for suppression of the pirate trade at Madagascar. The details of the deal between Bellomont and Kidd and several of the king's courtiers have never been made clear.

But Kidd, who had married a prosperous New York widow, Sarah Bradley Cox Oort in 1691, and who owned a large brick house at the corner of Hanover and Pearl Streets, went off to fight the pirates. The Assembly had voted him the gift of £150 for the use of his block and tackle when work was done on Trinity Church. He owned other property, and a ship named *Princess of Orange,* and a brig, and a sloop. He was a respected, well-established shipowner. Still, at Bellomont's urging, he sailed with a pair of king's commissions for Madagascar.

He ended up accused of piracy. He was convicted and sentenced in the most famous trial of its kind. It was conducted in London in 1701, and the penalty was death by hanging. There is little doubt that Bellomont and his other courtier associates betrayed him, for reasons of their own. The king's commissions that Kidd carried on his voyage were not produced in court, although he demanded them, and they were found 200 years later in the files of the Public Records Office.

Kidd's body rotted in chains on Execution Dock, above Thames-side. It was a powerful deterrent for seamen who had looked upon Indian Ocean loot as a means of rapid exit from the fo'c'sle. Men who continued as pirates after Kidd was hanged were mostly stupid, weak and lazy. The navies of the countries which suffered from their depredations sought them out and gradually exterminated them.

When Bellomont finished his term as royal governor of New York in 1702, Queen Anne appointed her nephew Edward Hyde, Lord Cornbury, to succeed him. The city was becoming wealthy, and her people were extravagant, and gay, and broad-minded. Lord and Lady Cornbury were pretty difficult to take, though.

Lady Cornbury, on her visits to various homes, expressed an immediate liking for expensive articles, vases, a piece of silverware, even a painting, a chair. These she asked for without hesitation, and was deeply vexed if refused. Her husband was less avaricious, but much more colorful.

He went to Albany on his first tour of inspection dressed in   *159* silk, satin, gold lace and an immense powdered wig. His sloop was newly painted for the trip in a brilliant combination of contrasting shades and giltwork. The crew wore fancy new uniforms designed by Cornbury himself.

The people along the river talked for months afterward about that voyage. Many of the indentured servants and the Indian and Negro slaves who were allowed to gather at the landings of the big manor estates to greet the governor had never seen anybody quite like him. They were accustomed to the eccentricities of some of the patroons, and the clothing of the manor lords which was imported directly from the most fashionable London tailors. But Cornbury walked, talked and looked like a peacock.

Later, in New York, he showed himself dressed in women's clothing. He paraded Broad, Beaver and Wall Streets delicately holding up his skirts and petticoats from the mud. His record as royal governor was poor, and he was accused of being dishonest. When he was recalled in disgrace, no New Yorkers and none of the Hudson River people who had seen him were surprised.

New York as a port of call was thriving. She received thousands of English settlers during the first half of the eighteenth century, and many Palatine Germans who had been forced by war from their homeland. They went to live and work in the Hudson valley, most of them as farmers. Wheat and corn and flax were very profitable crops. There was a great and steadily expanding fleet of river craft that moved them to New York for sale and shipment overseas.

Hundreds of sloops were in service, broad-bowed and heavily built, but some rigged with ninety-foot main booms. There were also faster, smaller boats called pinks because of their sharp ends, and hag-boats, and an occasional schooner. Rafts of timber were *160* floated down in spring just as soon as ice was out of the river.

The New York-Long Island ferry station in 1716–18 presented a busy scene from the Manhattan side. The square-bowed ferry, her sail secured, is about to dock with a load of cattle for the New York market. Horsemen and a wain with a double span of oxen move along the street, but the main activity is on the river. A Royal Navy cutter fires a salute near a pair of oarsmen, and deeply loaded sloops pass anchored craft.

Entire families sometimes occupied these, the man handling the steering sweep, his wife knitting or working at her spinning wheel near the lean-to shack, the children fishing and the dog barking at dogs ashore.

New York's rich merchants began to buy country places at Hoboken, across the river, and along the Hudson further up, and at Greenwich and Stamford, on Long Island Sound. The Peace of Utrecht, signed in 1713, brought forty years of prosperity with it. New York was now one of the "bread" colonies, in the same way as Massachusetts and Connecticut, New Jersey, Pennsylvania and Maryland. Her ships supplied the West Indies with an enormous and really vital amount of foodstuffs, in return for which she received the rum, molasses and indigo which were traded for mixed cargoes of all sorts in Europe and England.

The fur trade was still very important, although by 1700 most of the valuable animals in the New England region had been destroyed. The manor lords in their Westchester County and Hudson valley meetings after a foxhunt, a cotillion or a wedding talked more and more about the need to take Canada from the French. The same sentiment, they understood from their correspondents, was being expressed in Boston and Philadelphia and Baltimore, and in Virginia, the Carolinas and Georgia. For the first time, the colonies seemed to be unified.

The profit to be made from 300,000 beaver skins, the yield for a normal year's hunt in the New World, could not be ignored. The pelts cost very little except excess manufactured goods and cheap trinkets, and bartering for them furnished occupation for hundreds of men. Even as far back as Dutch times and the *bosch-lopers,* imitation wampum made of glass beads and practically worthless had been used in barter with the Iroquois. The barter, the work of transshipment, the sale of pelts, then manufacture into hats and the sale of those brought wealth in gold and silver to the nation that controlled the trade. This was true, too, with deerskins, which formed the chief supply of leather in Europe.

Two policies for war against Canada were advanced. New England and New York wanted it so they could take full possession of the fur trade. Pennsylvania and the southern colonies wanted to be certain that they reached the Mississippi before the French had secured the enormous riches of the region.

The population in Canada had remained practically static for years because of the home government's involvement in European wars. It was estimated that there were not much more than 2,000 families in the colony, and about 500 of their best men were in the woods, engaged in trade with the Indians. Conquest should be easy.

The war between France and England began in 1754, and was marked by severe Indian raids against the English frontier settlements, and defeats of the English forces. But the Royal Navy was powerful, and successfully blockaded the entrance to the St. Lawrence River. It was impossible for French reinforcements to get to Quebec.

Quebec fell to the English in 1759, and that decided the fate of France in the New World. Canada was ceded, and Louisiana, except for the town of New Orleans. Spain, which had been an ally of France during part of the war, relinquished her rights to Florida. The entire eastern third of North America was now English soil.

Still, there was no real unity among the colonies. They were opposed to each other on many issues, jealous and suspicious. Governor Jeremiah Dummer of Connecticut wrote as early as 1714 that the colonies were "so distinct from one another in their forms of Government, in their Religious rites, in their Emulation *163* of Trade, and consequently in their Affections that they can never be supposed to unite in so dangerous an enterprise as seeking independence."

Forty years later, Governor Glen of South Carolina wrote to Governor Dinwiddie of Virginia on the same subject. His letter was dated March 14, 1754, and held in consideration the gravity of the war situation: "The French are no way Strangers to the Superior Strength of the English Colonies on the Continent but I am afraid they have too good Reason to consider us a Rope of Sand, loose and inconnected, and indeed it is to be lamented that we have hitherto been so."

The Board of Trade was aware of this serious disunity, and was pleased. Colonies divided among themselves were much easier to rule. The home government firmly believed that it could enact almost any kind of legislation or tax impositions, and that, finally, they would be accepted by the colonists. Thomas Pownall, who came out from England in 1764, held the same belief. He was a supposedly shrewd observer, and served as secretary to Sir Danvers Osborn, recently appointed royal governor of New York. He wrote:

> Some say the colonies will revolt some day. No, their hearts are in England and England is their home, they would not risk losing the rights of Englishmen.

Pownall revised his calculation within a year. During the Stamp Act riots of 1765, the splendid Hudson River estate that belonged to Major James of the Royal Artillery was destroyed by a patriotic mob. The major had been careless in his expressions about the people who opposed the tax, and their lack of obedience to the Crown. Then, on Golden Hill, at the corner of Pearl and John

NEW YORK

Streets, a detachment of British garrison troops sent to destroy a liberty pole was stopped by a group of young men. The men belonged to an anti-British organization called Sons of Liberty, and had distributed a subversive broadside that was unsparing in its criticism of the king.

They defended the liberty pole against the British. The troops came forward with fixed bayonets. The patriots carried cutlasses and clubs. There were blows struck, and thrusts of the bayonet. Blood was spilled in the frozen ruts of the street. It was the first encounter of the Revolution.

Four years later, on an April afternoon tide, Captain Chambers brought the ship *London* into port. *London* was fully loaded with tea, and the tea tax was supposed to be in effect in New York. A group of patriots boarded the ship and convinced themselves that Chambers was lying when he said he had none of the stuff aboard.

The ship was visited again that evening. The hatches were opened and men went below into the main hold. Tea chests were hauled on deck and dumped over the side until the hold was empty. The Sons of Liberty and the members of the other New York patriotic groups were ready to join the rest of the aroused colonists in open rebellion.

But during the Revolution the city was forced to take a submissive role. New York was occupied by the British forces on September 15, 1776, after the Battle of Long Island had become disastrous for Washington's army. The British held it for seven years, and maintained it as their principal base on the Atlantic coast. The occupation troops made themselves very much at home there.

Grenadier Guards, units of the Royal Artillery, squadrons of dragoons, the Forty-second Royal Highland Regiment, and Hes-

165

sians and Loyalist ranger and cavalry detachments formed the garrison. The Royal Navy had vessels on blockade duty from Plum Gut, at the eastern end of Long Island, to Navesink, off the New Jersey bluffs past Sandy Hook, and patrol craft busy in the East River and up the Hudson almost to West Point.

The British outposts extended from King's Bridge to West Farms on the Bronx River. American outposts, with headquarters at Peekskill, extended from Mamaroneck on Long Island Sound to Dobbs Ferry on the Hudson. The area between was known as the neutral ground, and was roamed by thieving bands. Those who claimed Tory sympathy called themselves "Cowboys," or "Refugees." The rebel sympathizers had taken the name of "Skinners," which had reference to their ability to loot thoroughly, and leave little behind.

Sir William Howe, the British commander-in-chief, insisted that all citizens who had chosen to remain within the city swear allegiance to the Crown, or take the consequences. This applied also to people living outside the city in Westchester, and New Jersey, and Brooklyn, and further out on Long Island. They were ordered to apply to local military headquarters for what was known as a "badge of protection." It should be, the British order said, "a red rag to mount on their hats."

The badge served its purpose, and was respected by sentries and patrols. Red rags appeared on all kinds of hats, and as a result the supply of red-flannel petticoats ran very low as they were torn into strips for badges. Then the whole procedure became ridiculous. People who could afford it wore red feathers in their hats. But the British officers already had contempt for the local Tories. They called them the "petty-coat gentry."

Wearing a red badge and sometimes carrying a forged pass, Continental Army informers found their way quite easily into New

York City. They were dressed in civilian clothing, and they crossed on the Fulton Street ferry from Brooklyn, came over from New Jersey in a sloop that was loaded with vegetables, fish or oysters, walked the King's Bridge from Westchester and took the Bloomingdale Road to the city.

Morning parades were held on Broad Street. The Grenadier Guards units turned out with oboes, clarinets, horns and bassoons. Hessian officers in tight blue coats and eelskins on their queues were early patrons at the taverns. Some of the Loyalist ranger officers in green coats and red waistcoats soon followed them. Others from the Royal Artillery batteries and the Navy ships were unwilling to drink so early in the day, and passed their time in the bookshops. They bought copies of *Humphrey Clinker,* the newly published *History of Callifernia,* the second volume of *Progress of Vanity, or Virtue* and the latest London magazines and papers. The local Loyalist sheet, *New York Gazette,* they usually left untouched.

Around noon, sedan chairs and open chariots appeared in the streets. Negro servants in livery bore the heavy chairs, and wore red-and-blue coats, canary-yellow breeches and white stockings. The coachmen and the postillions also wore livery, but in addition wigs and tricorne hats, white gloves and red-topped boots. Their passengers were the most esteemed ladies in New York.

The ladies were brilliant in wide-panniered, stiff brocades. Their headdresses were very high, according to the London fashion. They had jewels at their throats and massive rings on their hands, and their fans sparkled with rhinestones. When they replied to a bow along Broad Street or Wall Street, they took great care with their headdresses; all the morning had been spent arranging those.

Officers of the Forty-second Royal Highland Regiment, the   *167*

Black Watch, were among the admirers who saluted the city ladies. They wore black-plumed bonnets, and lace jabots, long red coats. Their plaids hung from beneath the gold bullion of the epaulette on the left shoulder. The sporrans were trimmed with silver, made of otter skin. The kilt was dark-blue, with a green sett, but the stockings were gayly diced in a red-and-white design, and the slippers bore wide silver buckles. The sword hilt was ornamental, of filigreed basket shape, and made of silver. There were a number of ladies who admitted they envied the Highland officers their finery.

But the Scots and the Hessians were given guard duty aboard the prison ships that hung at the anchor in the Hudson, and in Wallabout Bay, off the Brooklyn shore. Men from the Continental forces, captured in action or taken from privateers overhauled at sea, filled the reeking and rotten hulks. The worst of the lot was *Jersey*, and each winter scores of her inmates died of pneumonia, the bloody flux or dysentery. During the fair-weather months, for a small fee, the guards allowed them up on deck to a vantage point where they could watch Royal Navy men row ashore to an afternoon of entertainment at Lispenard's Meadow, near Canal Street. Watching the Royal Navy sailors was the closest some of the American prisoners came to sexual expression for a period of seven years.

The meadow had been chosen as a recreation area by Lord Howe, and tents were put up there. The concession was handled by an enterprising pimp named Jackson. He had imported three shiploads of whores. Two were white, and from England, the third was Negro, and from the West Indies.

During the long years of occupation, the city was almost completely cut off from the usual sources of country supplies. This

created a great inducement for smugglers who tried to get past

New York harbor in 1796, a fine frigate in the foreground and the new ensign above the Battery tower. The ship, with her beautiful swan figurehead and high forecastle, has been at anchor for some time. Ashore, the lower Broadway area is thick with buildings, and St. Paul's Chapel is at the far left.

the American lines through back trails or woodlands, and down Long Island Sound by boat. So American headquarters authorized the use of whaleboats that mounted swivel guns.

Two or three of these boats could hide in a Long Island or Connecticut cove at dusk, make chase at night or during fog, capture the heavily laden and slower supply boats. Every man in a whaleboat crew was supposed to carry a commission from the Continental Convention, but many failed to obey the regulation.

There were former New York harbor pirates among them, *169*

and they began indiscriminate raids. Both Tories and patriots needed to keep a watch upon them, and Tory appeals to Admiral Howe brought no action. Royal Navy cutters, an aide explained at New York headquarters, had other duties than to pursue rogues whose crimes were no worse than stealing a boatload of cabbages, or possibly a cow. But the Continental Convention finally revoked all commissions and the raiding stopped.

Admiral Howe still was vexed by the problem of Royal Navy protection for New York harbor. With her many coves and backwaters and thirteen tributary rivers leading into the Hudson, the men of the British guard squadron were kept very busy. During September, 1776, before His Majesty's forces had taken Manhattan, there had been the madcap submarine attempt. That was against Howe's flagship *Eagle,* and might have succeeded if her bottom had not been sheathed with copper. Sergeant Ezra Lee of Lyme, Connecticut, was working hard to attach the bomb when Royal Marine sentries aboard the frigate heard him, and he escaped into the darkness in his hand-cranked craft.

Captain Adam Huyler was much more successful against the British. He had been the skipper of a sloop whose home port was New Brunswick. He was fully familiar with all of the New Jersey coast around Sandy Hook, and the harbor waters inside it. A good patriot, and a man who enjoyed the profit to be made from a night's work of privateer looting, he led whaleboat raids with great skill.

One of his most daring sorties was in October, 1781, when well inside Sandy Hook he sent his men to board five British storeships. He commanded a small gun-sloop and a pair of whaleboats. But their crews took the storeships after fifteen minutes of cutlass and pistol fighting. Wheat, cheese, dry goods, powder and 170 shot were dumped into the whaleboats while the Royal Navy escort vessel fired an ineffectual broadside, and a Royal Artillery battery on the beach at Sandy Hook also missed target.

Huyler later took the big British ship *Father's Desire,* seized her in the Narrows and brought her as a prize into the Raritan River. She gave him twenty hogsheads of rum and pork and fifteen prisoners before he had to abandon her because of pursuit. He and his men, carrying their loot and their prisoners, escaped in pulling boats through hidden channels in the marshes wholly unknown to Royal Navy coxswains.

During a night of full moon, on Friday, April 19, 1782, he shoved off with his gun-sloop and a barge for the Narrows. His lookouts had seen a British cutter, and Huyler's force took her although she was armed with six eighteen-pounders and ten nine-pounders. Her crew of fifty men surrendered to him, but tide and wind were adverse, and he could not keep her. So he set her afire, and on the way home captured a sloop which he later returned for a $500 ransom.

With the defeat of Cornwallis at Yorktown and the collapse of British military effort, it was decided to evacuate New York. This was done in the fall of 1783, and it meant the loss of everything they had owned for more than 28,000 Tory refugees who had gathered in the city. The New York *Morning Post* on November 7, 1783, carried an article that said in part: "the voice of the inhabitants is so universally against them that they cannot hope for a peaceful residence among us."

But the Tories were defiant to the last. They shouted from the decks of the transports, "Hell or Halifax!" The people on the wharves or aboard the harbor craft yelled back in derision, "Nova Scarcity!"

Among the evacuees was the owner of the King's Head Tavern, located on Fulton Street in Brooklyn. It had been known *171*

British troops under General Cornwallis made a difficult landing in 1776 on the west bank of the Hudson. They climbed the Palisades, hauled their artillery by hand, pursuing Washington's army from New York.

before the war as The Ferry Tavern, and less than a mile away from the front door, in plain sight in Wallabout Bay, were the black hulks of the prison ships that held thousands of Americans. But the occupation brought vast profit, and the change in name.

The King's Head was a favorite rendezvous for Tory "fashionables," Royal Navy officers from vessels in the bay and Royal Artillery officers who used the ferry to Manhattan. A caravan for the service of patrons was run between Jamaica and the Brooklyn Ferry on Tuesdays and Thursdays, and added to the popularity of the establishment.

NEW YORK

When the owner left, he tacked a sign on the door. It read: "Auction Sale. Paintings, pictures, pierglasses, organ, billiard table, 20 globe-lamps, flagstaff, ensign, pendants, and several hundred lamps (used for illumination) both transparent and made of tin. *The landlord intends for Nova Scotia immediately.*"

A Black Watch detachment formed the British rearguard. Pipers sounded as they marched aboard the transport on November twenty-first and she cast off and headed down the bay. The crowd at the Grand Battery jeered, then cheered and began to dance in the streets.

The thirteen colonies united as states under the Confederation of the United States, with title to the immense territory that stretched from the seacoast to the Mississippi River, and beyond. The Loyalists who stayed after the British evacuation were expelled from all offices that they held, and barred from the professions, forced to pay double or triple taxes. New York State collected more than $3,600,000 in this way, and Loyalist property was also seized and put up for public auction.

Freedom finished the Navigation Acts, but in 1783 a British Order in Council barred importation of meat, fish, butter and cheese from the United States into the British West Indian islands. It further confined trade in all other goods to British ships. New York shipowners had learned, though, how to avoid the effects of a blockade, and they had already decided that new markets overseas should be found.

The New York brig *Empress of China,* under command of Captain John Greene, cleared Sandy Hook on February 22, 1784, bound for Macao via Cape of Good Hope. She reached her Chinese port August thirtieth and was back home in May, 1785, with a cargo of tea and silk. The profit for her owners was so substantial that Boston, Philadelphia and Providence merchants quickly entered the trade.

PORTS OF CALL

While *Empress of China* was still at sea, another New York-owned vessel shoved off for the Orient. She was the North River sloop *Experiment,* and made the first direct run to China. Built for river work, she had a low freeboard, and was only 85.5 tons, with a very long main boom and bowsprit. She flew both upper and lower square topsails, and her crew of fifteen men and boys were kept busy. But her master, Captain Stewart Deane, was a Revolutionary War privateer veteran, and he brought her into Canton in four months, twelve days. She came home with a highly profitable cargo of tea, silk and ginseng, and New York was actively established in the China trade.

The port grew, and there was a lot of shipbuilding along the East River as the need for new and bigger vessels increased. The miserable, undeclared French War in 1799–1800 and then the war against the Barbary pirates that came right after it gave young, ambitious seamen plenty of battle training. They were not interested in Robert Fulton's attempt to put a steamboat in service on the Hudson River. But most of the sea experience they had gathered was wasted during the War of 1812 except for the privateer crews who were able to escape capture by the British.

The war brought almost incalculable harm to New York. It was for three years under tight British blockade. Some few vessels were able to slip away to sea, among them *Scourge,* which earned the right to her name as a privateer. Cargoes of beef and flour and other provisions were smuggled out occasionally for sale in Canada, or to the British squadrons cruising off the coast. But the rest of the time merchants, seamen, longshoremen, shipyard workers and draymen sat around and cursed President Madison as much as the British.

The odds against winning the war were at least forty to one, and the United States had started it. There were eighteen war-ships under the American flag, and more than 800 under the

NEW YORK

British. Since 1792, each major European nation had been defeated in turn by British fleets. And the American Army, so-called, could not win a battle.

But, in December, 1814, peace was made. The British had expended enough in money, ships and men. Napoleon was again a figure to be confronted in Europe, and Wellington wanted all available forces back on the Continent. Another victory celebration was held in New York. It did not last long, though; men were eager to return to work, forget the wasteful years of war.

New activity was begun on the Hudson. Various steamboat companies competed for the trade started by Robert Fulton and his partner, Robert R. Livingston. Men who were New Jersey residents resented the Manhattan monopoly. They pointed out that John Stevens and his sons, Robert and John, had as early as 1804 run the twin-screw steamer *Little Juliana* as a ferryboat between Hoboken and New York. A fair share of the business should be operated from across the river, they said.

Then Aaron Ogden, who had been elected governor of New

West Point as seen from across the Hudson about 1810, Fulton's *Clermont* headed upstream for Albany. The group of people in the foreground are about to board her with the child and their assorted luggage. *Clermont* has her accomodation ladder rigged, and some passengers have disembarked, started ashore.

PORTS OF CALL

Jersey on the anti-war ticket in 1812, entered the dispute. He built the steamer *Sea Horse,* and insisted that she had the right to dock in Manhattan. This, according to Fulton and Livingston, was an invasion of their monopoly rights, and they made an appeal to the New York State legislature.

There were rulings, and counter-rulings. Fares were lowered until rides across the river cost almost nothing. Cornelius Vanderbilt, who at the age of twenty-four had become the skipper of an oyster boat, was hired by a Jersey faction. He was already known as "Commodore" because of his ability to control harbor pirates, and he took command of the steamer *Bellona.*

He ran her over to Manhattan while she streamed aloft a banner that read "Jersey Must Be Free." When New York officials came aboard looking for him, he had disappeared. A very polite and pretty young girl was alone in the pilot-house. Vanderbilt was back at the wheel, though, as *Bellona* left the dock with a load of passengers. He had been hiding, the officials guessed, in a small closet in a corner of the pilot-house.

But passengers got weary with interrupted schedules, collisions in mid-channel, scalds from escape-valve steam, burns from stack cinders. Steamers on the run out of New York to the upriver ports sank at an alarming rate. One competitive-spirited captain was heard to shout as his vessel cut down another amidships, "There she goes—right in the goddamn ladies' room!"

Passengers made clear that such warfare must stop. They insisted also, due to the number of boiler explosions, that passenger barges be towed astern of the steamers. The river ride to Albany became both enjoyable and reasonably safe.

New Yorkers soon accepted the fact. Their port was about to overhaul Boston, handle the largest amount of tonnage in the nation. It deserved the best.

CHAPTER 7

Philadelphia

THEY SAW THE LOW, QUITE FLAT LAND when they were allowed on deck from the foulness of the immigrant ship hold. Sailors pointed out and named the capes for them, May to starboard, Henlopen to larboard. This was the Delaware, and the Philadelphia settlement was some thirty miles upriver. The immigrants stood on deck for hours while the ship tacked, then squared away with the incoming tide. They stared in fascination and with fierce hope at the land.

Most of them were peasants and, born in the seventeenth century, were illiterate. They did not know much about the New World. But they kept that knowledge clear.

Here was Pennsylvania. No other Atlantic coast colony was like it. This was the central arch between the northern and southern regions, and the richest of the lot. William Penn had just founded in 1682 his "City of Brotherly Love" under a charter given him by Charles II, the English king. Penn was a Quaker who practiced what he preached, and he had written that he wanted to "afford asylum to the good and oppressed of every nation."

His statement had been translated, and spread widely through England, Ireland, Wales and western Europe. Some of the immigrants knew it word for word. They could quote from what he had said further about his purpose: "I aimed to frame a government which might be an example. I desired to show men as free and happy as they could be."

Within a year after he founded Philadelphia, twenty-three ships loaded with immigrants came up the river and went to anchor. Those people were Germans, and Welsh, and English. When they came ashore on the sandy beach at Dock Creek they found most of the settlement located there, with only a few cabins at the edge of the huckleberry patches that reached inland to the great oak forest.

The newcomers were awed. The Quakers wore neat, sober gray, the men tall black "steeple" hats, and the women and girls tightly tied sunbonnets and plain kersey dresses. The houses of the settlement, even the new jail, were built of logs. Men came from the forest carrying freshly killed game. They handled their heavy, double-bladed axes with ease and skill. Out on the wide and smooth river, Indian warriors who wore only breechclouts and were daubed with paint bent from dugout canoes to cast grapevine fish nets.

The air bore the scent of the strawberries, the raspberries and grapes that grew wild. The dooryard flowers in front of the cabins were tulips, and pinks, and roses, lilies, carnations. The
178 newly arrived people were almost unbelieving. They had just

heard of six-inch oysters, and turkeys that weighed forty pounds.

There had been nothing like that in the war-torn Rhineland of the Palatinate, nor the bleak windings of the Welsh valleys, the close-walled Midland towns in England where for every man who worked ten did not, and they and their families nearly starved. The Palatinate Germans, slow and methodical, were stunned by the arrival. The experience followed too soon upon the weeks of confinement in the hold of the ship that brought them here. They were glad to surrender themselves to young Francis Daniel Pastorius, be led from Philadelphia to the settlement five miles away that was already called Germantown.

Pastorius explained patiently to them the laws of the colony. The fundamental guarantees of liberty were granted by a charter called "Concessions and Agreements." Rights of religious freedom, free speech, petition and trial by jury were assured. Capital punishment was made illegal, even in the case of traitors. Fighting and the issuing of challenges for duels were absolutely banned. The punishment was six months' imprisonment for any hot-head assailant or prospective duellist, with a fine of ten pounds. Nobody was to carry "pocket pistols, skeins, stilladers, daggers or dirks or other unusual weapons, save officers and strangers travelling upon lawful errands."

Swearing, lying, drunkenness and the drinking of healths, and obscenity, stage plays, cards, dice, masques, revels and bull-baiting were specifically forbidden, along with any other deed which might excite the people to "rudeness, cruelty, looseness and irreligion." Children who listened glumly to what Pastorius recited were told by him that conditions for them were much better than in the neighbor colony of New Jersey.

Over in New Jersey, the Assembly had recently declared, "Undutiful children, smiting or cursing their father or mother, *179* except provok'd thereunto for self preservation, should be punished with death."

The newcomer children in Germantown were deeply impressed. They slipped away from the cabins assigned to their families and talked with some of the offspring of the original settlers here. Pastorius was right, they were told. In Pennsylvania, it was hard to get killed. Only an Indian would do it, and that was when he had been drinking rum that came from New Jersey.

The children and their parents learned a great deal more about the colony in the next few days. William Penn, although a devout Quaker, was much less sober-sided than many of the settlers. He was an English admiral's son, and his father had been owed the sum of £16,000 by King Charles. Acquisition of the colony had taken care of the debt, and Penn was quick to use the grant.

He arrived from Sussex in October, 1682, aboard the 300-ton ship *Welcome*. A hundred of his Quaker friends were with him, and he first went ashore at New Castle, in the lower Delaware. His deeds were issued in the name of James, Duke of York, the king's brother. Penn formally presented them to the people at New Castle, and took possession by the solemn delivery of "turf and twig and water and soyle" of the Delaware and its west bank. Then he returned to *Welcome* and kept on upstream to the site of what was to be Chester and, above that, Philadelphia, his City of Brotherly Love.

Penn was thirty-eight, slim, handsome, energetic. When the plan for the Philadelphia settlement was laid out between the Delaware and the small river named the Schuykill which led into it, he went looking for a homesite for himself. He chose rolling, beautiful meadowland some miles further up the Delaware. He called the place Pennsbury, and built his home there.

But he was often on the river, to make tours of inspection of

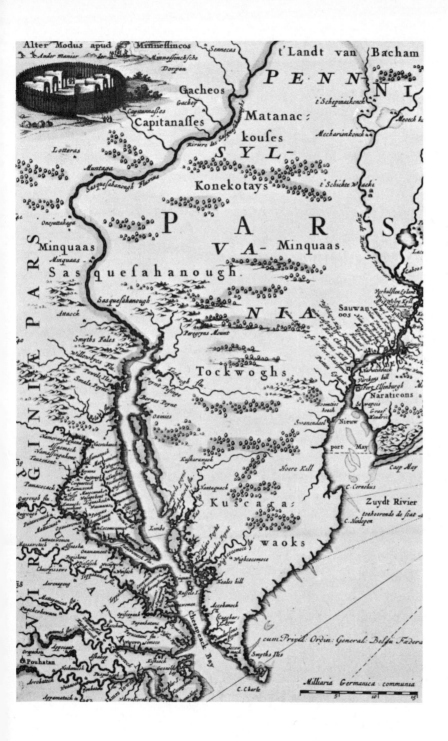

Alter Modus apud Minnessincos
Ander manier der Minnessinck sche Dorpen

Sennecas

't Landt van Bacham

PENN-
NI

Gacheos
Gachoy

't Schepinaikonck

Meoech

Capitannasses
Capitanasses

Matanac:
koufes
SYL-

Mecharienkonck

Lotteras

Rivure des Sassof

't Schichte Wacki

Muntaga

Konekotays

Sasquesahanough Flurius

P A R S
V A- Minquaas.

Onejuttabaga

Minquaas

Minquaas

Sasquesahanough.

N I A

Sauwan
oos

Verhulsten Eyland

Attaock

Sasquesahanough

Smyths Fales

Willowbyes Flu.

Parqeyns Mount

Nacratikonck
Verckes kill
Fort Elsenburgh
Swagois
Groot Eylandt

Powels Iles

Tockwogh
Flu.

Tockwoghs

Naraticons a

Smals Poynt

Poynt Pleasure

Bornes Poynt

Ozinies

Roomtias hoeck

Swanendad

Nieuw

port May

Caep May

Kushurawaock

Hoere Kill

C. Cornelius

Zuydt Rivier
toeboorende de staet

Lombe

Kuscaca:

C. Hinlopen

Cuttatawomen
Massawteck

Apploan Poynt
Badds Poynt

Accomack
Wighcocomoco

waoks

Keales kill

Russels I.

Accohanock

Oryhenk

Capahar How

VIRGINIÆ PARS

O Powhatan

Cheapeack Bay

Smyths Iles

cum Privil: Ordin: General: Belga: Foderæ

C. Charle

Milliaria Germanica communia

Philadelphia and the other settlements, and to treat with the Indians. He moved in true courtier style, lounging on the satin stern thwart cushions of a barge built in England to his specifications. Her narrow transom was emblazoned with the Penn family coat-of-arms. The hull strakes were painted blue, red and orange, with much gilt ornamentation around the bow. A canopy shielded him from the sun that burned away the summer haze from the river valley. The twelve oarsmen wore livery, and kept excellent stroke.

Penn's hat carried a plume, and had an uptilted brim. The curls of his periwig reached his shoulders. There was lace at his throat and cuffs. His stockings were sheer silk. He must have been conscious as he stepped ashore at Dock Creek that he was very much a part of English tradition. Not even the Duke of York approached Westminster Palace water-stairs with a finer-looking craft or crew.

Penn was very serious, though, about his plans for the colony, and meticulously fair in his treatment of the Indians. The tribes of the Delaware basin were called Lenni-Lenape. Their principal sachem, the man with whom Penn dealt the most, was Tamend, whose name the English changed to Tammany. The Indians were big, and strong. They painted themselves with red and white clay, wore bark-fiber waist garments. The warriors were expert hunters, fished the river constantly, used weirs to catch the immense run of shad that came upstream from the sea each spring.

Penn remarked that the Indians "tread softly—and mostly walk with a lofty chin." Their skins were swarthy, their eyes small and black. They greased themselves with bear fat against the mosquito swarms, and could always be identified as they came downwind on a warm day. The warriors' wives, Penn reported, were "true servants of their husbands."

PHILADELPHIA

He met with the chiefs at a place called Shackamaxon, which later became Kensington. Peace calumets were smoked under a great tree, and gifts exchanged. The tree came to be known as the Treaty Elm, and Penn was pleased. The early history of Delaware before his arrival was a series of frustrations, defeats and tragic failures.

Dutchmen had driven out Swedes who in 1638, with the aid of some tough Finns, had tried to take over the entire Delaware region. The Finns, who were fine axemen, built the first log cabins in America. But the marshland mosquitoes were sufficient to discourage a Swedish attempt to build a fort on the east bank of the river.

Along in 1655, the Swedes were almost ready to leave. Then Governor Peter Stuyvesant of New Amsterdam sent a fleet of seven ships to the river. The Swedes surrendered without a fight. The garrison of Fort Christina, their main installation, was allowed to march from it with "drums and trumpets playing, flags flying, matches burning."

The Dutch had not lasted here, though. The English had taken the colony from them in 1664 with little trouble. Both the Dutch and the Swedish attempts suffered from the fact that the home governments had not supplied them with enough people to build towns, and fishing and trading fleets, and to till the soil, make the colony self-supporting.

Penn dealt carefully with the Indians. He needed their friendship, and a lot more land than he at present owned. Still, he gave most of his effort to the planning of Philadelphia. He was America's first town planner. He mapped out a gridiron of streets to fill the space between the Delaware and the Schuykill. This would not only be a great city, but a leading port of call.

The original settlers had been forced to live in caves dug   *183* in the river bank, or in tents made from old sails. Then, with Penn's arrival, as the town began to take shape, a small boat basin was dug where a creek entered the river. A drawbridge was built at the entrance, and it connected with the Blue Anchor Tavern. The tavern had been in business before Penn's arrival aboard *Welcome,* and was the center of social and business life along the entire stretch of river.

River traffic had been of extreme importance to the colony right from the beginning. England keenly needed ship timber for the Royal Navy. There was some trouble with the Indians because of their shad weirs in the reaches above Philadelphia, but that was solved by negotiation. Ship and boat construction was started at a number of yards on the lower river at Marcus Hook, Chester, New Castle, Lewiston and Wilmington. Timber came downstream in great quantities, and was a prime harvest for the colony.

The Dutch in their time had called the river Zuydt, meaning "South," with the Hudson River known to them as "North." The Swedes called it *Sodre Reveriet, Swenskes Revier,* and *Nya Sweriges Revier.* Englishmen had named it the Charles before it became the Delaware.

But Penn was determined that the Delaware name should stay. The colony was a success. His appeals for settlers had been passed all over western Europe and the British Isles. The people were arriving by the shipload, even during the severe winter months when the river was filled with a jagged litter of ice and the pilots took days to navigate the thirty miles upstream to Philadelphia.

The immigrants were a strange and often a sorry lot. Penn's shipping agents had collected hundreds of Germans who belonged
184 to peculiar pacifist religious sects. Prominent among them were

the Mennonites, and these followed the word of Menno Simons, a Dutch reformer, although there was a dissident group that chose Jacob Amman as their leader. They kept apart from the Moravians, and the Schwenkfelders and the Dunkers. The Dunkers were vegetarians. The men wore beards, and long white gowns; some of them thought that the use of buttons was sinful. They communed with spirits, and mumbled to themselves as they stumbled over the Philadelphia ruts and newly laid cobblestones in their rough wooden clogs.

Many of the immigrants landed sick, or dying. Ship conditions had been extremely unhealthy in the lightless, heatless holds. What was commonly called "ship's fever," and pneumonia and dysentery killed a considerable percentage during the weeks at sea. The people were almost without hope. They had been tricked into giving what were for them huge sums of money to buy passage, and in addition had agreed to work for seven years, unpaid, to make good the balance owed. Food was in short supply aboard the vessels; one shipload had arrived at Philadelphia after living for a week on the rats caught in the hold.

The Germans accepted this without much protest. All of their sects maintained beliefs similar to the Quakers. They would not meddle in the affairs of others, even when it meant the loss of members of their families, and their friends. It was also forbidden among them to bear arms aggressively, and to take an oath. They were sedate, quiet, willing to move forth to the dangers of the frontier if only because that life would offer them some sort of sanctuary from the world.

Quaker merchants in Philadelphia whose affairs had begun to prosper with the expansion of the colony were whole-hearted in their praise of the German Lutherans. But they were less happy with the Welsh immigrants. These people were Baptists, and very   *185* determined in their views. The wiry and quick-moving Welsh-men told the Philadelphia authorities in plain, harsh language about the sufferings of the voyage, and how, when and where they had been cheated by the shipping agents. It was quite difficult to get some of the Welsh out of Philadelphia and located in distant settlements.

But the Scottish Presbyterians who came in from North Ireland were the worst. They knew their rights, they said, and they would have those satisfied before they stepped foot out of Penn's town of brotherly love. Most of the Scots were big, rangy men, with blue eyes, red hair and extraordinarily short tempers. A number of the families had been proscribed, driven from their homes in Scotland for refusal to join the Church of England. Then, in Ireland, they had fought the native Catholics, and, for practice, fought each other.

They took over the Blue Anchor Tavern as their temporary headquarters. Men who were recognized as shipping agents were chased, caught and thrown in the river. Songs were sung in the Blue Anchor taproom. There was dancing to a bagpipe. But the leaders who met with the colony authorities were canny, adroit in their dealings. When the Scots left for the frontier, retribution for the various losses suffered during the voyage had been made, and the groups were happy. Pipers marched ahead along the forest trails in the leaf-dappled summer sunlight, playing gay tunes. Life on the frontier promised well. There would be no more trouble with landlords or leases, like that in Ireland. Each man was given enough space for himself here, and a chance for some fighting should the Indians turn ugly.

While the frontier was settled, and forts and trading posts and cabins were built far inland past the set of steep falls at
Trenton, the colony gradually became rich. A number of the

towns prospered because they were along the sixty-mile stretch of the Delaware on the well-travelled route from New York to Baltimore. The trade supported taverns that were reasonably free of lice. Food was palatable, if plain; rum, gin and cider were in plentiful supply.

Families such as the Coopers, who maintained a twenty-four-hour service across the Delaware at what was to become Camden, took care of stagecoaches, pack trains, single horsemen and farmers' carts. Three horses working on a treadmill propelled the ferry, with the help of the crew using poles and sweeps in the winter ice. Philadelphia, just below Cooper's Ferry, handled a great share of the traffic and took steady profit from it.

The town was the center of activity for all of the colony. Immigrant ships that were still malodorous from their Atlantic passages lay at anchor alongside West Indian trading shallops and coasters. The Dutch had introduced the shallop to the river early, brought them over from the Netherlands in knocked-down condition. Their broad beam and shallow draft made them excellent river craft, and they carried many different cargoes.

Philadelphia kept several shipyards busy with orders for brigs, brigantines, schooners and shallops. Blacksmiths turned out nails, spikes, chain plates, block sheaves and rudder irons from local bog iron. Anchors were fashioned at special forges. Ropes, made at first at open walks, were later produced under sheds, but out of town where the highly flammable hemp and flax would not cause a general fire. Sailmakers had originally worked for individual shipbuilders or merchants. But then they were hired by the owners of the yards in the same way as the ship-wrights, carpenters, riggers and block-makers. Along the river, within range of tidewater, practically every creek of any size held a boatyard. Farmers built boats for themselves or their neigh-

The 36-gun frigate *Philadelphia* was built there in 1799 for service against the Barbary pirates. A Navy inspector stands serenely watching sawyers and carpenters who fashion out the ship's timbers. The Swedish Church is in the background, and at the far left a woman bends to gather chips in her apron.

bors during the long winter months. One of the principal colonial products was flour. The farmers brought their rye and wheat to the mills at the Schuykill, the Brandywine and the various swift-flowing creeks that were tributaries of the Delaware. Then they hauled the flour to Philadelphia in their shallops for sale or further shipment.

An enterprising miller named John Harding had built a windmill on a sand island in the middle of the river opposite Philadelphia. It took the name of Windmill Island, and barges, gundalows and sloops tied up there with cargo until it finally became a menace to navigation. But Harding made a fine living meantime, and the island kept the name for years after the mill operation was discontinued.

Tough, snuff-chewing rivermen dressed in buckskins supplied the Delaware shipyards with timber. They handled the huge rafts which each spring came downstream from beyond Trenton Falls, some out of the narrow, turbulent headwater reaches in the Catskill Mountains. When they had tied up and were paid, they found their way to the Blue Anchor Tavern. Their initial evening's entertainment usually meant full redecoration of the taproom, and the rest of their stay in town was passed in jail. Then, urged by the sheriff, they started the long walk home.

The rafts delivered at the shipyards contained white pine, spruce, cedar, oak and fir. Others carried cherry, birch and walnut logs. Those were cut up for the manufacture of furniture, and gunstocks. Red maple was used for spinning wheels, and handles, and wooden tools.

Coopers got a good share of the raft timber for barrel staves, heads and hoops for the same sort of container use as in New York and the New England colonies. Flour and biscuit went into the barrels and hogsheads for the West Indian trade, and meat, *189* and fish, and for a time some of the tobacco that William Penn grew without much success. Philadelphia was actively engaged in the rum and molasses and indigo barter with the island planters, but Penn's tobacco could not match the Virginian product, or bring him anything like equal prices.

Philadelphia also shipped out a great quantity of dressed leather to England and western Europe, for shoemaking purposes, and saddlery and harness, and furniture, and house frames for the West Indian sugar-plantation owners, who were rapidly becoming wealthy. But Philadelphia ships, the open and undefended Delaware and the peaceful habits of the Quakers attracted pirates. It was all too easy; more loot could be taken off the Delaware capes than in the Caribbean, and without retaliation.

The towns along the lower bay were raided often during the 1680s and 1690s, although the loot to be taken was small. Lewes, because of its exposed position on Cape Henlopen, was a favorite target. Many of the pirates were Caribbean veterans who had transferred their base to Madagascar, but returned to this coast to get rid of their loot. They had sold their fighting ships in the Bahamas or South Carolina. They appeared off the Delaware sailing nondescript coastal vessels. But those were loaded with the pick of the Red Sea plunder.

The pirate leaders quite openly approached the Philadelphia merchants. Men in the grubby little counting-houses that flanked Dock Creek were offered bales of magnificent Oriental silks at extremely tempting prices. Among the rest of the stuff for sale were pearls, loose gems, bars of gold and silver, and large amounts of "Arab gold" that included moidores, pistoles, guilders and pieces of eight.

While the leaders dealt patiently with the merchants, the
190   pirate crews cruised the bay. It had been reliably reported that

one contingent of sixty Red Sea outlaws had arrived with belts stuffed with gold coins that amounted to between £1,000 and £1,500 a man. They had no need to pillage Lewes, seize family silverware and even pewter. For the same reason, though, they chased fishermen offshore, and endlessly caroused, gambled. All of them were very deeply afraid; they suffered from "Tyburn ague" and felt beneath their chins the rapid tightening of the hangman's knot. If they stayed inactive, fear would wholly consume what was left of their courage.

Scores of the Madagascar men, prodded by that knowledge, decided to settle in Philadelphia or in the other port towns, and give up life outside the law. They spent money carefully in various bribes, and were welcomed. The Quaker authorities were reluctant to take action against them, as the pirates were well aware. And Penn was in England, occupied with affairs which were to him much more pressing than piracy.

One of the pirates, a handsome young man, became engaged to the daughter of Edwin Markham, the governor of the province. When the marriage plans were announced, some of the Philadelphia people spoke critically to Markham about it. They said that Parliament had recently passed an act making piracy a major crime in all of the colonies. It was well known, they added, that Markham's prospective son-in-law had served as a member of the crew of Captain John Avery, a notorious Red Sea pirate, and that Markham was friendly with Avery and a number more like him. These other men, former members of Captain William Kidd's crew, had also been given refuge in the colony.

Markham answered that the pirates had always been civil to him, and brought in money, "which was an advantage to the country." He did nothing to block the marriage, and in fact gave *191* his blessing to the event. The angry citizens appealed to the Assembly, and that body summoned the prison warden. He was charged with allowing two men arrested as pirates the liberty to stroll around Philadelphia. The warden admitted the charge. "But," he said, "they never go out of jail without my leave and a keeper, which, I think, may be allowed in hot weather."

Then William Penn returned and was confronted with the problem. He delivered an eloquent proclamation. There were at the time a pair of reputed pirates on trial, one of whom was alleged to have served with Avery, the other with Kidd. It was Penn's intention to have his proclamation studied in London, and he took care to defend himself:

> I leave to those who have been so elaborate and elegant in representing weakness in the Province of Pennsylvania since my arrival; who, if they will do me justice will have less to say to my advantage. I confess I think my interest in these cases ought not wholly to be overlooked, who as Lord of the Soil, erected into a Seigneury, must needs have a royalty, and a share in such seizures, else I am in much meaner circumstances than many Lords of Manors upon the seacoasts of England, Ireland and Scotland. . . . I do not write this to dispute any right with the King, resolving to obey his commands and submit myself to his further consideration.

His Majesty was moved to take action through Parliament, and after 1700 piracy was no longer a source of public distress and enormous hidden profit along the Delaware. An act of Parliament had really finished it in the North American colonies. This nullified the necessity of transportation back to England for the accused in a case of felony, *i.e.*, piracy. Special courts were established in the colonies to handle the work.

Commissions were created under the Great Seal or the seal of the Admiralty, with the powers of trial, conviction and sentence. Men were tried "before the silver oar"—the famous device placed in front of the bench when the Admiralty Court was in session. This was twenty-one inches long, and weighed twelve ounces, bore the British coat-of-arms, and a crowned anchor, the seal of the Admiralty.

It served much the same purpose as the royal mace, displayed when the House of Commons was in session, gave a great sense of legality to the proceedings. The trial commissions were allowed to extend to quorums of seven officers aboard Royal Navy ships, or civilians designated to act as judges. The authority granted by the home government enabled the establishment of a Vice Admiralty court in any province, and each court had full hanging powers.

This was done, though, a bit too late. Quaker pacifism and laxity still looked like corruption in high places to many of the people who had suffered from pirate raids. An anonymous subscriber to a Philadelphia paper reported on June 1, 1699:

> To the Lords of Trade—There is arrived into this Government about 60 pirates in a ship directly from Malligasco. They are part of Kidd's gang. About 20 of them landed in this Government. About 16 more of them are landed at Cape May in West Jersey. She is a very rich ship—all her loading is rich East India Baile Goods to a very great value, besides abundance of money.

Then, on June 6, in the same newspaper:

> The Pirates that are in this Government of West Jersey are at Liberty, for the Quakers there will not suffer the Governor to send them to Goale. Thus His Majesty may expect to be obeyed in all places where the Government is in Quaker hands.

193

PORTS OF CALL

Pennsylvania, the key arch in the structure of the North Atlantic colonies, suddenly showed herself weakened, badly hurt by religious dissension that had taken severe political overtones. Quaker was hated by Baptist, by Dunker and Mennonite and Presbyterian, who in turn had no use for each other. Philadelphia was a Babel where many languages were spoken, and few were understood. Beyond, out in the counties, the various sects remained aloof, and intransigent.

Fifty years after Penn first arrived, the population had not become homogeneous, and actually was growing more diverse. Both New England and Virginia, by rigid governmental and religious restrictions, had enforced some degree of uniformity among their residents. But Penn had invited, and accepted, everybody. The colony was a weirdly mixed, chaotic collection of nationalities, languages and religions. There were more than a thousand Swedes and Welsh who still used their native speech. The Hollanders knew a little English, but talked together in Dutch. The Palatines knew nothing except Low German, and made no attempt to improve their knowledge. The Assembly meetings in Philadelphia were often serio-comic as bearded Dunkers shouted at wildly yelling Welshmen who paid no attention to broken Dutch-English protests and calmly delivered Quaker "thees" and "thous."

That overwhelming desire for self-determination was to work sorely against the colony during the Revolution, and already men who could think objectively were aware of the gravity of the discord. Meanwhile, though, Pennsylvania prospered.

The population increased until in 1730 it was 50,000, and by 1763 there were 200,000, mainly because of the continued flow of Scotch-Irish and Germans. Philadelphia lay in the middle of a wide and fertile agricultural country that included West

194

Jersey and Delaware. The colony's commodities were sent to the West Indies, to western European ports and to ports in the British Isles along the famous triangular trade route that had proved so successful for the New England and New York merchants.

Benjamin Franklin, when he arrived in October, 1723, at the age of seventeen, found an already prim, well-built town. Dock Creek was about to be filled in and become Dock Street. The Blue Anchor Tavern was very much in business. Market Street led straight from the wharf where he landed to the grassy square at the center of town.

The houses were built almost entirely of brick, and generally three stories high. Row after row were built in the same manner, with marble doorsteps, identical ironwork and window structure. The streets were paved with flat footwalks on each side, and meticulously clean.

Franklin had come to the town of brotherly love in the traditional fashion, penniless and hungry. Some weeks before, with very little money, he left Boston for New York in search of work. He was in trouble with his older brother James for articles he wrote and published in James's paper, the *New England Courant,* while his brother was in jail. Benjamin chose to write facetiously about the lack of action on the part of the Bay Colony authorities to catch pirates who preyed on local vessels. This was the same topic that had led the authorities to arrest James, so upon release he advised Benjamin to go elsewhere to finish his training as a printer's devil.

There was no job for Benjamin in New York, and, almost out of money, he started for Philadelphia. He boarded a sloop that would take him across New York harbor to Perth Amboy in New Jersey. A squall hit the craft while she was partway to the New Jersey shore.

PORTS OF CALL

The sloop was driven over against the Brooklyn shore, and the rotten sail torn to pieces. Franklin described the scene in his autobiography. He wrote: "In our way a drunken Dutchman, who was a passenger, too, fell overboard; when he was sinking, I reached through the water to his shock pate and drew him up so that we got him in again."

Franklin, the pilot and the Dutchman rode out the night at anchor in the sloop. He reached New Jersey the next day and went along the main highway to the Delaware. Boatmen gave him passage there, but he was forced to row for a day and most of a night to get to Philadelphia. He wrote about that arrival: "I was very hungry, and my whole stock of cash consisted of a Dutch dollar and about a shilling in copper coin, which I gave to the boatmen for my passage."

He soon found work, though, and stayed in Philadelphia while it grew to the size of the second largest city in the British empire. A lighthouse was built at Cape Henlopen in 1725 as a very badly needed aid to navigation for the increasing number of vessels that used the port and also touched at the lower river towns.

The State House was begun in 1732 on Chestnut Street, and in 1735 the state assembly occupied Assembly Hall before it was finished by the builders. Water Street was built out in front of Front Street. The windmill on Windmill Island lost its sails in a gale in 1751, and was not rebuilt. There were in 1753, either at anchor or alongside the wharves, 117 seagoing vessels. The major exports were wheat, flour, corn, flaxseed, barrels, casks, skins and furs, and ginseng. Most of the imports were manufactured goods, and came from England.

Robert Morris had a spectacular rise in the shipping business. He was the son of poor Liverpool immigrants, and got only a few years of education after his family's arrival in Philadelphia. Then he joined the powerful mercantile house owned by Charles Willing, serving as an apprentice. He was in 1754 and at the age of twenty a full partner in the firm with Willing's son. He was able to boast a few years later that he "owned more ships than any other man in America."

The firm drew a great part of its wealth from the West Indian trade. But it dealt also in the immigrant traffic. The 250-ton brig *Wilmington* sailed regularly from the company wharf in Philadelphia for Belfast, carrying a cargo of flaxseed. The ship's holds on the homeward-bound passage were filled with Ulster "redemptioners" who had mortgaged their future for seven years to get away from the Irish landlords. *Wilmington* stayed in the Belfast trade for fifty years and took generations of Scotch-Irish to America.

New Castle was the first port of entry for ships coming up Delaware Bay from seaward. The redemptioners spent little time below after that. They watched the river scene, guessing at the size of the oysters being pulled aboard a tonger sloop, and the depth of the channel, the welcome they would be given in Philadelphia and how long they would stay there before they could get away to the frontier country.

There were very few of them who were disappointed by the city. This was much more of a place then Belfast, and that was praise enough. Arch Street Wharf, where the ferry from Camden tied up, was clamorous with activity. Windlass pawls clacked as sailors heaved cargo up out of ships' holds and then it was lowered away to waiting draymen and wagoners. Those men shouted at their teams and each other and were quiet only when an Admiralty surveyor in a cocked hat, powered wig and brass-buttoned coat asked them bruskly who their employers were.

Philadelphia was in the middle 1700s a rapidly growing port which attracted all kinds of traffic. A shallop approaches Windmill Island for a cargo of flour, and a well-loaded Durham boat is at center. A canopied

The redemptioners stood closely together, even the most brash of the Ulstermen shy. The city, with its red-brick houses and church spires and narrow streets, was not unlike those in the British Isles. But here on the river were evidences of wealth which were astonishing in their abundance.

There were boats that the local people called "batteaux," but were really enlarged, sturdily built skiffs. They came down-

rowing barge splendid enough to belong to the governor is at the right near the big warship. The city shows its prosperity in the many fine brick buildings and the State House, on Chestnut Street.

river so laden with cargo and passengers that only a few inches of freeboard remained. Men wearing buckskin shirts and fur caps propelled them with long oars, or sweeps. The cargo, usually corn or wheat in sacks, was stowed two and three tiers high at the bow, and in the same fashion right abaft the oarsmen. A canopy stretched over the stern section to protect the passengers and the captain. The captain, distinguished by a beaver hat, *199* blew often upon a strident tin horn. That horn was used, too, the redemptioners understood, to summon the crew and passengers from shore. Bound upstream against the current, the crews pushed the craft along with "setting poles," and progress was slow. Passengers brought their own blankets for overnight stops, and their own food, and rum.

But more impressive than the batteaux were the Durham boats. One of the oldest iron works in Pennsylvania had been founded in 1727 at Durham. The only way for its products to reach Philadelphia was by water, along the Delaware, until in 1745 a road to Bristol was built. Robert Durham designed a flat-bottomed boat capable of carrying fifteen tons of cargo down the swift upper river.

The Durham boats were from forty to sixty feet long, with a six to eight foot beam, and a two or three foot draft. Their ends were pointed, somewhat like a canoe, and the tiller extended well into the boat. The rudder was huge. They could be rowed, sailed or poled. Headed upstream, they needed a crew of five men, one steering and two on each side pushing with iron-shod poles as they walked along the boards which extended the full length of the boat.*

They brought out bar iron to be used by blacksmiths and anchor-makers, and slit iron to be fashioned into nails, and tools and implements of all sorts, including thousands of cutlasses to be delivered to the sugar plantations in the West Indies for field-hand work at cutting cane. Pots, pans and kettles were turned over to the Indian traders, or to peddlers who sailed the shallow back creeks in canoes or trudged the trails and visited lonely cabins where the nearest neighbors were miles apart.

* This was the boat Washington used to cross the Delaware to Trenton.

PHILADELPHIA

But Durham boats handled other cargo whenever there was space, bales of pelts or deerskins and the wheat and corn which all farmers cultivated. Ironmasters lived very well back in the ore-bearing country, the redemptioners were told. They built themselves fine mansions on the hill crests above the forges, and usually they were in charge of what was known as an iron plantation. That meant a blast furnace, at least one forge, houses, a sawmill and a grist mill, and all the equipment, and the fleet of boats. The whole investment was around £7,000, if not more. There were in the 1760s just as many blast furnaces and forges throughout the colonies as in both England and Wales.

The Pennsylvania mines were the best, though, and gave the greatest amount of ore. Blacksmiths were important people in the colony. So were whitesmiths, who worked in tin plate, and made kettles, coffee pots, saucepans, sand-shakers, lanterns and Dutch ovens, for which there was a big demand. Block tin was brought in from South Wales in cargo consignments for the whitesmiths, unloaded at Philadelphia and then tinned iron sheets were hammered at plating mills.

Right across from Philadelphia, on the Jersey side at Wistarburg, a man named Caspar Wistar had started the manufacture of glass in 1739. He sent for expert glassmakers from Rotterdam, and for forty-two years he and his son Richard carried on the business. They made window glass, bottles, pitchers and other products that were shipped coastwise as far north as Maine, and to Baltimore, and Charleston, and Savannah. Then Heinrich Wilhelm Stiegel came from Germany around the middle of the century and set himself up as an ironmaster near Lancaster. He shifted over later to making glass, and built several glass houses. His exquisite transparent and deep-blue, and amethyst, and green and wine colored glass was in wide demand. But his ideas got ahead of his ability to finance them, and he finally failed, clinging onto his self-presented title of Baron.

Pottery made in southeastern Pennsylvania was another coastwise cargo item from Philadelphia. Her tanneries were kept active to supply the overseas and domestic markets, and she also turned out silverware, and pewter, and brass buttons, and sperm-oil candles for the West Indian trade. William Bradford, the printer, had joined David Rittenhouse, a Dutch paper-maker, as early as 1690 in building the first paper mill in America on the Wissahickon Creek near Philadelphia. Other men soon followed their example, and in 1756 the first pulp engine was introduced from Holland. Bookbinding was begun as a shop industry, and Pennsylvania books went along in coastwise ship cargoes with bundles of Benjamin Franklin's *Pennsylvania Gazette,* and the *Pennsylvania Packet.*

When the redemptioners left Philadelphia and started for the frontier, they used the Market Way. For a time, the belvederes, the superb country estates of the rich merchants, flanked the road, their lawns and gardens and orchards extending down to the river. But, while the State House clock tower was still in sight, the road became bad.

The redemptioners' guide said that there were stretches ahead that were filled with mud-holes, roots, rocks and fallen trees. Rivers were often crossed by fording them, or by ferries moved by ropes or sweeps. The big and strongly made Conestoga wagons, painted bright red and blue, the body curved upward at each end and covered with a coarse cotton cloth stretched over hoops, had been introduced by German settlers who lived in the Conestoga valley of Pennsylvania. Those, when they were deeply loaded, though, mired down to the hubs, or snapped an axle, gave spavins to the team that tried to pull too hard.

A boatyard gang is hard at work under William Penn's famous Treaty Elm, Philadelphia beyond downriver. A tarpot smokes at center, men rig sails and new timber while visitors lounge in the shade with their dog. Ships wait below to get to wharves, and at one a vessel is careened for bottom cleaning and repair.

The redemptioners passed on their way along the river road the famous Treaty Elm at Kensington. A boatyard was built on the bank beside it. Sawyers worked beneath the spread of shade from the immense branches. Their guide said that it cost around £2 a ton to haul iron from Reading to Philadelphia. That was about fifty miles by road, and the price of iron at the furnace was only £3 a ton. So Philadelphia grew bigger as a port every day. Anything that could be hauled by water was sent there.   *203*

But, with all her prosperity, Philadelphia for ten years before the signing of the Declaration of Independence felt extremely bitter antagonism towards the home government. The imposition of the Navigation Acts and the other restrictive regulations on trade had become almost intolerable. Any loyalty or respect for the Penn family was lost when the two brothers who were the then proprietors refused to speak to each other in public. The king was the butt of comic writing in the *Pennsylvania Packet* that had satirical reference to the queen mother. The paper reported:

> It has been observed that the French king, an old man, is governed by a young woman, while the k—— of ———, a young man, is governed by an old woman.

One year, soon before the Revolution, St. George's Day, traditionally observed in a merry manner by all loyal Britons, could muster up only twenty celebrants. Slate House, the fashionable tavern, the Queen of Otaheite and the other coffee-houses, the dancing schools and the fencing schools were frequented by young macaronis who slavishly copied the latest London styles. They wore a large knot of artificial hair fastened at the nape of the neck, a very small cocked hat and tight-fitting clothes, and carried walking sticks that were almost head-high and decorated with silk tassels. But they failed to celebrate with the Britons.

The Royalist group was forced to go to the theater and interrupt a performance there to get attention. Flushed with wine, and belligerent, they made the audience sing "Rule, Britannia," "Britons, Strike Home" and "God Save the King."

The long-expected crisis came early in the summer of 1773, when the East India Tea Company attempted to land taxed tea cargoes in America. People all along the Delaware protested to London and made their position very clear. If the tea was sent, they said, both ships and cargoes might be burned.

There was no government answer to these letters. A Philadelphia mass meeting was held in the State House yard. It was resolved there by unanimous vote that no tea tax was to be collected. The tax, the resolution said, "had a direct tendency to render assemblies useless and to introduce arbitrary government and slavery. Whoever shall directly or indirectly aid or abet in unloading, receiving or vending the tea is an enemy of his country."

A warning was issued in the form of a broadside to the Delaware pilots by the Philadelphia "Committee for Tarring and Feathering." The pilots were told to look out for a tea ship named *Polly*, under the command of Captain Ayres. Ship and master were described in the broadside as "an old black ship, commanded by short, fat Captain Ayres."

When *Polly* took in her topsails and closed with the land at Gloucester Point, a public-protest meeting was held. A couple of the pilots boarded her. They talked with Captain Ayres, and advised him to stay out of the Delaware. Should he bring *Polly* into the bay by himself, they said, they would put a halter around his neck, dump ten gallons of liquid tar on his head and lay upon the tar the feathers of a dozen wild geese. Captain Ayres decided that he had chosen the wrong time to enter, and told his mate to alter course and send *Polly* away from the land.

News of the Boston Tea Party reached Philadelphia by courier on Christmas Eve. The famous companies of mummers in their gaudy costumes were out collecting Christmas "dole" from house to house, reciting doggerel and singing carols. The bells of Christ Church had rung all afternoon and evening and, with the Boston news, were kept clanging until dawn.

205

PORTS OF CALL

A year later, though, the brig *Greyhound* put a cargo of tea ashore at Greenwich, in southwestern New Jersey. The stuff had been consigned for Philadelphia, but the master, a man named James Allen, was unwilling to make the upriver run and try to deliver it. He slid inside the bay at night, when mist covered the Jersey marshes. Then he found his way along narrow, mud-banked Cohansey Creek, constantly using the sounding lead.

He stored the tea in a barn that belonged to a Tory. This backwater was a former pirates' hangout, and among others Blackbeard Teach was supposed to have used it to stay safe from the law. Allen hoped that he could hide here long enough to get rid of the tea in small lots, smuggle it out through Tory sympathizers.

But the local clergymen aroused the farmers. Forty of them dressed as Indians broke into the barn on the night of November 22, 1774, and took the tea chests to the middle of a field, made a bonfire. Henry Stacks was the only one of their number whose patriotic fervor weakened. He filled his pockets with tea, and was called "Tea Stacks" for the rest of his life.

When war came, the old dislikes, the unsolved feuds and claims between religious and language groups, widened, became a very serious threat to any chance for unified action. The province was in a condition of near-anarchy

Swedes and Dutchmen and Palatinate Germans were reminded of the slights, imaginary or real, that had been inflicted upon them by the "smart Quakers" in Philadelphia.

The proud and sensitive fair-haired Welsh reminded themselves that they were of ancient Cymric stock. Their ancestors were the *Bonheddig*, who had ruled centuries ago over *Gwynedd*, the White Land, and most of Britain, too. They were not in any way ready to take orders from a set of English fops, Philadelphians *206* in particular.

PHILADELPHIA

The Scotch-Irish along the back creeks and the wild mountain ridges of the Cumberland country recalled the broken promises in the days of the Indian raids. Because of those, wives were scalped, children killed or stolen, cabins and crops burned. The Philadelphia people had kept right on making money, and more promises.

But now in Philadelphia the Quaker fops were quick to join the Continental Army, although for that most of them were excommunicated from their church. Men heard about it in the interior, and met at crossroads taverns, or at a bend in a creek where a Durham boat could be boarded. They left the mines, the forges, the glassworks, the mills, the fishing boats and farms, and came at last to Philadelphia as volunteers. Other men were already mustered aboard the Philadelphia privateers like *Alfred,* and at sea.

There was between all of the groups a great common denominator, a permanent bond. They or their parents had made the immigrant passage across the Atlantic. That fact alone had profoundly changed them. The Atlantic separated them from the past, gave shape to the future.

They were Americans, and they were Pennsylvanians. So they went to war against the forces from overseas who in the name of King George III would drag them back into the past.

CHAPTER 8

⤳ *Baltimore*

SHE WAS A BERMUDA-BUILT SCHOONER, with a cedar hull, a pair of tall, tapered masts and sharp lines. Joshua Barney liked her. She promised to be fast, even with those ten carriage-mount cannon put aboard. Her new name, given her by the Marine Committee of the Continental Congress, was *Hornet.* She was looking for volunteers, lacked a crew of any kind.

Barney left the shipyard where the carpenters hired by the Marine Committee worked at entering gun-ports in *Hornet's* bulwarks. He found her master, Captain William Stone, and said that he would like to serve aboard the schooner as master's mate. Stone, a veteran seaman, was quick to accept him although Barney was not yet sixteen. This was Baltimore, in December, 1775, and the recently convened Congress had extreme need of men to take 208 to sea what it called, with some optimism, the Continental Navy.

BALTIMORE

But Barney, at the age of fifteen, was an experienced ship-master. His strutting, and the way he wore a stock, slanted his hat, were forgiven. If he wanted to act like a cockerouse, which was common Maryland talk for somebody of importance, he rated it.

Barney had proved that during the voyage he had just finished. He had started it as an apprentice aboard a schooner owned and commanded by his brother-in-law. He learned navigation while the ship was outward-bound with her cargo of bulk wheat for the Mediterranean port of Nice. Then, hundreds of miles from land, the captain died.

The ship had sailed short-handed, without a mate. Joshua Barney was the only member of the crew with any working knowledge of celestial navigation. The rest of the crew, grown men, held a meeting and discussed the problem. It was their unanimous and almost immediate decision that Joshua serve as master for the remainder of the voyage. He could only accept, and began his duties.

His brother-in-law's quadrant was heavy and unwieldy, but a reliable instrument. The navigation book in the cabin, printed in London in 1760, opened with the statement that it was "The Pathway to perfect Sayling." It was "published for the Common good of all Masters, Pilots and other Sea-men whatsoever." Added to it was "A Nautical Discourse necessary to be knowne of all Sea-men to prove the way of a Ship (upon the Superficies of the Sea) outward and homeward to be both one, returning by the opposite Point of the Meridian Compasse. And also to prove the East and West directed by the Meridian Compasse to lead in a Magneticall parallel."

He made sense out of this, and used the accompanying logarithmic tables. He checked the error of the "magneticall" compass by sun amplitudes and lunar sights with the quadrant, laid off courses that brought the schooner accurately to her European landfall on Cape Finisterre. Then he sailed her into the Mediterranean past the immense brown thrust of Gibraltar, the crew openly awed by his skill, and took her to Nice.

Nice, a small and chromatic Italian port on the Riviera, was in need of wheat for the manufacture of spaghetti. Joshua ordered the schooner's hatches opened; the cargo lay intact, dry, unspoiled by mould or sea sweat. The Italian merchant who was the consignee went down in the holds and sifted through his fingers the golden, hard kernels, grown in the back Monocacy country by frontier farmers. He chewed some of the kernels, and admitted that the quality was excellent.

Joshua talked with the man through the ship's agent. He got a good price, and sold the entire cargo. Then he loaded rock ballast, headed for Baltimore.

But, inside the Virginia capes, the schooner on a fine point of sailing and with Old Point Comfort almost abeam, the big British sloop-of-war *Kingfisher* pulled over, and made a signal. That was for the schooner to heave-to, without resistance. The man-of-war had her gunports triced. Her gunners bent over the pieces with lit matches, ready to fire.

A launch came away from the king's ship. The crew was armed with pistols and cutlasses. The ensign who boarded from her brought a bosun's mate and half-a-dozen sailors. He said he wanted all of the arms aboard this vessel. Great Britain, he explained to Joshua, was at war with "the rebels."

Joshua knew the meaning of "rebels," and did not argue. He surrendered the small supply of arms aboard the schooner. Then he stood at the side expressionless while the Royal Navy men went back to their ship. He shaped his own course between

BALTIMORE

Horseshoe Shoal and Middle Ground, proceeded up the bay to Baltimore.

He was furious with rage, his hatred of the British, held since the Stamp Act period, fully inflamed. It was only by luck that the schooner had not carried contraband cargo homeward-bound. The British would surely have seized that. And the *King-fisher* ensign had been careless—he didn't take the schooner's strongbox. The gold from the sale of the wheat was in it. Joshua's widowed sister would be in real trouble without the wheat money, and again he was lucky.

Joshua visited his bereaved sister. He made the accounting for the voyage, and paid off the crew. Then he went to inspect *Hornet.* His fury against the British had not subsided. He wanted to get to sea and fight them. He would be very foolish to trust only to his luck with the Royal Navy. The odds were too great.

One of the first Continental flags came from Philadelphia to Baltimore right after Joshua Barney was accepted for Navy service. He was sent out with the flag, a drummer and a fifer to rally a crew for both *Hornet* and another Baltimore vessel, the ten-gun schooner *Wasp.*

He paraded the muddy, ice-encrusted streets for several hours with his detachment. Baltimore was small, and as recently as 1750 had contained only twenty-five houses. But it was the center for the back-country German and Scotch-Irish farmers, and the trade from the upper rivers. A number of men and boys in their older teens had already been recruited for the Army. They drilled in the fields on the edge of town, learned the care and handling of the musket and squads right, squads left. Barney told his musicians to play loud. He was in need of a crowd.

He went down Light Street to the waterfront, and along it, past the sailor hangouts. Then he went back up to Market Street

Baltimore was still in 1752 a very small port. Men fished the cove with nets, worked as farmers. Then they began to build clipper-lined vessels. The design became popular because of its speed. Baltimore vessels were the fastest on any ocean. Privateers, frigates, slavers were launched. Shipyards spread out wide around the harbor. Lombard and Market Street merchants grew rich. Clipper ships broke the records to Canton. They broke them again, homeward-bound.

and halted the detachment at the taproom door of the Indian Queen tavern. The flag was boldly displayed, and soon there was a crowd. Men argued about the thirteen stripes, and the Union Jack in the upper right-hand corner. Joshua Barney talked to them about enlistment in the Navy. A recruit would have plenty of prize money if he served under this flag at sea.

Baltimore was unused to martial music, and the flag maintained interest for the crowd. Barney ordered rounds of cherry flip from the taproom. A waiter brought a table, a quill pen, ink, a sander and long sheets of paper. Barney talked to the bigger boys in the crowd, and then the men. Before darkness, and before it was too cold for him to write any longer, he had enlisted full crews for *Hornet* and *Wasp*.

BALTIMORE

There were merchant ships gathered in the Patapsco and out in the bay that waited for escort to take them to sea past *Kingfisher*. A convoy was formed with the two armed schooners ready for the Royal Navy ship. But *Kingfisher* gave no trouble, and the American ships stood on their separate courses at sea. Barney, busy as master's mate aboard *Hornet,* was pleased. His ship and *Wasp* were the first Continental Navy vessels to get offshore.

He found little glory, though, in the duty that was given *Hornet.* Her orders were to make rendezvous with a squadron that was being assembled off the Delaware capes. It was to cruise the southern coast under Captain Esek Hopkins, the commander-in-chief of the new Navy.

Hopkins decided to attack New Providence Island, in the Bahamas. He passed an order for the squadron to keep formation and follow his flagship there. But at night, in bad weather off the coast of South Carolina, the schooner *Fly* fouled *Hornet. Hornet* was quite badly hurt aloft. Her rigging and square topsail gear needed repair; she asked for and received permission to proceed into port. Barney lost his chance to take part in the assault on New Providence, and keenly regretted it.

He was still eager for action when *Hornet* moved up the coast weeks later and tried to get inside the Delaware capes. She was sighted and pursued by the forty-four-gun Royal Navy frigate *Roebuck.* There was just one thing for Captain Stone to do; he ran as fast as he could put extra canvas on the schooner. But across the bay she met another Royal Navy ship, *Maria.*

Barney was eager to fight. He loaded one of the broadside cannon, trained and aimed it, held the burning end of the long slow-match over the touch hole to ignite the charge. But Captain Stone told him not to fire. Stone said that he had "no inclination for shedding blood." Barney turned from the piece in disgust and threw the slow-match at the captain. This greatly hurt Stone's sense of naval decorum. He kept off the deck most of the time afterward.

Hornet ran aground and for several days beat herself cruelly on a Delaware sandbar. She smashed her rudder while she lay there, but somehow the lookouts aboard the British patrol craft missed her, and Barney was able to work her off and conn her upstream to Philadelphia.

Captain Stone left her without reporting the slow-match incident to the Marine Committee, withdrew from active service. Barney was regarded favorably by his superiors in the port. When *Roebuck* and another of His Majesty's frigates, 28-gun *Liverpool*, started up the river towards Philadelphia in May, 1776, he was given command of a row-galley.

This was a craft built and outfitted by the State of Pennsylvania in the fashion adopted by several of the former colonies anxious to maintain their own navies. She was fifty feet long, with a thirteen-and-a-half-foot beam and a shallow draft. Her armament was an eighteen-pounder in the bow and four brass three-pounders mounted on stocks along the after-rail and on the stern.

The crew, most of them Durham boat veterans, slept in bunks under the side decks and the center-line gangway. Barney and the other officers shared a small cabin aft. Tarpaulins covered the hatchways at night and in foul weather. Cooking was done in a brick fireplace on the gun platform forward, or ashore if that was possible.

She was equipped to carry a lugsail on a pole mast, but Barney relied on his twenty oarsmen. He waited for *Roebuck* and *Liverpool* in the lower river, surprisingly patient. Their pilots, he knew, were unreliable. When *Roebuck* grounded in mid-channel, he was ready.

214   He opened on the frigate with the eighteen-pounder, kept

A furious action was fought in the Delaware off Mud Fort in 1777 between American and British forces. The Americans defended the river with frigates, rowing galleys, fireships, and the fort's guns. The fireships were effective, and *H.M.S. Augusta* set ablaze, *Merlin* burned to avoid capture.

Roebuck between him and *Liverpool.* He delivered grapeshot and canister, concentrating his fire along the main gun deck. Then he ordered his gunners to lift it, and they swept the rigging where the Royal Marines in their shellacked shakos clung and used long-barreled muskets. There were more Marines in the fighting tops, and some of them sent musket and swivel gun rounds whip- 215 ping into the water around the galley. The gunners who had been killed or wounded on *Roebuck*'s main deck were replaced. The twenty-four-pounder shot they fired came through the air with a whine that changed into a rough, enormous roar. The cannon balls flung geysers high where they struck the river, and the men who worked the row-galley were drenched. Vapor rose from the barrels of their guns. They were forced to check their powder.

But they laughed. They were winning. Other American craft were here, and pounded *Roebuck*. Her fire was weak. *Liverpool*, caught on the wrong side of the channel, was of little help to her. The morning tide let *Roebuck* float clear, and with *Liverpool* she headed downstream, in retreat.

Barney got his commission as lieutenant a few weeks later. He had distinguished himself in the attempt to land powder from the American brigantine *Nancy*, chased ashore by the British. This was taken into consideration when Robert Morris gave Barney the commission. Morris was the fiscal agent of the Continental Congress, and a leading figure in the war against the British. The procedure was a bit unusual because Barney, although still seventeen, was the thirteenth of his rating on the naval list.

Barney went home on leave to Baltimore early in 1776. Out at the Point, where he could use deep water, George Wells was building a twenty-eight-gun frigate under government contract. Her name was *Virginia,* and she was 126 feet long on her gun deck, weighed according to her plans 681 tons. She looked as though she would be as fast as the merchant ships which had made the local shipbuilders famous, and Barney hoped to get assigned to her.

There was difficulty in finishing her, though, because of the British blockade of the Chesapeake. She was not ready for sea until the spring of 1777, and James Nicholson had been appointed to command her a year before. Meantime, the crew had disappeared. Baltimore clipper schooners, very fast because of their concave lines and severely raked masts, were popular as privateers, and the pay was a great deal better than that offered in the Continental Navy.

Nicholson rated just below Esek Hopkins, the commander-in-chief, and tried to gather a crew in Baltimore through impressment. Governor Thomas Johnson objected so vigorously that for a time Nicholson was suspended from his command. The Marine Committee assigned Joshua Barney to *Virginia,* and he reported aboard, was put in charge of recruiting.

Barney went to Bordentown, where the remnants of the Continental Navy were held after the British seizure of Philadelphia. He collected enough men for the new frigate and two merchant vessels that waited in the Chesapeake loaded with valuable tobacco cargoes but short of crews.

He marched the sailors overland to Baltimore, and they took his orders, and none of them deserted. Along the way, he halted the column at Valley Forge while he paid his respects to General Washington. It was in the midst of the terrible winter of deprivation and despair for the Army, and Barney's lot did not have to be told that they would be much better off at sea.

Virginia sailed from Baltimore in January, 1778, and Nicholson cautiously took her into the lower bay. British cruisers were reported off the capes, and he was afraid of capture. He made a sortie towards the end of March, trusted the pilotage to the master of a locally owned brig. The wind was fair and strong, and *Virginia* began to show some of the speed promised in her lines.

But the master of the brig was a poor pilot. *Virginia* hit with violence on Middle Ground. The following wind hurled her repeatedly onto the shoal and before she could work off it she had   *217* broken her rudder. The only maneuver that would save the ship was to drop anchor. Nicholson gave the order, and Barney immediately obeyed.

When dawn came over the bay, the Americans found a pair of British frigates almost within cannon range of *Virginia*. These were *Emerald* and *Conqueror,* and once he had identified them Nicholson ordered his barge hoisted out and held ready alongside. He put the ship's papers and ten men aboard her, asked Barney to join him.

Barney refused to desert the ship, and the other officers would not leave her. But when he tried to persuade them to cut the anchor cable so that the ship might drift onto the beach and destroy herself, they were unwilling. They said that to wreck *Virginia* would not save them captivity in a British prison hulk. The crew had already broached ship's stores and passed around pannikins of rum. The officers, all except Barney, sought their share.

A boarding party from *Emerald* came over the side at ten o'clock and took possession of the ship. The crew was shouting, raving drunk. Barney kept aside from them although his brother William was one of the Marine detachment and caroused with the rest.

Joshua Barney was treated with dignity as the senior officer aboard *Virginia*. When he was transferred, he was given a berth in the captain's cabin on *Emerald,* brought his meals there. But the next morning he suffered deep humiliation. Captain Nicholson, under a flag of truce, boarded the British man-of-war and asked if he could get his personal clothing from *Virginia*.

Nicholson made the request in the captain's cabin. Joshua Barney was in a corner of the big cabin where sunlight reflected 218 off the water entered through the stern gallery windows in dazzling beams. It was possible that Nicholson failed to see his former lieutenant as he came from on deck. But he certainly heard all that Barney had to tell him.

Barney cursed Nicholson. He did it with great thoroughness and a choice of several well-known Maryland oaths. The British officers in their crimson, gold and lace did not pretend to listen. But they did not speak until Barney was finished with his description of Nicholson's shortcomings. Nicholson was given permission to take his clothing, and a file of Royal Marines marched him to the side.

That was the last satisfaction Barney was to have for five months. He spent them in the hold of the prison hulk *Jersey*, in New York's Wallabout Bay, and all around him men died miserably, or went insane. Then he was offered a promise of parole, signed it and was released.

He went back to Baltimore, but not for long. The sea called him, and he took privateer service aboard the fast clipper schooner *Charming Molly*. He had need of money, and now, more than ever, a compulsive desire to fight the British.

But *Charming Molly* was captured at sea in 1780 after a long chase. The British, as they inspected their prisoners, recognized Joshua Barney as a parole violator. The usual penalty for that, the senior British officer said, was hanging. But Barney had the reputation of a brave enemy. His life was to be spared, so that he might serve an indeterminate sentence in a dungeon at the Old Mill Prison in Portsmouth.

Old Mill was situated between Portsmouth and Portsmouth Dock. It was an immense structure, built of granite and given in wartime to the confinement of several thousand American privateersmen captured in waters around the British Isles. The warden was proud of his record of very few escapes.

But Old Mill was considerably better than *Jersey*. Prisoners were allowed to govern themselves, and established their own rules of conduct. There was a prison library, and a man might borrow books. Ship models carved by inmates from bits of bone or wood were sold on the outside by the guards.

It was through the guards that Barney's escape was arranged. He shared none of the amenities allowed the other prisoners, remained solitary in his almost lightless and heavily barred dungeon until the release plan was completed. A number of English liberals who profoundly disliked the war had involved themselves in securing his freedom.

Guards were bribed. Barney was supplied with a pair of boarding pistols and a rope that would help him over the prison wall. The boarding pistols were cruel weapons. They were equipped with short, grooved bayonets set on the muzzles. These snapped back when a lever was moved. The butt plates were broad, made of brass, designed to split a man's skull at a single blow.

Barney got out of Old Mill Prison without undue delay. He cleared the wall, and then was met by members of the "underground" who kept him in various hiding places for weeks. Contact was made with a Dutch smuggler crew. He went aboard the smuggler craft at night off the southern English coast and was taken to the Netherlands. The American privateer *Cicero* brought him home. He was given, early in 1782, command of the Pennsylvania State cruiser *Hyder Ally*.

She was armed with sixteen guns. Her name came from that of the leader of a revolt in India against British rule as represented by the Honorable East India Company. There were British ships off the Delaware capes, and Barney went after them

220   with *Hyder Ally*.

BALTIMORE

His Majesty's sloop-of-war *General Monk* lay close alongside the big British frigate *Quebec* past Cape May. She was a thirty-two-gun vessel, but that meant very little to Barney. He attacked her on April second, and seized her, sailed her away before *Quebec* could bring effective fire to bear and stop him.

Barney held command of that ship for the rest of the war, her name changed to *General Washington*. Then, with the peace, his Continental Navy service was finished, and he returned to Baltimore. He was unhappy ashore; he found that he could not be successful as a civilian.

Baltimore was booming, and it increased his unhappiness. There should be something here which would pay him enough to support his family and save them from the long absences while he was at sea. He was the town hero, and in all the taverns and coffee-houses, and where the merchants gathered along Lombard or Market Street, he was greeted with the greatest respect.

But, once he was away from the waterfront, the complex activity of the town confused him. The town had become too big for him. That was his trouble.

Even before the war, Baltimore had begun to change over from the tobacco economy dominated by the Tidewater planters. Tobacco prices were too fluctuant on the London market, and many of the planters were irretrievably in debt to their English agents. The town was now a center of trade for the back-country farmers, who each year sent down more grain for export in the schooners built on the bay. The despised "wool hats," smelling of cow dung and thoroughly chewed snuff, were the men responsible for most of the prosperity. But the shipbuilders held great prominence.

Some of them had memorized and could quote from Ebenezer Cooke's poem about the Potomac:

PORTS OF CALL

Materials here of every kind
May soon be found, were Youth inclin'd,
To practice the Ingenious Art
Of sailing by Mercator's Chart. . . .

Nothing is wanting to compleat,
Fit for the Sea a trading Fleet
But Industry and Resolution.

What was true about the Potomac was doubly true along the upper bay, and the Baltimore shipowners had kept the poem well in mind. The town was a conglomerate of English Catholics, French Huguenots, Scots Presbyterians and German Lutherans and a broad scattering of other sects. But Maryland held an extraordinary heritage from the original proprietor. Lord Baltimore had insisted upon religious tolerance, right at the beginning. Even the witchcraft scare, which spread over the entire Protestant world in the seventeenth century, left the Chesapeake region untouched.

Baltimore shipbuilders were able to find men who would work together without factionalism and bickering, and the resultant slow-downs. Crews for the vessels came from the town itself, or those nearby on the bay. Their sailors took part in brawls with men from foreign ships, and often sought out English crews, but they rarely fought each other.

Baltimore ships became famous for several reasons. The white-oak and pine that went into their construction were of the finest quality. They were exceptionally fast. The designers had got away from the centuries-old belief that a ship's beam must be a third of her length. The clipper schooners with their lean, long hulls,

Baltimore, because of her geographical position, became a great port of call where inland cargoes were shipped overseas. The National Road extended west to the Ohio Valley farms, brought wheat to Baltimore that was locally milled to produce flour. That was by 1827 more than half the port's export trade, with coffee from Brazil generally the main cargo on the return voyages.

flared bows and raked masts where topsail yards were crossed, were the favorite craft for men like Joshua Barney.

The town paid honor to Barney in April, 1788, when the Constitution was ratified. Baltimore held a celebration, and every trade and profession and business interest in the community was represented. The march started on Philpot's Hill, overlooking Fell's Point. It moved east on Market Street to Charles Street, and *223* south through Frenchtown, and then east again to John Smith's Hill, on the south side of the harbor basin. The hill there became known immediately afterward as Federal Hill.

A miniature full-rigged ship had been built by the town's shipwrights as their gift for the occasion. It was mounted on a suitably decorated float, and the dainty little vessel, about the size of a ship's boat, was called *The Federalist.* The shipwrights insisted that Barney ride aboard her and "sail" her during the parade.

Barney put on his Continental Navy uniform and his sword. He climbed up onto the quarterdeck of *The Federalist* and the float was hauled to the top of the hill by a crowd of admirers. There were 3,000 celebrants after all the floats were passed in review and the parade was disbanded. Supper was served, and large amounts of punch, and patriotic songs were repeated. Near dawn, most of the people went home.

But Barney stayed. He had been given a new command, and he was determined to sail her, and not on a float but in Chesapeake Bay. His appeal for a launching gang gathered a number of men and boys. They carefully slid *The Federalist* down the hillside under Barney's direction and, with dawn breaking, put her in the water.

Barney went aboard. He trimmed braces, and sheets, took a strain on halyards. Then he went aft to the tiller. The dawn breeze rippled the water, filled the small, beautifully cut sails. Barney squared her on her course out into Middle Branch, bore away towards Sparrows Point, the Patapsco and the bay. The crowd cheered. Barney answered with a formal salute. He was off the beach; he was a sailor again.

Astern, back there in the town, were the doctors, the lawyers, the dentists, the midwives, teachers, ministers and mechanics. And the hatters, the tailors, the boot- and shoe-makers, the stocking weavers, the milliners and mantua-makers. And the brick-makers and nail-makers, the glaziers, the blue-dyers, the coverlet-makers and the folks who worked in the woolen mill, the fulling mill, the tannery, the dye-works, the stove-works and at the shop where the Bible was printed. And he had left out the merchants, the apothecaries, the veterinaries, the wig-maker, the man who made combs and the man who sold drums. And the tavern-keepers.

He touched the helm, changed course a bit. The breeze increased, and spray leaped the knight-heads, flicked the deck and his face. Ahead, gleaming, the bay stretched. This was the world he knew.

He met all sorts of craft on the immense tidal expanse of the bay, and each of them was familiar. Men hailed him from gundalows and schooners loaded with heaps of freshly dredged oysters. A log canoe carrying a Baltimore-bound cargo of vegetables from the Eastern Shore sailed close aboard while the boy at the tiller inspected *The Federalist* and Barney. Sloops, ketches, an occasional brig breasted the current, and the men on deck waved or shouted, recognizing him and what this meant.

Inshore, muddy-hocked teams of horses dragged the great seine nets up onto the bank. The catches of shad and cod glistened when they were dumped. Gulls gave up looking for crabs in the shallows, cried at each other and dived for the fish. Ferry horses tethered at a crossing neighed and stamped with the sting of fly bites. A post-rider who waited for the ferry yelled loudly in greeting to Barney over the water.

Here along the Eastern Shore were the enormous plantations. The old English term of a "Hundred" was still used. It was given to a district that contained ten families and ten estates, and originally supplied a hundred fighting men to the colony. Tobacco kept the estates going, although every year more planters went bankrupt, or sold for what they could get, and moved to Annapolis and Baltimore.

When a London ship arrived fifty years ago and started to go alongside her wharf at Oxford, a cannon was fired to summon the planters. That was still the period of great prosperity. Eight firms of British merchants kept agents in the town. More than 200 deepwater ships used the harbor. Every ship trading on the Eastern Shore was required to clear her cargo at the Oxford custom house.

Seven or eight ships were often in the port together, taking their turn to discharge or load. The local merchants boasted that they could load a ship with 500 hogsheads of tobacco within twelve days. They talked less of the load of passengers that came ashore in 1747 from the English ship *Johnston.* Those were Scottish Highlanders, men from the army of Bonnie Prince Charlie, taken prisoner at Culloden Moor. The Scots had been eagerly bought as slaves, though, both in Oxford and in Annapolis.

Joshua Barney put *The Federalist* on a course for Annapolis out of the bay. He sailed her around into the Severn at the invitation of the governor of the state, General Smallwood. A state vessel met him at the mouth of the river and escorted him to the capital. Word of his voyage had reached the governor, and Barney was to be General Smallwood's guest.

Barney stayed for three days in Annapolis. The handsome little town joyously welcomed him, and he was the principal figure at banquets, offered successions of toasts that sometimes carried over until late at night. Then he boarded *The Federalist,* cast off, set his canvas and took an outward-bound course in the bay. He was headed for the Potomac and a visit on General Washington at Mount Vernon.

BALTIMORE

The stocky, dark-haired sailor went slowly up the broad river. This was historic country, and he was ready to enjoy it. From Chotank, on north along the Virginia side, were the Brent family plantations, and then the Mercers, around Potomac Creek; and Carters, and Lees, and Washingtons. Across on the Maryland shore were Smallwoods, of the governor's family, and a lot of Hansons, and Semmes, and Stones.

Every planter who was wealthy enough to afford it kept his own fleet of sloops or rowing barges handled by trained Negro crews in uniform. The famous ferry operated by the Hooe family ran from Pope's Creek on the Maryland shore to within two or three miles of Mathias Point in Virginia. It was on the shortest route from the capitals of Maryland and Virginia, and linked the upper and lower Potomac settlements.

But Barney gave his complete attention to putting *The Federalist* alongside General Washington's wharf at Mount Vernon. He was not certain of the reception he would be given by the national hero. His decision to present the miniature ship could appear not only mistaken but slightly foolish.

Washington received him politely, and without warmth. Barney did not stay long. He presented *The Federalist* as a gift of the merchants of Baltimore, and was given a correctly phrased letter of acceptance by Washington. Then Barney left. Washington noted the visit in his diary without comment.

Barney, back in Baltimore, recognized that if he were to make a living, he must go to sea.

The War of 1812 found him still the town's outstanding hero. His reputation had diminished very little during the years of peace. Baltimore was war-minded. War assured tremendous profit to the merchants, the shipbuilders and shipowners. Her privateers would bring home cargoes worth millions of dollars, even at

227

government-supervised auction. Seamen filled the shipping offices, signed articles for voyages aboard ships they had never seen. The town passed a resolution on May 21, 1812, and sent it to Washington. That was an appeal for an immediate declaration of war, against either England or France. The enemy did not matter.

When war was formally declared by President Madison on June eighteenth, the first privateer commission was issued to Barney. He had been in semi-retirement from the sea, and living on a farm owned by his wife in Anne Arundel County. There was a splendid clipper schooner waiting for him, and he came to Baltimore at once to take command of her.

She was named *Rossie*. Her principal owner was Isaac McKim, who was to build later the first square-rigged Baltimore clipper. McKim and his partners gave Barney the best. *Rossie's* bottom was freshly copper-sheathed, and she was outfitted with new sails, and new standing and running rigging. She carried ten twelve-pounder carronades as broadside weapons, and three long guns. Her crew of 125 men had been picked from a long list of highly qualified volunteers.

Barney got to sea twenty-four days after war was declared. He was back in Baltimore ninety days later, having seized four ships, eight brigs, three schooners and three sloops. There had been hard fighting for several of them. The action on August ninth with the British privateer *Jeannie* had lasted two hours. And the British government packet *Princess Amelie* would not surrender on September fifteenth until she was fiercely battered during another two-hour battle, fought in moonlight. But the approximate worth of Barney's prizes was put at $1.5 million.

His share of the prize money much more than paid the debts he owed in the town. Then he arranged for the disposition of the 217 men from the ships he had captured. He took his time.

BALTIMORE

He was in his fifties, and the strain of the voyage just completed had consumed a great deal of his reserve energy.

The Navy sent for him, though, and he went to Washington and accepted the rank of commodore. Then he returned to sea in what he recognized could only be for the American naval forces a disastrous war. The British had proclaimed on December 26, 1812, a state of blockade that stretched from New York to Savannah, and that was soon extended to New England as far north as Maine. The American ships were once more caught in their own ports, as they had been during the Revolution. Fast privateers would still operate, but from foreign ports, and could not get home.

There were by 1814 a total of fifteen Royal Navy 74s, twenty-seven frigates and many small ships of war on blockade station along the Atlantic coast. Two 74s, six frigates, a brig, five transports and eight schooners operated off the Virginia capes and in Chesapeake Bay. When the British came up the bay in July, 1814, Barney tried to defend the approaches to Washington with the small fleet of gunboats given him.

His defense ended ashore, behind a hastily built road block in farm country near a town called Bladensburg. It was on the British attack route that would take them to Washington. He commanded a force of 400 men, most of them sailors, the rest Marines. A battery of five twenty-four-pounders had been dragged into position and were manned by Navy gun crews. They covered a wide field of fire along the flat, open road.

Fifers and drummers played the British troops forward. It was a force of 4,000 men, and they were told to drive out the Americans from the barricade with the bayonet. Barney's gunners kept them back for half an hour, helped by Marine musket volleys. Then the sweaty-faced, wild-eyed British were close, and the sailors

229

The bombardment of Fort McHenry by the British fleet on September 13–14, 1814, was unsuccessful. The garrison took it, and held out against the plunging fire bombs from the enemy mortar ships. Baltimore, the British objective because of her many privateers, was saved, and the fleet withdrew.

who had been using spare muskets and pistols cleared their cutlasses.

Barney was wounded before he surrendered. The commanding British officer said that he knew who Barney was, and regretted having to take his sword. Barney said nothing. It was the third time he had been captured by the British, and his wound hurt him.

But Baltimore successfully and brilliantly defended herself. When Barney was released and got back there, he found that it was the only Chesapeake community which was able to hold off invasion, and that Washington had been sacked and burned. He was through with the sea, and reconciled to life on his wife's farm.

He closely examined the Baltimore privateer record before he left for Anne Arundel County. The victories reported keenly interested him. His own prize-money earnings had at first been very much overestimated.

During the thirty months of the war, federal licenses had been granted to 250 privately owned vessels. Baltimore syndicates or individuals operated 126 of these. Most of the Baltimore vessels were letter of marque ships, which because of the limitations of their licenses made few captures. Twenty-one ships, including the famous *Chasseur,* had served as both letter of marque ships and as privateers.

The British had captured or sunk fifty-four ships. Altogether, though, the 126 accounted for 556 enemy vessels. Their activities, along with the other American privateers, were a great aid in supplying the country's need for imported goods. Some of them for a time had blockaded the British Isles. It had been necessary for the Royal Navy to escort merchant ships in convoy from the Channel ports to Ireland. Maritime insurance rates in London were driven up to forty percent.

Chasseur, Lion, and *Prince of Neufchatel* were the big prize-money ships that had sailed out of Baltimore. The toast of the town was Captain Thomas Boyle, who was Marblehead-born and master of a ship when he was sixteen. His exploits as commander of a Baltimore privateer named *Comet,* and then of *Chasseur,* were legendary. Barney was eclipsed, almost forgotten.

The town was harassed at the end of the war, though, with the crippling lack of trade that affected all of the Atlantic ports. Her principal shipbuilders, William Fell, for whom Fell's Point was named, and George Wells, who built *Virginia,* and Thomas *231*

Kemp, who built *Chasseur,* and Isaac McKim, the major partner in the syndicate that sent Barney to sea in command of *Rossie,* were forced to lay off hundreds of workers.

It was the worst depression the town had suffered since 1729, when the original charter was issued. The neatly kept brick houses, the wide, tree-lined squares, the churches of almost every denomination, the fine shops, and the library, the theater, had attracted many of the Tidewater families who wanted no more of plantation life. Robert Carter, the owner of Nomini Hall on the Potomac, had made his residence in Baltimore after his forward-looking ideas were rejected by his planter neighbors.

Carter had questioned the validity of plantation civilization. He began in 1791 to free his slaves. According to his elaborate calculations, each year the fifteen slaves nearest forty-five years of age were to be freed, as well as any boys reaching twenty-one, or girls reaching eighteen. He estimated all of his female slaves would be freed by 1809, and all of his male slaves by 1812. His neighbors' complaints were so vigorous, though, that he had to give up the idea, close Nomini Hall and leave the Potomac.

There were other men of Carter's type in Baltimore. They, too, were able to forecast the eventual ruin of the tobacco plantation system. The future in their terms meant the expansion of trade to the Ohio, canals, new roads, steamboats and faster clipper ships. Still, a large portion of Maryland businessmen clung to the past; they were traditionalists, and proud of the fact. Without perhaps full awareness of the fact, they considered themselves English country gentlemen of the early eighteenth century, even the cavalier period, and attempted to live in that manner.

Colonel Edward Lloyd of Wye House, on the Eastern Shore, was prominent among them, and representative. The colonel, who had ordered a new yacht built, wrote to his London agent:

BALTIMORE

Be pleased to send me a compleat sett of American Colours for a Pleasure Boat of about 60 Tons burthen. Ensign and Pennant with 15 stripes; my Arms painted thereon, the Field azure, the Lion Gold; let these Colours be full-sized. Six brass Guns with hammers, screws, &c. compleat to fix on swivels and to act in such a manner as to give the greatest report; with the letters E.Ll. thereon, fitted to fire with Locks, Powder-horns, pricking-wires & charges, showing the quantity of Powder for each gun; and 200 ball, fitted to the size of the Bore. Have the guns fully proved before purchasing.

Colonel Lloyd also wanted:

A phaeton to be built by the best maker in London, fashionable, handsome carriage with two setts poles, wheels, harness for four horses, fitted to drive with or without postilions. It must not be too high, I being a gouty man.

Sky-blue cloth sufficient for six Servants Coats and yellow ditto for Breeches and Waistcoats, besides best blue and yellow Livery Lace.

Two pairs of Gentlemen's silver Shoe Buckles of the most elegant patterns . . . fashionable hats for the Family by Wagner of Pall Mall; morning caps for Mrs. Lloyd; four dozen Ladies' white kid gloves for a small hand; two quarts of the finest milk of roses in small bottles; twenty pounds best perfumed hair powder.

Then, for Wye House itself:

An elegant Watch Clock proper to fix on a Chimney Piece; also a Sett of Fashionable Decorations to set off a dining or supper table that will accomodate 20 people—with a sketch showing how the Images are to be placed on the Table according to the Vogue. The cost of the ornament not to exceed 100 guineas.

PORTS OF CALL

Baltimore responded to the influences of men like Robert Carter, and also Colonel Lloyd, and a compromise of sorts was achieved in the direction of the affairs of the town. But, in the decade after the War of 1812, shipping became the dominant factor. There were renewed orders from all along the coast and from overseas for clipper schooners. Expansion of the Ohio valley became secondary. The tobacco trade was no longer important. Bankers, merchants, shipowners were interested in the tea trade with China, and in the African slave trade, and in the piracy that still flourished in the Caribbean, particularly around Cuba and Hispaniola.

A vessel built for slave-hauling was built on the same model as a privateer, and so was one used by pirates. Plenty of excuses could be given for turning out a vessel of that class, although the United States was not of course at war. Men in the Lombard Street offices of the Baltimore shipping firms reminded each other that early in the colony's history "picaroons" had been active. The picaroons were the original Chesapeake pirates. Their spirit stubbornly persisted.

It was quite remarkable how privateering, slave-running and piracy were all bound together to make the Baltimore clipper popular. Without a doubt, trouble and unrest were her foster parents.

CHAPTER 9

Charleston

THE YOUNG MEN WHO RETURNED to Charleston in the latter decades
of the eighteenth century after completing their education overseas brought with them a great feeling of nostalgia, some very
sharp curiosity and a sense of superiority which they very soon
lost. Charleston represented home for all of them. Their pursuit
of education had taken them to Oxford, Cambridge, London,
Edinburgh, Leyden and Geneva, and yet they found upon landing at Gadsden's Wharf that the South Carolina city was just as
beautiful and sophisticated as any of those they had visited, and
actually possessed a strong individual quality that made it unique.

The young men, sons of wealthy planters and merchants,
were met by their families, and closely inspected. Boots, hats and
the latest style in London coats approved, they were driven home,
once their luggage was secured from the ship, and again they fell
deeply in love with these familiar surroundings.

235

Charleston harbor circa 1770 when it was the wealthiest colonial port, shipping cargoes of rice, indigo and naval stores. Ships loaded and discharged at Gadsden's Wharf, upper center, and the fine early homes were built along the East Battery. The city defended herself fiercely during the Revolution, but was captured in 1778 by a powerful British force of 14,000 men. It was the

Charleston at noon lay under an almost cruel blaze of sunlight. It was so brilliant that the shadows were purple-black. St. Michael's spire gleamed against an azure but cloudless sky. The delicately designed woodwork of the piazzas that stretched the full length of the great houses was painted a decorous white that shimmered with sun. Dogs, horses at hitching posts, cats which usually stalked the alley rats and even stray chickens were still.

The air smelled of heat. The narrow streets were laved with
236 it, as though by a tide. The high-walled gardens, the broad, tall

most severe American loss of the war: four Continental Navy ships were seized, and 5,400 troops taken prisoner. Charleston never quite fully recovered from the war, as the British government withdrew the large indigo crop subsidy. But the city remained lovely, unique in its architecture and famous for its cotillions, receptions and race meetings.

gateways and doorways that led to them, formed bastions of coolness for the houses. The pastel shades of the wall plaster, and the brick, faded by sun and long exposure to sea air, were accentuated by the vast clusters of mimosa, the smooth, neat trunks of palmettos, and the grayish-green spill of Spanish moss from the limbs of live-oaks.

Charleston had a great deal of resemblance to a West Indian port town. The heavy, supposedly hurricane-proof roof tiles, the wide piazzas, the fretted ironwork and the jalousied doors and   *237* windows all belonged there. Charleston, it was to be remembered, had been founded by Barbadians. Many of the older generation of planters persisted in the belief that to live in the West Indian style was the best existence possible.

But Charleston was in practically every other way an English city, and prided herself upon the fact. The coachmen who handled the smart rigs in front of the royal governor's mansion at 34 Meeting Street not only looked as if they had negotiated Hyde Park Corner; they had done exactly that, and for years, only been spirited out of London at grossly inflated wages. The houses on the old, original streets, Broad, and Tradd, and Elliott, and Church, and Stoll's Alley were filled with family heirlooms, pieces carefully transported from Sussex, Kent and Devon. Out past the East Battery, where the finest of the early houses stood, the shipping flew British colors, and most of the vessels were owned right here.

Charleston took her wealth from indigo, for which the home government paid a large subsidy, and from rice that was a staple always in demand on the English market. The city was located on a peninsula where the estuaries of the Ashley and the Cooper Rivers met. Seven-and-a-half miles across the harbor, beyond the clusters of islands, some of them still in thick forest, was the Atlantic and the sea road that led to England, and branched off coastwise and to the West Indies.

What was known as the Low Country reached inland along the rivers. That contained the rice fields which made the Carolinian planters among the wealthiest in the world, but bred the malaria that each year killed several hundred whites, and thousands of the Negroes who worked the crops. Each planter maintained a town house in Charleston where he lived during the highly dangerous summer fever season, and where he passed a

238

good part of the winter just to escape the boredom of country existence.

They left overseers to run the plantations, and the low, rambling, white-walled homes were shut. The planters and their families went aboard their prized river boats for the trip down the Ashley, the Cooper, the Santee or one of the tributaries to Charleston. The boats were built from cypress, out of three tremendous logs, one for each side, the third for the bottom and keel. Some were fifty-five feet long, and all of them were named, and contained collapsible, movable cabins for the use of the passengers.

Negro crews rowed the boats. There were usually six men in a crew, but at times as many as twelve. They were extraordinarily powerful, and wore white straw hats with long ribands attached, red flannel jackets, and wide-bottomed white cotton trousers. The slaves sang at the oars. They had created boat songs that were part chant, part spiritual.

The most popular was "Roll, Jordan, Roll." They liked also "Where, Oh Where Are the Hebrew Children?" It was customary for the verses to this to be sung solo, and by the stroke oar. He had learned the tune at Anglican service on the plantation, but changes in the melody and the words had been made during praise-house sings in the slave quarters. When the chorus was reached, all of the crew let go: "Away over the Promised Land!"

There were trips to Charleston that ended after dark. The planter group sat quietly amidships in the boat on the cushioned seats. Mosquitoes buzzed, whined, bit. The resinous flame of the torch at the bow seemed very dim against the night. Mist was on the water, and the city could not yet be seen. The crew were too tired to sing. There was just the regular, rhythmic plash of the oar blades, the creak of thole pins against the leathers and, *239* off in the darkness of the marshes, the subdued but vibrant choruses.

The trained ear could distinguish quail, and snipe, and the ducks, teal, blue wing, ring necks and shovellers. An opossum slithered through mud; a raccoon plopped scrambling in reeds. A killdeer-plover flitted down with a thin, quick wail and grazed the boat canopy, made the tassels swing.

240

CHARLESTON

It was at such a time that the returned scholar was acutely conscious that he was a Carolinian. There were, all told, no more than a hundred young men who went from Charleston to be educated in English or foreign institutions of higher learning. But they had a tremendous and lasting effect upon the life of the colony.

Carolinians had contributed generously to the colleges at Philadelphia, and Princeton, and Providence. The most substantial sum of £7,000 was given by John Mackenzie in 1771 for the express purpose of "founding an institution of higher education in the province." There were, though, several reasons why it failed. Principal among these was the dislike of sectarian religious influence in teaching, as practiced at Princeton, for example; and, even more, the profound belief that "real education" could only be gained abroad.

Before the Revolution, the citizens of Carolina were much too prejudiced in favor of British customs, knowledge and manners to imagine that elsewhere than in England anything of value could be found. A free school for boys had been started in Charleston in October, 1724. But it was not until around 1750 that Latin and Greek were taught. The majority of students who belonged to prosperous families went straight to England.

Charles Pinckney removed his entire family to England in 1754 so his sons could be educated there. Henry Laurens took his three sons abroad when the youngest, Harry, was only seven years old. The members of the Rutledge family transferred directly from the Charleston schools to the English universities, or to the Inns of Court. The Carolinian contingent was the biggest of any colonial representation which entered the Inns in search of legal education.

There were altogether, during the quarter of a century pre-

Bull Frog

ceding the Revolution, thirty some young Carolinians who attended Middle Temple, Inner Temple or Lincoln's Inn. Only a few of these took up law as a profession. But they found their legal training extremely useful when they started in trade in Charleston as merchants and shipowners. It was also of great aid to those who went into politics. Charleston's leaders in the last years of the colony were nearly all Inns of Court graduates.

This group was quite consciously aristocratic, and felt a decided sense of responsibility for the welfare and future of the colony. They completed their educations with the definite intent of coming home to a very full and active, public-minded life. Young John Laurens, when he went to the Middle Temple in 1774, was already thoroughly trained in Greek, Latin, Italian, French, belles-lettres, physics, mathematics, experimental philosophy, geography, riding and fencing. John Rutledge planned an even more strenuous campaign at Middle Temple for his younger brother Edward.

Edward should first learn shorthand, so as to be able to take notes of everything at court. He was to go to court often as an observer, and to the House of Commons. While there, he would carefully remark the speakers, and the various styles of delivery. He should "master French, and be able to read or speak it offhand, and go fully through the classics." He was to read the purist English authors, to acquire an "elegant style and expression." Further, he was to study history, logic and surveying, get a familiarity with lawbooks, reports, statutes and cases in all branches of the law. He could, for recreation, attend the theater, especially when David Garrick was playing. He should mark Garrick well, and "profit by him."

242   More than twenty doctors were listed in Charleston before

1700, some of whom may have been quacks, or apprentices. But, between 1732 and 1738 the *South-Carolina Gazette* named thirty-six. These men were educated either at Edinburgh or Leyden, and most of them in the Scottish city. There was until 1765, when the medical college was established at Philadelphia, no source of such education except overseas. Two early Leyden graduates, Thomas Dale and William Bull, became prominent in the colony, and Bull was the first native-born American to obtain a degree in medicine.

Dr. John Moultrie, Sr., who had trained at Edinburgh, emigrated to Charleston right after his graduation, in the first decade of the eighteenth century. His reputation as an obstetrician was so great that when he died many Charleston ladies went into mourning. He was followed in the profession by his son John, who attended Edinburgh University in 1749, was awarded a degree there and proved a thesis on yellow fever.

The returned scholars, gradually accustoming themselves to the more placid and heat-dominated life of Charleston, found they talked less and less of their English or European experiences. There were evenings, of course, when fog swept in from seaward and the bells of St. Michael's and St. Phillip's sounded, that the Oxford graduate was reminded of Tom, the great bell at Christ Church. That was in what was called Tom Tower, and at ten minutes past nine in the evening it began to ring. Tom had a booming, deep-throated quality that carried far beyond High Street, over the Meadows, and across the river to Marston Moor and to Elsfield, and Chipping Norton.

Lincoln's Inn graduates during the same sort of evening smelled in imagination the sourness of the Thames at low tide, and the raw pungency of the Newcastle coal that would only smoulder in the grate, heard the chimes of St. Paul's dimmed *243* by the clatter of traffic in Chancery Lane. The Edinburgh men had memories of the vast, dark rise of Arthur's Seat, and the turrets and the ramparts of the Castle caught within the fog off the Firth of Forth that flowed upward along Leith Road like a strange river; the bells of St. Giles sounded the hour in crashing echo, and in a wynd of the Old Town a startled child cried. Leyden men recalled the willows, dripping smooth, silver beads of moisture, and the street cobbles shiny, too, under the fog, and the staid, geometrical rows of the university buildings. There was in the distance ruminant, not at all loud, yet containing unmeasured strength, the North Sea surge against the dikes.

It was inevitable for the men who had lived overseas to gather by themselves. They were abruptly bored by Charleston. The winter rounds of assemblies, balls, receptions, dinner parties and concerts, even the stage performances by English companies became very stale. They after all had been extended *entrée* at the great country houses, were entertained by the nobility. They had seen Garrick in many of his Shakespearean performances, met him at the Turk's Head tavern in Gerrard Street with Samuel Johnson, and Reynolds, Burke, Goldsmith and Boswell.

Concerts at the Orange Gardens were charming. But they could hardly compare with an evening spent at Vauxhall. The Jockey Club meetings, the various races and cockfights and bouts with cards and dice were supposed to hold the intense interest of even the most sophisticated. Still, those counted very little against New Market and Ascot, the prices paid for thoroughbreds at Tattersall's and the bets made at White's or the Cocoa Tree. For those who boasted of gay night life and the allure of certain octoroon beauties, the answer was a description of the activity at Tom King's coffee-house in Covent Garden.

244   That was not really a coffee-house. It was a whoreshop, and the most famous in London. King came from a good Wiltshire family, had gone to Eton and then to King's College, Cambridge. Following a protracted visit to London after graduation, he set himself up as a pimp, and married a very popular whore. The exhibitions at King's began when "Leather Sides," the huge porter, lifted a naked and saucy whore over his head while she poised on a silver platter. William Hogarth, the squat, lumpy-nosed painter, was present at King's nearly every night. Charleston keenly lacked both kinds of men.

These moods of longing for the life abroad did not last, though, and the young men were once more greatly satisfied by what Charleston had to offer. The best bookshop in the colonies was here. Robert Wells, the owner, had opened it in 1754, and later printed and edited the *South-Carolina & American General Gazette*. He announced that he had established "proper correspondences" in London, Paris and Amsterdam, and within a reasonable length of time could procure any book. He also offered to obtain any British magazine "with all convenient speed," and a few months after its publication he had Samuel Johnson's *Dictionary* on sale in his shop.

Thomas Whitmarsh, who founded the *South-Carolina Gazette* in 1732, had served as a journey-man printer in Benjamin Franklin's shop. He stated in an early issue that his paper would take both sides on almost any issue, because men's opinions were "almost as various as their Faces." All parties should be "educated in the Belief, that when Men differ in Opinion, both sides equally to have the Advantage of being heard by the Publick."

This was in general accepted and supported in Charleston, and a large amount of latitude was permitted until a controversy over a sermon preached by an English clergyman almost led to several duels. But discussions of all sorts were heard at the local *245* taverns and coffee-houses, and the Charleston Library Society bought a wide diversity of books. The society was started in 1748 by a group of seventeen Charlestonians who created the idea of a common fund for importing current pamphlets and periodicals. The list of members grew to 130 in less than two years, and the society began to purchase its large stock of books, along with scientific apparatus for experimental purposes, and hired a librarian at a good salary. It became the meeting place of Charleston's most distinguished and cultivated men, and was the center of intellectual life in the colony.

Charleston's young ladies, though, were not offered many cultural sources. They were discriminated against because of their sex in the same fashion practiced in all of the other colonies, and abroad. The best education available to them was given at the various "dame schools." Classes were devoted to "dancing, music, and French," and every "lady of quality" had to show skill in embroidery, needlework and drawing.

Several of the dame school proprietors advertised in the *South-Carolina Gazette*. Jane Voyer taught young ladies embroidery, tapestry work, drawing and French. Elizabeth Anderson boarded young ladies and gave similar instruction. Mrs. Elizabeth Duneau, "a gentlewoman late from England," opened in 1770 a very refined boarding-house for the accomodation of the daughters of affluent local families in need of "finishing." She said in her advertisement that before her arrival in Charleston she had brought up "many ladies of rank and distinction."

A Charleston lady, Mrs. Sophia Hume, expressed herself vigorously on the subject of so-called polite education for women. She said, "And now to finish and compleat a modern education, it requires the following Accomplishments, *viz.* To be expert in Dress and Dancing, Omber or Gaming in general, to be able to make judicious Remarks on Opera Airs, and Stage Plays . . . and reading Romances and other pernicious Books. Add to all this, the Art of Writing, where after those present are much flatter'd and complimented; the Absent on the contrary, are as ungenerously dealt with, and severely handled."

The young ladies took a considerable amount of pleasure from their music. Lessons were given on the violin, and the harpsichord, German flute, English flute, cello and spinet. Charles Theodore Pachelbell opened a "Singing School" for young ladies in 1749, and the principles of harmony were taught. The St. Cecelia Society was founded in 1762 in Charleston. It was the first musical organization in America, and supported an orchestra of paid musicians. They in company with several amateurs gave regular fortnightly concerts for the members of the society during the winter and spring seasons.

But it was one of Charleston's young ladies, Eliza Lucas, who despite the narrow confines of her education achieved the greatest technical development in the colony. She experimented in the years 1741 to 1743 with the extraction of dye from the West Indian indigo plant. She discovered the deceit of an expert sent from the island of Monserrat, and was able to establish indigo as a major crop for the colony, and a large source of its wealth. She later, as the wife of Charles Pinckney, tried to manufacture silk at their plantation, "Belmont," although with nothing like the same success.

The culture of indigo had been introduced into the colony as early as 1723, and the legislature encouraged its production by granting a bounty. Then, in 1744, Eliza Lucas proved that on the fertile bottom land of St. Andrew's Parish the crop could be produced profitably with slave labor. Growth was further stimulated by a British government bounty of sixpence a pound on all indigo shipped to England. Next to rice, it became South Carolina's chief crop.

b.b.b. Bunches of the Seed, or enlarg'd in Fig.II.
The whole Plant is from 4 to 8 Feet in height.

Fig. I.
One of the Pediculæs, enlarg'd to its natural Size.

Fig. II.
A Bunch of Seed, enlarg'd to its natural Size.

Indigo culture in South Carolina in the pre-Revolutionary period, the crop being carried from the fields and processed. Dye taken from the indigo plant was in great demand by English cotton and woolen goods manufacturers, and found a ready market. This scene was drawn by an artist with Scottish bias; the figure at right wears a kilt, and his English companion is a midget.

Rice had been introduced into the colony almost at the beginning of its history. Dr. Henry Woodward was given a couple of bags of good seed rice by Captain Thurber, the master of a ship that had called at Madagascar on her way to Charleston. Some of this seed was planted by Woodward, and he gave the rest to friends. The new crop took so easily to the Low Country soil that by 1690 it was an important trade element. Ten years later, there were not enough ships in Charleston harbor to haul the crop brought downriver in barges and bateaux from the plantations.

CHARLESTON

The planting of rice on a large scale demanded wide acreage, and the use of creeks that could be dammed and released to flood the fields. The sons of middle-class Charleston families who could not afford educations abroad often went to work on the rice plantations in some sort of supervisory capacity. It was, for those who were not sea-minded or content to serve as a minor government official, better than being a clerk, an artisan or a mechanic, and paid more.

A revealing insight of life in the colony was given in the advertisements printed in the *South-Carolina Gazette* between 1732 and 1775. Navigation instruction was popular. Fourteen courses were offered. John Wilson was qualified to teach arithmetic, geometry, trigonometry, algebra, accounts, surveying, mensuration, logarithms, navigation, gunnery, fortification, mechanics, hydrostatics, optics, hydraulics and astronomy.

If a man could live through a few Low Country summer seasons, the surveying, mensuration, accounts, hydrostatics and hydraulics might come in very handy. There was, of course, always the fever to be considered. Summertime, the owners of the plantations were away in the North, at Newport—"the Carolina hospital." Overseers ran the work. They were tough and usually embittered men, frustrated in their ambition to own land, and quick to take out their wrath on subordinates and slaves.

The management of a plantation demanded a continuous use of immense amounts of water, and a thorough knowledge of hydraulics. During the early stages of growth, the rice crop was submerged. Water was let in through a complex series of locks and canals, ditches, dams and gates from ponds and streams. Then it was drained off by gravity. A big force of field hands was necessary for the planting and hoeing, and repairs, and the gathering of the crop.

PORTS OF CALL

The overseer commanded a man he called his "driver," who was actually the foreman. Then there was the "trunk-minder," in charge of the irrigation work. Bird-minders shot or chased off the rice birds that threatened the crop. Carpenters and blacksmiths and bricklayers had their specific jobs, and the boat and barge crews. There were shepherds, and cattlemen, and swineherds, and grooms and stablemen and postillions under the orders of the coachman. An old and wise, greatly trusted nurse was in charge of the sickhouse, and took care of the young children while their mothers were at work in the fields.

The butler and the rest of the house servants went with the owner's family to Charleston in the season, and the big house, known as "the hall" was deserted for as much as several months at a time. It was possible for a young assistant bookkeeper or a surveyor working temporarily on the property to enter the house and look around without being detected.

The furniture was covered with sheets against dust and moisture. The window jalousies and all doors were closed to keep out sunlight, and a candle failed to show the details of the rooms. But the visitor could see enough to excite his imagination and make him dream.

The family sat at the immense mahogany table while dinner was served. The silver candelabra were used, and the silver spoons and knives and forks were all solid silver; the china, the glassware, the napkins, the tablecloth, all of that came from England. The butler hardly made a sound as he moved around the table. Footmen who wore livery just a little less fancy than the butler's served the wines. Grace had been said by the master, as the head of the family, before a bit of food was touched.

What these folks ate kept the servants going for more than an hour. There were in season local shrimp, small, and very sweet, and oysters, and duck, and venison. They also liked calipash, and okra daube, and jambalaya, and panygetta, and Pompey's head, bops, espetanga corn bread and tipsy pudding.

Brandy or Madeira came with the coffee, and after the ladies left the room the men talked horses, gambling, shipping news and the last reports from their correspondents in New York, Boston and London. Books were discussed, too, and the theater, and there was some mention of philosophy and comparative religions. These were cultured men; they had not forgotten the years of education abroad. Then, in the next room, their womenfolk played the spinet or the harpsichord, and the men rose and joined them.

The unasked visitor to a Low Country plantation house could promise himself, stirred by ambition, that he would marry into one of the wealthy families. When he was ready for it, he would pick a Drayton daughter, or a Wragg, a Bull, a Huger, a Mazyck or Manigault or Pinckney as his bride. That meant a home in Charleston.

The town house would be built of brick, and three stories high. The floor plan was conventional, square or rectangular, but great care was given to the cornices, the window trim, the interior panelling, the mantels and staircases. The first floor was

elevated because of dampness; the high ceilings gave more air, and better circulation. The drawing room was on the second floor and led out onto the piazza on the south side of the house. This offered protection from the sun in the middle of the day, and a place to sit in the evenings and enjoy the prevailing breeze from the southwest. The garden within its high walls was below the piazza, and past it the quarters for the servants, and the stable. The best section to build a house was on White Point, close to the harbor, where the ships' bells could be heard all night long, and the breeze moved away most of the mosquitoes and flies.

The ambitious young visitor promised himself further that he would have his wife's portrait painted, and quite possibly his own, by Jeremiah Theus. He would join the St. Andrew's Society, and the Friday-night Club, and the Monday-night Club, famous for cards, feasting and the drinking of wine. He would open an account at Robert Wells's bookshop and subscribe to all the best British periodicals, and make a habit of stopping by for a rum punch at Kerr's tavern, or Dillon's or Shepheard's, on his way home from the counting-house at the end of the day.

That was where the small but very wealthy and powerful group of Charleston merchants met. Charleston was the port town for an immense trade area that stretched north to Virginia and south as far as Spanish-held Florida. The lucrative wholesale trade was mainly in the hands of factors, men who represented large British firms. They dealt in banking and brokerage, and in shipping. A lot of money was made in supplying stores to the Royal Navy, turpentine, and tar, and pine for spars, and planking. Some of the merchants engaged in that, as well as slave-running, but most of the business of the port outward-bound was the shipment of rice and indigo.

252

CHARLESTON

There was in Charleston little of the dislike of the mother country that every year became more of a problem in the northern colonies. She did not compete, in the fashion of Boston and New York and Baltimore, with British shipbuilding. Her only interest was to supply the British market and the West Indies, furnish them commodities and stores that they could not get elsewhere for the same sensible prices. The Navigation Acts did not severely affect her, and her population were not fervent tea-drinkers. Taxation on the part of the home government was considered in the main to be justified.

The young men of the town who believed themselves gay blades did not actively enter politics. They were much more interested in the punctillio of the duel, and took instruction from James Cliquet. He taught them the use of the saber, the sword and the epée. They also spent hours of their time at dancing school. Dancing was not simply a form of popular expression, but an art to be mastered. It was a definite part of a gentleman's education and social training.

There were, in addition to the various country dances, hornpipes to be learned. The complicated measures of the minuet were formidable. And with those mastered, the louvre, the paspied, the rigadoon, the new cotillion and other fashionable dances came next. It all seemed worthwhile, though, when the violins began to throb at the beginning of a ball, and the gentlemen in powdered wigs, lace at their throats and cuffs, stepped forward across the gleaming parquet into the light of hundreds of candles and bowed to the ladies. The ladies, in tight-fitting, low-cut silk or satin, held forth their hands and were led out to take part in the graceful, slowly and meticulously executed measures.

Standing beside the immense punchbowl and the rows of bottles aligned behind it, the Negro servants in formal livery did not appear to watch the dancing. Still, the keen, thoughtful glances followed each step and gyration, and some ladies' maids rested half-hidden in the ballroom doorways, and at the tall windows children crowded each other in the darkness. A full description of the ball would be given later in the slave quarters of various town houses, and a report of the winnings made at omber by the gentlemen not inclined to dance, and the losses suffered by those who had mistakenly left the floor.

The Negro population of Charleston, much greater in number, kept a close and constant check on the white. Paternalism was practiced, and a certain form of benevolence. But there had been short and cruelly repressed slave revolts in the early years of the colony. The freed slaves, and the privileged few among the house servants who had been taught to read, learned the history of Carolina. They had also heard their masters talk of it; the main facts were well known.

The colony was founded in 1670 by an English expedition that came to the mainland from Barbados. There were two principal reasons for the settlement. King Charles II wanted a trading post that would supply the West Indies with foodstuffs and timber, and Barbados had become much too small for the size of her population since the importation of Negro slaves. New land was needed, and the Carolina grant would furnish it.

Sir John Colleton discussed the colonization idea with his close friend, Anthony Ashley Cooper, who became the first Earl of Shaftesbury, and who died in exile in 1683 after various changes of allegiance. They formed a group of Lords Proprietors, which included the Duke of Albemarle, the Earl of Clarendon, the Earl of Craven, Sir William Berkeley and Sir George Carteret. The king gave them a stupendous tract of land that reached from the southern boundary of Virginia to the mouth of the St. John's *254* River in Florida, and westward as far as the Pacific Ocean.

CHARLESTON

The grant was made in 1663, but the Lords Proprietors were not happy. They wanted more land. Colonization was delayed until they received several hundred more miles of territory along the north and south boundaries. The charter expressly forbade the use of English titles, so a new form of nobility was created.

This was done by Ashley's secretary, John Locke, who later became famous as a philosopher. His colonization plan was very badly designed, though, and could never be put into effect. He gave as his reason for it the need to sell land at a penny an acre.

The titles he conceived were barons, cassiques and landgraves. Each proprietor of the original group would have 96,000 acres, or eight "baronies" assigned to him. A landgrave would have 48,000 acres, and a cassique 24,000 as his share. Locke believed that the sale of land to title-hunters would prevent the growth of "a too numerous democracy."

The expedition that left Barbados in 1665 mustered less than one hundred men and was under the command of Sir John Yeamans, who had been recently knighted, then commissioned governor of Carolina. He found the people of the Cape Fear colony in trouble, but there was little that he could do for them. He turned over command of the expedition to Captain Robert Sandford and went back to Barbados.

Sandford was a veteran shipmaster. He followed the preliminary survey of the region made by Captain William Hilton. He cruised Port Royal Sound off Hilton Head Island, then moved up the coast to the Ashley River to establish the site of the colony. A young London surgeon named Henry Woodward who served under Sandford volunteered to stay behind alone with the Indians they met, learn their language, create friendship and trade.

The Indians treated Woodward well, and he quickly adapted himself. The local chief's nephew had decided to leave home with the English expedition, and in reality Woodward was a hostage. *255*

But the mother of the departed young Indian came into the wigwam that Woodward occupied and enlisted as his squaw. He was living very happily when a Spanish raiding party from St. Augustine seized the village and took him prisoner.

Woodward spent some time in solitary reflection in a dungeon at St. Augustine before an English buccaneer named Searles raided the place. The buccaneers needed a surgeon and, out of gratitude and with the hope that he might somehow get back to Barbados, Woodward joined them. Searles, though, had no liking for Barbados, which was often patrolled by Royal Navy ships. It was not until 1669 that Woodward was able to get away from the buccaneers, and only then after the ship had been cast ashore on the island of Nevis by a hurricane. One of the colonizing ships found him there and took him to Carolina.

He came to the Carolina coast a mature and hard-bitten man. He was among the first to recognize that the site of the new settlement, known as Charles Town, was unhealthy. The settlers discovered that they were menaced by the Spaniards, and bands of Indians who descended in swift forays from the interior, the ravages of fever and the indifference of the Lords Proprietors. The lack of concern on the part of the Lords Proprietors was due to the fact that the large island of Jamaica, taken from the Spanish during the Cromwell period, was being opened to colonization. The Spaniards had already done a good deal to develop Jamaica; a fortune could be made faster there than in Carolina.

The original settlers of the Carolina colony were never to forget the early vicissitudes suffered because of the ignorance, carelessness and greed of the Lords Proprietors. They had carried with them also from Barbados a profound hatred of those who held power and willfully misused it. Most of them were dispossessed people, small planters who had lost their land when huge combines had been formed in court circles in London to start the wide-scale cultivation of sugar. Others were former indentured folk who had paid bitterly, through years of long servitude, for their freedom. Their hatred of absentee landlordism and the corrupt practices of court favorites was to last until the days of the Revolution, and play a great part in Carolina's decision to demand her freedom.

Ten years after the settlement was begun on the muddy, low-lying bank of the Ashley, the move was made to the juncture of that river with the Cooper. The new location was much better, and the town began to grow. But the population was still only 700 people, and it did not expand vigorously until the arrival of a contingent of French Huguenots. These came in the 1690s and numbered more than 400, and were warmly welcomed by the predominantly English population. The town was still less than 5,000, and Dr. Woodward was absent on long and dangerous journeys into the interior.

He dealt with the tribes, mainly the warlike Yamassees, and continued his work of fraternization among them. He sought furs and deerskins to stimulate the Charleston trade, and was successful. Those, sent as exports to England, along with the shiploads of foodstuffs and timber sold in the West Indies, kept the colony alive, secured its future.

The famous sea wall was begun in 1701, and by 1704 a system of wide, intersecting streets was designed. There were several hundred houses, a number of them of brick construction, and churches of various denominations, large public buildings and, along the waterfront, taverns kept busy by merchants, shipowners and sailors all day long.

Planters were emerging as the dominant commercial class, as indigo and then rice were introduced as crops. Rice culture only   *257* needed the importation of sufficient slaves for field work to expand into large-scale industry. The Church of England was established by law in 1706, and gave impetus to the intellectual life of the community, and also transmitted English culture to the colony. Charleston was, more than Boston, more than Portsmouth or any other New England town, London overseas.

The Carolina planters were able to buy large quantities of British goods, among them many luxury articles. This, with the sale of thousands of slaves, meant big profits for the British merchants and their Charleston factors. The brutal Yamassee War in 1715, though, showed the colonists the almost total lack of interest in their problems on the part of the Lords Proprietors. When the Indians were driven back and the colony again made safe, the Assembly asked the Crown for a royal charter.

It was finally granted in 1729, when the king purchased the interests of the Lords Proprietors. The colony was divided in half, and afterward known as North and South Carolina, the northern capital at Albemarle. Charleston and the Low Country were in a few years well ordered and prosperous.

Their prosperity was announced when Charleston opened her first dramatic season January 24, 1735, with a production of Thomas Otway's blank-verse drama, *The Orphan*. The prelude to it was written by a local, anonymous poet who recalled the enormous wilderness inland, and "the hideous waste" in which there were "Men more Savage than the Beasts they chac'd." Then the poet boasted of "peace and plenty," and used really rousing lines:

What various Products float on every Tide?
What numerous Navys in our Harbours ride?
Tillage and Trade conjoin their friendly Aid,

CHARLESTON

T'enrich the thriving Boy and lovely Maid.
Hence we presume to usher in those Arts
Which oft have warm'd the best and bravest hearts.

Charleston was on her way to wealth. News of the affluence of her mercantile class reached London, and in the early 1730s accommodations for passengers to the colony were taken by people who sought some of it for themselves. They were goldsmiths, and silversmiths, and peruque-makers, and portrait artists, who were known locally as "face painters." Still, Charleston remained a small city. Her population in 1742 was slightly more than 6,800, of whom not more than a third were white, and the majority of them were tradesmen, shopkeepers, artisans, mechanics, shipyard workers and sailors.

The ruling class was compact, came from the rich planter families, the merchants, the government officials, lawyers, doctors and clergymen. It was they who controlled the colony, and more often than not told the royal governor what action he should take. This had been true when both of the Carolinas had been bothered by a plague of pirates.

Edward Teach, known also as "Thatch" or "Thach," alias "Drummond," alias "Blackbeard," was a huge, sloven blusterer who liked killing almost as much as drinking rum. He was born in Bristol, went to sea early, jumped ship in Jamaica, where in 1716 he received the attention of a pirate captain named Benjamin Hornigold. He was given command of a sloop by Hornigold, took several prizes, then turned most of his effort to a change in personal appearance, and marriage.

Teach let his bushy black beard grow long, then braided it with bright ribbons. He thrust long wax tapers into his hair, and *259* to frighten the timid or his rum-hazy shipmates, occasionally lit one in a darkened room. He carried a number of pistols stuck in sashes and his belt, and a cutlass, and a dirk. Twelve women were so impressed by him that they became his brides in West Indian ports. Then, tiring of them and the persistent pursuit of his ship by the Royal Navy, he began to sail off the mainland coast near Charleston. Loot was less than in the Caribbean, but so was the danger.

The big, foul-smelling pirate was often ashore in Charleston with his crew. The king's pardon had been offered all pirates, and Teach was surreptitiously welcomed by certain merchants who bought the loot he offered at very low prices. When he went back to sea again, he visited Bath Town up the coast where he fell in love with and married a sixteen-year-old girl. He spent a considerable amount on her wardrobe, and more on rum and food for himself and his shipmates. It was necessary for him to take the sloop offshore and seize a prize.

But in Cape Fear harbor, waiting for a suitable vessel to loot, he met Major Stede Bonnet. The major was unique among pirates. He had left the life of a prosperous sugar planter in Barbados and invested all of his available funds in a pirate ship to get away from his wife. He was an almost complete innocent when Teach came upon him, although the crew he had recruited were veteran renegades.

Teach taught Bonnet fast, and for a price. He let the major witness his handling of the prisoners from a ship he captured on her way into Charleston harbor. Among the passengers were Samuel Wragg, a member of the Charleston city council, and Wragg's four-year-old son William. Men in Teach's crew were sick with malaria, and he needed medicine for them. So in the message he sent to the governor, Robert Johnson, he demanded a fully supplied medicine chest. If it was not received soon, he said, he would send the heads of the captives to Charleston.

The boat carrying the medicine chest appeared just as Teach prepared to use his cutlass on the kneeling and tightly bound prisoners. He showed his contempt for the governor by robbing the boat crew and putting them on the beach almost naked. Then he sailed off north to visit his bride.

Bonnet decided to cruise the waters near Charleston and make his own deals with the governor. But Colonel William Rhett, with a record of action against the Spanish, resented the threat to the port made by Bonnet. He equipped two ships, recruited crews for them and started after the major.

Bonnet's ship, *Royal James,* ran aground when he tried to evade pursuit. He and his men fought for five hours, though, after Colonel Rhett opened fire. Half of the pirates were killed or wounded, and Bonnet chose to surrender.

Rhett took the lot to Charleston. They were put in irons in the guard-house at the head of Broad Street, and held for trial. The major remembered the names of some of Blackbeard Teach's friends among the citizens. Messages were passed, and it was arranged that Bonnet and his sailing master should be allowed to escape. They got out a week before their scheduled trial, and hid on Sullivan's Island in the harbor.

Colonel Rhett took a detachment of men, though, and re-captured them. They were closely guarded while another volunteer force from the city, this time under the command of Governor Johnson himself, went offshore and fought and captured a pirate ship. The pirate captain, a famous desperado named Richard Worley, and most of his men were killed in the action. The twenty-four who remained alive were brought back and tried with Bonnet and his men.

PORTS OF CALL

The presiding justice at the trial was Nicholas Trott, known as the codifier of the laws of the colony, and also as the friend and legal consultant, if not business associate, of a long list of pirates. But the trial was brief, and summary; all of the men tried were found guilty, and sentenced to be hanged. They were hanged at White Point, facing the harbor. Their bodies were buried the same day, November 12, 1718, at low-water mark.

Charleston was not bothered again by pirates. Teach was caught soon afterwards by a Royal Navy sloop-of-war while he and his crew were in Ocracoke Inlet. A young lieutenant named Robert Maynard engaged Teach in a cutlass fight and killed him after he had inflicted twenty-five wounds. Then Maynard severed Teach's head from the immense body, lashed that to the bowsprit of his vessel and sailed into Bath Town in broad daylight so that there would be no misinformation possible about what had happened.

As Charleston continued to thrive, Governor James Glen reported to the Board of Trade in 1749: "It will perhaps surprize your Lordships to be informed there is annually imported considerable quantity of fine laces of Flanders, the finest Dutch linnens, and French cambricks, chintz, Hyson Tea, and other East India goods, silks, gold and silver laces, etc." Glen was honestly alarmed by the extravagance of the citizens, did his best to warn them.

CHARLESTON

His alarm was unwarranted, though. Charleston during the years just before the Revolution was the most prosperous city in all of the colonies. The *South-Carolina Gazette* stated in the issue of March 7, 1774, that Gadsden's Wharf on the Cooper River was "reckoned the most extensive of the Kind ever undertaken by any one Man in America." The weekly also praised Prioleau's new wharf with its docks and stores, the new Assembly Room, the elegant new theater on Dock Street, the number of fine new homes on White Point and in other sections of the city and the excellent scholastic standards of the academies that had recently opened. The article spoke further about the encouragement given by "many Gentlemen of Taste and Fortune" to music and the fine arts. Charleston was extremely proud of what it had achieved.

The city was at that time a hundred years old, and at the peak of its material and cultural prosperity. For the past fifty years, the rice industry had brought increasing wealth. Two generations of merchants, shipowners and planters, their fortunes assured, had devoted themselves assiduously to the arts, to culture in general, and what they recognized consciously as the amenities of graceful living. They built beautiful houses and stately churches, rested content in the fact that their society was in many respects as sophisticated and brilliant as any to be found in the Old World.

But, by 1770, the political thinking of the colony was almost wholly given to what was seen as the inevitable break from England. Liberty was the constant topic of conversation. Charleston merchants joined with other colonial groups in a general non-importation association as a protest against the added taxation. They would not handle British goods of any sort. And Charleston was the last American port to resume trade with the mother country.

PORTS OF CALL

The editor of the *South-Carolina Gazette* wrote on October 4, 1770: "Indeed, should any merchant here Attempt to imitate those of New York the Landed Gentlemen and the most considerable Planters seem determined to withdraw their custom from those Houses never to be restored."

It was the temper of the Carolina aristocracy which was finally responsible for the break from England. The men of wealth and position were willing to disregard economic considerations, even at the risk of losing their fortunes. They were confronted with a problem unlike that in New England, where the new British regulations threatened the entire commercial life of the colony. The decision to be made in Virginia was strongly influenced by the fact that the tobacco planters owed enormous debts in England; if the colony severed her ties, those could be forgotten. South Carolina, though, would suffer an almost incalculable loss by seeking independence. Her prosperity was dependent on the mother country, and her cultural and social bonds were extremely close.

Still, when the ultimate choice was made, the Carolina aristocracy were nearly unanimous in their support of the cause of independence. There was no community, with the possible exception of Boston, where the patriotic feeling was as strong as in Charleston. Christopher Gadsden, an impassioned orator, rallied the local artisans with the power of his language. But the men of wealth like the Laurenses, Hugers, Pinckneys, Middletons, Heywards and Rutledges were not swayed by oratory. They were convinced that they maintained the tenets of basic English law, and what John Locke had called "the inestimable Rights of Life, Liberty and Property."

The past was for them very clear. They held memories passed down verbally from generation to generation, and also some few written records. Seated on their piazzas in the dusk while over the bay the breeze quickened and rattled the palmetto fronds, they carefully recalled that past.

It led to Barbados. The big planters had begun to take over the island in 1640, and they showed no mercy to the small. Freedmen living in the colony were forced to sell themselves temporarily as slaves. A planter named Richard Atkinson owed another planter, John Batt, for 2,000 pounds of cotton. He made a written agreement with Batt: "That if the said two thousand pounds of Cotton shall not be paid upon the day aforesaid, that then and immediately upon default of the said payment, it shall bee for the said John Batt, or his assigns, to take the body of me Richard Atkinson, servant for the term of six yeares, without any further trouble or sute of lawe."

A freedman named George Haddock fell in love with and married an indentured woman who was the chattel of a planter named William Light. So Haddock entered into an agreement: "Lett all men know by these present that I, George Haddock, doth Covenant and promise to and with, William Light, Gent., for to serve him for and dureing the terme of two yeares fully to compleate and end from the day of the date thereof; which two yeares I and doe serve for Anne Mitchell, who is now my Wife, being the remainder of her four yeares for which she came over for, as by her Indenture."

It was Oliver Cromwell, the Lord Protector, who started the white-slavery trade. He had ruthlessly suppressed the Irish rebellion in 1649, and afterward transported great numbers of Irish soldiers to Barbados for life servitude. He described the storming of Drogheda in simple language: "When they submitted, these officers were knocked on the head, and every tenth man of the soldiers killed, and the rest shipped for Barbados."

PORTS OF CALL

The next year, after the defeat at Dunbar, thousands of Scottish prisoners were transported. They were joined a year later, in 1651, by other Scots taken at the battle of Worcester. Felons were also sent out by the shipload to empty English prisons, and pirates who had been caught on the high seas and held in jail in Dorchester and Plymouth. Many of them could not stand the effects of the sun; Barbados was nearly on the Equator, and they were exposed to it in the fields from dawn to dark. They died of exhaustion, sunstroke, malnutrition and the beatings given by the overseers.

A bell summoned them to work at six o'clock in the morning. They worked with the cutlass in the cane rows, or in the grinding mills, or the rooms where the sugar syrup was boiled until eleven o'clock. Then even the overseers admitted that the heat was too great. A break was taken and a meal served to the workers. This was loblolly, Indian maize mixed with cold water, eaten in paste form on a piece of plank. Work began again at one o'clock and was finished at six. Supper, served in the huts, was more loblolly, or potatoes mashed in water.

Richard Ligon, who was in Barbados from 1647 to 1650, wrote: "To this, no bread nor drink but water. Their lodging at night a board, with nothing under, nor anything on top of them. . . . If they be not strong men, this ill lodging will put them into a sickness; if they complain, they are beaten by an Overseer; if they resist their time is doubled. I have seen an Overseer beat a Servant with a cane about the head till the blood has followed for an offence that is not worth speaking of."

Scots and Irish and English decided in 1648 that they could take no more. They conspired with the former pirates and London footpads, and the Negro slaves who were being better treated than themselves. But, at the last moment, one of the plotters informed

Thousands of New England horses were sold to turn a sugar-cane press endlessly in the West Indian heat. The fires are stoked with canes, sugar is scooped from the pans and raw juice runs into the vat at left.

a local official, Judge Hethersall. The dragoons moved in, and reinforced the overseers. The ringleaders were caught; eighteen men were executed.

Negroes were afterward preferred as workers. A Negro slave was a permanent possession, so it was to the advantage of his master to preserve him. A white man, held for a limited period, was worked to the utmost. When a white man became too ill to work, he was thrown off the plantation as a worthless burden. A law passed in Barbados in 1661 read:

Many masters, when their servants grow sick, and unable to perform their daily Labour, will seem to remit some part of the Time to be cleared of them, or turn them off, to the intent they may not be chargeable to them for their Recovery, whereby many of the said Servants most miserably perish, or become a charge of the Parish where they first happen to be laid up.

It was calculated in Barbados that for the cost of maintaining a white man for ten years, a Negro slave could be bought for life.

The Charleston aristocrats caught in the middle of the swiftly moving events leading to the Declaration of Independence brought back the almost forgotten past. They made vivid once more the Barbadian memories, related that historical circumstance to what was happening now, and here. The memories helped.

They were the descendants of proud and desperate people, most of whom had died in degradation. Freedom was not possible for those others. Some had died gasping, bloody, pitched into an irrigation ditch at the side of a cane field by an overseer who disliked the sight of corpses. Some were taken by the fever, babbled during the last hours in the fly-noisy, dung-smelling huts of the nine glens of Antrim, and of Glengariff and the cascades and waterfalls, cool, cool, and clean; and of Ballynahinch, and Dunluce, on the crag; and the mavis in the heather on the Highland moors and the red, tall deer standing there.

TO BE SOLD, on board the Ship *Bance-Iſland*, on tueſday the 6th of *May* next, at *Aſhley-Ferry*; a choice cargo of about 250 fine healthy

NEGROES,

juſt arrived from the Windward & Rice Coaſt. —The utmoſt care has already been taken, and ſhall be continued, to keep them free from the leaſt danger of being infected with the SMALL-POX, no boat having been on board, and all other communication with people from *Charles-Town* prevented.

Auſtin, Laurens, & Appleby.

N. B. Full one Half of the above Negroes have had the SMALL-POX in their own Country.

CHARLESTON

The Charleston aristocrats decided to fight. Freedom was a very precious thing. Nothing could matter more.

Charleston defended herself gallantly against the British in the Revolution. When a task force under General Henry Clinton tried to take the port in June, 1776, it was beaten back with the loss of 200 casualties. The palmetto-log fort on the island that was the center of the harbor resistance was later named for the commander, General William Moultrie.

But two years later the British were back. Clinton with 14,000 men attacked and took the city. The American garrison of 5,400 men was captured, and four Continental Navy ships. It was the heaviest American defeat of the war.

The British stayed in Charleston for more than a year. There was great suffering and poverty in the town. Trade was completely stopped. The British deported the wives of paroled and imprisoned American officers. Men were accused of being spies, and a militia colonel named Isaac Hayne was tried and hanged by the British when he refused to swear allegiance to the Crown. The war dragged on outside Charleston while Royal Navy ships harried the coast. Then peace was made, and, finally, the British were gone.

The citizens started to rebuild, and first cleared away the litter of destruction. Most of the houses had been damaged by enemy fire, those in the section around Broad Street by ships' guns, and those in the northern half by field artillery and siege weapons. Many of the great plantations had been burned, and it was estimated that 25,000 slaves had been taken away by the British.

Charleston gathered her strength fast, though. The population in 1790 was over 16,000, and she gave a great welcome in that year to President Washington. He was making a triumphal tour of the South, and stopped at Thomas Heyward's house on Church Street. A concert and ball were held in his honor, where the ladies who were present wore bandeaux bearing the president's portrait and a motto of welcome.

A few Hessians from among the British occupation force had asked for discharge in Charleston, stayed on and became citizens, were assimilated. They were simple men who had served as mercenaries, clumped around for years in eight-and-a-half-pound boots, brass caps and thick, tightly buttoned woolen uniforms. Their peacetime occupations were as carpenters, bricklayers and masons. They had none of the dramatic quality of the Haitian refugees who came ashore in the late summer of 1791 and told terrible stories of the slave revolt in Hispaniola.

These were the planters who came from what had been France's richest colony, and the wealthiest colony in the world. They were shaken by horror, subdued by shock or hysterically shrill. All summer long, they and their families, and a surprising number with their household slaves, had been arriving on the mainland coast. Baltimore held 1,000 of them; they landed from fifty-three ships that had sailed in convoy from Hispaniola. The sum of $12,000 had been raised in Baltimore for their relief.

Ships from Cap François, Saint Marc, Gonaives, Port au Prince and the other Haitian ports appeared in Charleston harbor almost daily. The Frenchmen came ashore magnificently dressed, and the boatmen who brought them in from the ships said that many carried strong-boxes which were filled with gold. This was confirmed by local merchants who met the Haitians at the Exchange and were asked to get them established. No matter how frightened they were, most of the Haitians were still rich.

Then, gradually, from the merchants who heard it first, the detailed account of the Haitian slave revolt was learned in Charleston. That had begun on the night of August twenty-second, with a meeting of the slave leaders at Gallifet, in Bois Caiman. Drums called them through the darkness, and where they gathered on the property known as Choiseul le Marquis was only a kilometer away from the Great Road.

The Great Road stretched across the Plaine du Nord, and along it were the finest of the plantations. The owners of 200 of them heard the drums, and were aware of the murmuring, the stirring in their slave quarters, and knew that their people were armed, could only be waiting for a signal.

The drums gave it before dawn. The revolt spread through the lush, blue-green and flat Plaine du Nord. The owners of the 200 plantations abandoned their property and fled to the coast, or they were killed. Within a week 600 coffee plantations and 200 sugar plantations were destroyed. Fire swept an area of 2,000 square kilometers.

The slaves in revolt took the Great Road to Cap François. This was the capital of the colony. Here runaway slaves when captured had been burned in iron cages, suspended above hardwood fires in the Place d'Armes. Frenchmen, white troops, stood in rank with fixed bayonets beside the fires.

Some of the slaves who attacked Cap François were *marrons,* wild ones, who had hidden for years in the mountains. They were crazed with hatred of the French, and they knew nothing about cannon. They crawled up to the fortifications under musket fire, then thrust themselves into the barrels of the big pieces. The French gunners blew them apart point-blank.

But the slaves seized the city. They drove the French out of Hispaniola. All of the colony belonged to them.

The Haitian story was retold countless times in the Charleston slave quarters. They were the Gullah folk, and supposed to be happy, even gay. But when their masters had won against the British in the war called the Revolution, nothing came down to them. Their condition was just the same.

The street ditty went:

Buh Rabbit, wha' you fuh do dey?
I does pick oshta fuh young gal.
Oshta does bite off muh finguh
An' young gal does tek 'em fuh laugh at.

Most of the Negroes in Charleston had accepted what life gave them. They were slaves, and aware of the fact that their children would be slaves. Still, it meant a lot that the Haitian planter folks were here.

Sometime, the Negroes would have their day. Then freedom would be more than a word whispered in darkness, with the doors of the quarters shut tight.

Mocking Bird

CHAPTER 10

≈ *Savannah*

IN ENGLAND IT WAS CALLED the "Great Experiment." Thousands of prayers went with them, the people aboard *Ann* knew. This was supposed to be a crusade.

Church congregations all over England and in many parts of western Europe had taken up contributions to make the expedition possible. The House of Commons had voted £10,000 to assist the colony. The Bank of England gave £350 in a remarkable expression of charity. Lord Jekyll's gift of £500, while extremely generous, was just one of a great number from private citizens.

But the description furnished by the colonizers in England did not match reality. The scene here was no part of a "veritable paradise." Alligators lay grunting, snarling in the red-clay shallows of the river. Mosquitoes that seemed as big as English sparrows came in hordes out of the canebrakes across from the steep bluff.

PORTS OF CALL

When the rain stopped and the fog lifted a bit, the 112 colonists on *Ann's* main deck could see the top of the bluff.

The Indian warriors who stood there held little resemblance to the noble redskins reported in England. Their coarse hemp capes, their loose drawers and the puttee-like wrappings on their legs gave them a comical effect. This was increased by the battered European hats they wore. The women wore calico jackets and skirts, and badly bedraggled sunbonnets. Trade with Charles Town must have been quite brisk, the new arrivals decided. Their own visit to the place on the way here had impressed them; the South Carolina folks were surely sharp in a barter.

Now the *Ann's* master, with an anchor down, told his passengers to leave the ship. That was General Oglethorpe coming down the bank, he said. The shipmaster turned away and ordered the mate to fire a charge from a small brass cannon. The date was February 12, 1733, he informed the mate, and the mate should enter the firing of the cannon in the logbook. It was a salute demanded by Oglethorpe and the Board of Trustees.

The colonists gathered up their gear and went over the side into the waiting boats. General James Oglethorpe and his Charles Town friend, Colonel William Bull, stood on the bank to greet them. The name of the colony was Georgia, the colonists repeated, and that made sense, because it was named after the king. But they did not know why this place was called Savannah.

General Oglethorpe, a large and long-faced man, met them on the bank with solemn words of greeting. He sounded very much like one of the English ministers who had described Georgia as a second Eden. But, the colonists noticed, Oglethorpe wore a steel corselet and casque; a sword was at his hip. Oglethorpe was a soldier first and last, and somewhere in between was a philanthropist interested in helping poor folks build a colony in the New World.

274

SAVANNAH

During his youth, Oglethorpe had served under Prince Eugene of Savoy on the Continent. He came home to enter Parliament as a Tory. His family were landowners who had suffered a great deal because of their support of the Stuart cause. He was by background and training a conservative.

But then the tragic death of his friend, Robert Castell, brought forth a strong humanitarian quality in his nature. Castell was a dreamy intellectual who was sent to prison in accordance with extraordinarily strict English laws against debtors. He died there of smallpox, at first mistreated and afterward completely neglected by a brutal jailer. Oglethorpe led an investigation authorized by Parliament. He found that thousands of people, many of them the victims of temporary bad luck, were in jail for failure to pay their debts.

Oglethorpe's investigation created a sensation in England. Reforms followed it. Debtors were turned out of jail by the hundreds. Oglethorpe saw among them future colonists for an ambitious, idealistic venture in North America. He enlisted the support of leading churchmen and philanthropists and, through courtier friends who were close to the king, was promised a royal grant.

A Board of Trustees with twenty-one members, including Oglethorpe, was established. The royal grant gave the colony land lying between the Savannah and Altamaha Rivers, and embraced the coastal islands. The territory had been originally ceded to Carolina, but Oglethorpe did not look forward to any trouble from the people at Charles Town. He expected, though, almost immediate raids from the Spanish in Florida, and the French who held New Orleans.

News of the Georgia venture had been widely spread. The Spaniards and the French, thinking of their own colonial plans, keenly observed what was going on. It had aroused a tremendous 275 surge of religious fervor, and an increasing stream of cash donations. There had never been so much publicity and such enthusiasm for a similar project. Now the enthusiasm, the hopes and charitable instincts of almost the entire English population were involved. Men and women who could never see America, and did not even dream of going personally to Georgia, were excited to a fever of charity. Europeans made their contributions, too, and joined in calling it a crusade.

The term, Great Experiment, was commonly used for it in England. Pamphlets were written about it, and poems. It was the subject of conversation among fashionable people, and at court. England was proud of herself. She was aware that Europeans regarded the project as a source of hope, an assured future for the oppressed but worthy poor.

Oglethorpe and the other members of the Board of Trustees, hard-headed and completely without emotion in their judgment, recognized that the proposed colony held two principal elements to make it successful. It would create a very badly needed buffer between the Spanish and the French and the Carolina colony. It gave at the same time a release for the humanitarian impulses always present in any age or population, and quite easily aroused. The hundreds of sermons about Georgia preached by English ministers were to be taken along, and space found somehow in the colony's supply ship for the 3,000 religious books that had been sent along with the gifts of cash.

There was another great source of interest in the Georgia colony. English merchants saw it as a market where their manufactured goods could be sold. The colony would also produce raw materials and luxury items which England was now forced to buy elsewhere, silk, indigo, wine, rice and spices among them.

A number of highly educated Englishmen had held high hopes

for years that tropical cultivation might be achieved in an overseas colony. Lord Clarendon, Sir Hans Sloane, Dr. Benjamin Worsley, John Evelyn and Samuel Hartlib had experimented in their own gardens at home. They tried to grow ginseng, and cacao, and senna, and pineapples. Those had all failed, along with the attempt to grow tobacco.

But the unemployed who haunted the slum streets of London like the wraiths of a bad conscience would do more than ease the domestic crisis once they were in Georgia. They and the freed debtors would work on the silk plantations, grow indigo and rice. While they built the forts, then the schools and churches, they would develop strong physiques. They should be fit to meet a raid from Florida.

The long lines of applicants who waited for hours to be interviewed in London found there was quite an emphasis on physical requirements. Oglethorpe's humanitarianism was tempered with caution. His purpose was to help unfortunate Englishmen, but he did not intend to take any derelicts. Criticism about the benevolence of the founders was heard. It was claimed, and never disproved, that only six applicants who were former jailed debtors were accepted. The men who were taken were assigned at once to military training. Sergeants of the Guards regiments drilled them outside Buckingham Palace every afternoon.

There were thirty-five families in the group that landed from *Ann.* They and the rest of the colonists slept in tents for the first few nights. The town site that Oglethorpe had picked was along the rolling expanse of ground that stretched inland from what the people called Yamacraw Bluff. They found the local tribe of Indians, who were of the Yamacraw tribe and related to the Creeks, affable, indolent and greatly interested in the casks of beer hoisted out of the ship.

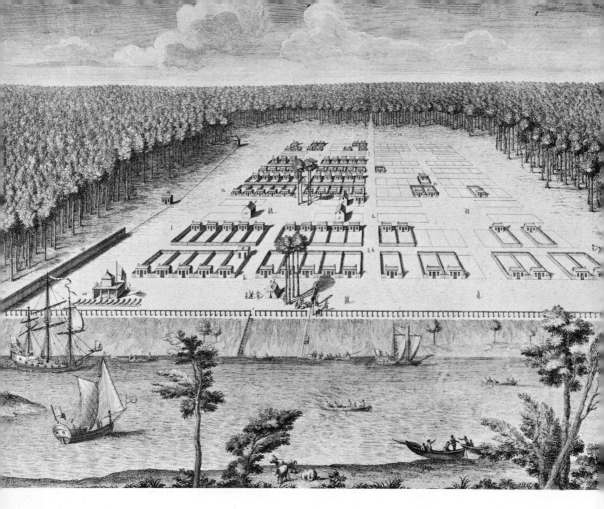

General Oglethorpe laid out Savannah with great care. The city plan has never been changed from the original. Early ships anchored in the river with the alligators. Colonel Bull of Charleston helped locate the colony. So the main street was named in the colonel's honor. The bluff presented problems until steps were built. A heavy-duty crane at the top handled ship cargoes. Tall warehouses were later built along the river front. They were three stories high, and resembled forts. Their thick brick walls survived British bombardment. They were still standing at the end of the Revolution.

A hand-cranked crane was built and set up at the edge of the bluff to get the cargo out of the ship, and the Yamacraw braves, their squaws, their children and their scrawny, tick-ridden dogs
gathered there all day long. Oglethorpe was very careful to keep

his temper with them, and maintain friendly relations. The old Yamacraw chief, a man named Tomochichi, received Oglethorpe's almost immediate respect, and among the tribal group was a half-breed woman who was extremely useful to the English. Her name was Mary Musgrove. She had been educated in the Carolina colony, then married John Musgrove, an English trader, moved with him to the Savannah River region.

Oglethorpe clearly understood how much Mary Musgrove might help him, and treated her with ornate cavalier courtesy to which she, large, greasy but romantic, responded. Oglethorpe was busy, though, in organizing the colony, and had little time for gallantry. He laid out the town by careful design.

It was eighteen miles inland from the sea, and within reach of the tide. He saw it as a port where deepwater ships could tie up at the wharves to be built below the bluff. He named the principal street Bull Street after his Carolinian friend who had helped him pick the site. All of the streets led at right angles away from the river. Simple houses, twenty-four feet by sixteen feet, made of rough, sawed timber were built along these, and at regular intervals were large squares to be used as market-places.

Each family was allocated a building lot in town, and a garden plot outside it, with a total of five acres, and forty-five more in the country for general farming. The fifty-acre limit was enforced for all indigent colonists, but there was a provision for people of means.

Oglethorpe realized that the regulations of the colony were often in conflict. People who could afford it, and a number had the money, were permitted to buy as much as 500 acres of land. This was a direct violation of the spirit of the Great Experiment, for it set up separate classes according to wealth.

No slaves were allowed, but white indentured people were *279* being steadily sent out by the Board of Trustees. Their terms of service extended from seven to fourteen years. Then, if they agreed to stay for four more years in the colony, they were promised twenty-five acres of land. It was a long time to wait, though, and a tremendous hatred of the more fortunate could be created meantime.

No rum was allowed in the colony. But beer and wine were permitted. Traders using the inland trails to Charles Town brought back large quantities of rum. They insisted that it was for barter with the Indians.

Oglethorpe knew that the annual shipment of deerskins to Charles Town had gone over the 50,000 mark. Deerskins had become the main source of shoe leather in Europe. Pack trains came out of the interior each week with fresh skins; Indians moved over the trails carrying an average load of thirty skins. They worked for a couple of knicknacks, or a yard or two of duffel cloth. The same kind of ridiculously small wages were paid to the crews of the flatboats that took the loads of skins to Charles Town.

The flatboats were loaded upstream on the Savannah River at what was called Savannah Town and later became Augusta. It was a four- or five-day trip from there down to the coast. Then they went along the inland channel across Port Royal Sound and among the islands to Charles Town. The return from Charles Town, with the final, upriver leg against the current and tide, took twenty days, often almost a month.

The crews were at first a mixed lot. There were indentured white men, and Indians, and former Negro slaves who had bought their freedom in Carolina and migrated to the new colony. The flatboats were commanded by white men who were expert pilots and responsible to the owners, most of whom were Charles Town merchants.

SAVANNAH

For the flatboat crews to drink rum upon reaching Charles Town and to bring a supply back with them was only sensible. Oglethorpe, who liked a glass of Madeira himself, permitted it without comment. What was good for trade was good for the colony, and England.

Then, after the Board of Trustees turned over the colony to the Crown in 1752, the crews became entirely Negro. The rice trade had expanded tremendously, and with it the size of the plantations. Some of the Low Country holdings near the mouth of the Savannah and on the coastal islands were as much as 2,000 acres. Tobacco was also grown on them, but the really profitable crop was rice.

That was the cargo the flatboat crews hauled. They brought it in bulk to the deepwater harbors at Savannah, Beaufort and Charles Town, where it was put aboard ship for England. The outstanding figure among the slaves on a wealthy rice plantation was the chief boatman. He held a highly regarded post. The flatboat crews were chosen by him from among the young, husky and smart field-hands. He was called "the patroon," and deserved the title.

His knowledge of boat work was vast. He was familiar with the coastal channels, the bays, creeks and sounds between Savannah and Charles Town. He knew the approaches to the Savannah River, and the river itself to the head of navigation. The channels constantly shifted due to the action of storms or extreme tides, and he kept detailed information about them, in preparation for his next trip.

The coastal marshes were crisscrossed with shallow waterways that spread out in an elaborate, confusing network. Clumps of live-oak hung with long, gray, thick streamers of Spanish moss marked some of the larger islands. But most of the time a patroon

steered his course through mile after mile of marsh grass where water fowl squawked and splashed and the blue bottle flies and the mosquitoes and the gnats were unrelenting.

The crew used poles, and sweeps; when the wind was right, the patroon set a crude squaresail on the stub mast. He checked his bearings for newly shifted sandbars, conned the boat around them, standing straddle-legged at the long tiller, then filled the sail again for the next long reach.

None of the boats navigated at night. It was too dangerous in the lightless, winding channels. They anchored, or they went alongside at some plantation wharf. There was singing and dancing and a little rum-sampling after supper. But, with dawn, the patroon had his crew back in the boat, had cast off the lines and started the day's haul towards port.

Oglethorpe, who was forty-three, and vigorous and keen when the colony was founded, worked very actively to strengthen it. He considered Spanish attack inevitable, and prepared wide-scale defense. A battery of five cannon was emplaced on Yamacraw Bluff for the protection of Savannah. He built Fort Argyle southwest of Savannah on the Ogeechee River. It was located at a ford where southern Indians friendly to the Spanish usually crossed on their way to raid in Carolina.

He built a line of forts on the coastal islands, and went as far south on a tour of inspection as the St. John's River, near

St. Augustine. Then he laid out the town site of New Inverness, where he hoped a group of Highland Scots would settle. His forces were thin, and scattered, and he repeated the fact often in his correspondence with the Board of Trustees.

While he waited for the Scots, who were being recruited in the Highlands, he built a road from Savannah to Augusta, and others that connected St. Simon's Island and New Inverness. But before the Scots arrived, a large contingent of Germans entered the colony.

These people were Salzburgers, who came from the Austrian mountains by way of France, then England. They were sturdy, and thrifty, and God-fearing. The pastors of their congregations held tight control over them. They settled at a place called Ebenezer, found too much malaria there and moved to a second site that was promptly named New Ebenezer and proven to be healthy.

The Salzburgers were followed by Moravians, who were supposed to settle south of Savannah on the Ogeechee. But they were opposed to the idea of carrying arms. They stayed in Savannah and refused to go to the frontier. This created bad feeling against them; they were called cowards and shirkers by some of the other colonists. So they moved out, and started a search for a home site that finally ended in Pennsylvania.

The Board of Trustees was able to collect 130 Highlanders who had no scruples about bearing arms. They were accompanied to Georgia by a group of about fifty women and children, and settled at New Inverness as Oglethorpe had planned.

The settlement was on the Altamaha River, near the mouth. The Scots chose to call the surrounding region Darien. This was in memory of the Scots who had lost their lives in the tragic enterprise at Darien, on the Isthmus of Panama.

283

PORTS OF CALL

An expedition backed by practically all of the available capital in Scotland had attempted to found a colony on the isthmus. It was made in 1698, with the Spanish established in strong garrisons at Panama and Cartagena. The Spanish troops, their Indian allies, malaria and dysentery and the losses suffered in several battles forced the Scots to surrender. But the Spanish commander allowed them to march forth from the fort to their ships carrying their flags, and with the bagpipers playing. Now, at New Inverness, were men who were veterans of the Darien campaign, and they had forgotten nothing.

Oglethorpe used the Scots in an attack he launched in the winter of 1739 against St. Augustine. It was disastrous, and the Scots and the rest of Oglethorpe's troops were severely defeated. Then, early in the summer of 1742, the Spanish chose to come north with a fleet of fifty ships.

Thirty-six of the Spanish ships managed to maneuver past Fort William without damage, and entered Cumberland Sound. Word of their arrival was spread by Oglethorpe, in command of the defense on St. Simon's Island, and he sent a special messenger to muster the Highlanders. Then he met the Spanish attack with all the ships and troops he could collect.

He ordered his own schooner into action. She carried fourteen guns, and with her went a merchant ship named *Success* which had been at anchor in the roadstead, and eight York sloops. Oglethorpe fought the Spaniards from the ships until the weight of the enemy fire became too severe. He gradually withdrew his men, local militia and Indians, and told them to hold the fort on the beach. They went ashore and manned the guns there long enough to give covering fire for the ships they had just left.

Oglethorpe had ordered the crews aboard those to fight clear of the Spanish fleet if possible and head for Charles Town. Helped by the shore fire, they were able to get away to sea; a number of the Spanish ships were small and lightly armed, failed to make a close pursuit. But Oglethorpe could not hold the fort.

The Spanish commander put 3,000 men on the beach at St. Simon's, landing them from ships' boats. They attacked the fort boldly, crawling through the sea-grape and over the sand dunes slowly in their bulky boots, then rising up to shout, "Lutheran dogs!" and rush at the gun embrasures with their pikes, halberds and musketoons.

Oglethorpe retreated into the jungle behind the fort. His total force, without the Highlanders, was 500 men. He could not afford to stand up to the Spaniards. But a kilted messenger came jogging along the trail to tell him that the Scots were on their way.

The Scots deployed scouts to watch the Spaniards. They stayed close to them but out of sight in the jungle until July seventh, when the ambush was fully prepared. Then they gave the harsh, wild Highland yell and jumped the Spaniards in a swampy clearing on the main trail.

Some of the Scots were veterans of the campaign in Panama. Other, younger men had only heard of that. But all of them had left their cherished homeland because of extreme poverty. The Spaniards on St. Simon's represented power, wealth and a chance at retribution. The Scots leapt at the slow-moving, fly-pestered files with terrible ferocity.

Their weapons were the Claymore sword, the great Lochaber axe and the dirk. They kept on yelling while they fought. Their heavy woolen kilts swirled as they swung and hewed and stabbed; their bare legs were splashed with blood and mire. Glaring around at each other after the Spaniards were dead, mortally wounded or prisoners, their eyes showed red-shot and not quite sane.

The Spanish detachment smashed by the Scots was only a

part of the force on the island. But the defeat was so severe that the Spanish commander decided to give up the plan to invade the colony. He embarked his men and sailed for St. Augustine.

It was the last real threat ever made by the Spaniards to break the line of the Savannah River and seize the colony.

Oglethorpe went home to England the next year. He had spent ten years in Georgia, and considered his work done. But even in the remoteness of the easy, country-gentleman life he recognized that the Great Experiment was about to become an absolute failure.

The elaborate agricultural program designed to sustain the colony was discarded as worthless. The exotic plants sent out from England for experimental purposes and put in gardens along the banks of the Savannah had withered away and died. The vineyards that were to grow in abundance were a dream. The rows of mulberry trees reaching in geometrical avenues to the horizon to provide food for millions of silkworms were a reality only in the ambitious engravings made in England. Some indigo had been planted, and rice was a profitable crop; and that was all.

The colonists had begun to desert Georgia early, while Oglethorpe still served as governor. Some went across the river to Carolina, and others to Virginia, or further north. Savannah held 5,000 people six years after it was founded. Before Oglethorpe left, the population was down to 500, most of them newly arrived immigrants.

Oglethorpe understood that two-thirds of the settlers for whom the Board of Trustees had provided a home at no expense were among those who chose to go elsewhere. But there was further bad news.

The attempt to keep rum out of the colony created crime and
286 lawlessness. It was smuggled without hindrance. Grogshops

operated openly on street corners in Savannah. No citizen would go to court and testify against his neighbor.

When the Board of Trustees finally allowed the sale of rum in 1742, they insisted that it be purchased only in exchange for various products. This requirement was ignored. The agitation for abandonment of prohibition had been led by a group of Savannah merchants who were sharply interested in the profits of the liquor trade.

Oglethorpe, in retirement in England, could remember the titles of several of the books among the lot of 3,000 shipped to the colony with the first settlers. There were copies of *The Great Importance of a Religious Life Considered,* and *Friendly Admonitions to the Drinkers of Brandy,* and *The Duty of Man.*

But the colonists did not like working in the fields under the fierce sun. They wanted slaves, so they could be gentlemen in the fashion of the Carolina folks across the river. They wanted rum for their own consumption, and cheap barter with the Indians. More than anything else, they sought more land, which would make them rich.

Oglethorpe refused to accept slavery. He fought against it with all his ability. There were people in England, though, who found a way around the restrictions of the Board of Trustees. They arranged for slaves to be imported from Carolina on leases that would last for a hundred years. The Board of Trustees became tired of the struggle. They offered in 1748 a compromise which the settlers recognized as an admission of defeat. Slaves would be allowed in the colony, but the number was to be held to four slaves for each white indentured servant.

The Board of Trustees gave up completely in 1753, allowed the Crown to take the colony. They had spent over a million dollars in promotion of it, and gained very little in return.

287

An eighteenth-century plantation scene, with the ship, the tidewater mill, warehouses, slave quarters and mansion.

But Georgia prospered almost at once under the Crown with the various restrictions removed. During the next few decades, the Savannah River valley and the adjoining seacoast to the southward were given to intensive rice cultivation, and Georgia developed her own planter aristocracy. The slave forces on the plantations were constantly expanded, and renewed. Malaria in the marshes where the slaves worked made life short.

Savannah became a very active port of call, in direct competition with Charles Town. She built for the first time a decent wharf below the bluff. The anchorage space for the shipping out in the river was widened, deepened and marked by buoys. The warehouses at the foot of the bluff increased in height with the prosperity of the owners. Their brick construction, narrow, barred windows and buttressed walls gave them the appearance of fortresses. Pilots still complained about the difficulties of navigation up the crooked, tricky river from Tybee Island at the mouth, but they kept on collecting their fees and handling the vessels.

Georgia had begun to export in the 1760s a great variety of products. Ships' manifests presented at the Custom House in Savannah listed silk, leather, lumber, staves, and hoops, pink root, Sago powder, indigo, and rice, peas, corn. Most of these were for the West Indian trade, and with them went oxen, cattle, sheep, hogs, and turkeys, geese and chickens.

Purchasing agents for the Royal Navy ordered large amounts of handspikes, oars, spars, pitch, tar and turpentine. London wholesalers bought all available deerskins, and beaver, raccoon and otter pelts. The deerskin supply was almost exhausted; hunters had driven the last of the species beyond the Cherokee Mountains, out of range of pack trains that could reach the coast.

The old, rough-sawed wooden houses were now gone from the central squares of Savannah. Neat, pale-yellow-brick houses replaced them. The squares were grassy, cool, flanked by palmettos, live-oaks and magnolias. The houses were set within gardens, and the fragrance of their flowers was pervasive.

Churches of various denominations were along the streets that led to the bluff. Many of the merchants' offices, the taverns and coffee-houses were located close to the waterfront. Narrow, cobbled alleys between the warehouses served the draymen, the carters, the drovers and pack-train gangs on their way to the harbor.

PORTS OF CALL

The favorite tavern was at Broughton and Whitaker Streets. This was started in 1766 by a Swiss named Peter Tondee. He had come out early to the colony with his parents. They were settlers who succumbed soon to malaria and left him and his younger brother as the first teenage charges of the Bethseda Orphanage.

Peter Tondee was trained as a carpenter, and helped build the orphanage. Then he met and married an Acadian widow. She was of great assistance to him when he opened his tavern. What he and his clientele called the "long room" was cool, quiet in summer and warm in winter. It was the center for the All Saints Quoits Club, and the Union Society, and a number of other organizations, which in 1774 included the Sons of Liberty.

The first meeting of the Sons of Liberty was held July twenty-seventh at Tondee's, with a lot of speeches and no action taken. The second meeting was held on August tenth, and secrecy was strictly enforced. Tondee stood at the door and checked every man who asked to enter. The royal governor, James Wright, was well liked, but kept from the meeting.

Some of the New England settlers, Puritans who had come from Massachusetts in 1752 to Georgia, took a prominent part in the meeting. They were prosperous men whose 32,000-acre holding was at Midway, between the Savannah and Altamaha Rivers.

Their principal crops were rice and indigo, which they shipped to England. They had built their own port at Sunbury on the coast. The harbor was busy with the vessels that took the settlers' products to England and returned to them the finished goods they needed. A force of 1,500 slaves worked the holding, and at Midway a typical, thin-spired Congregational Church reared high above the palmettos. Still, the Puritans were fervent in their desire for independence.

SAVANNAH

The August tenth meeting at Tondee's achieved definite results. A resolution of grievances against the home government was drawn up, and signed. A vote was taken to send supplies to the rebels in Boston. The news of Lexington had arrived in May, and given the Georgians the incentive which they had lacked. Georgia, a considerable group of citizens argued, was isolated, did not belong in the conflict. She owned only a few ships. Her grievances were not severe, and taxation did not seriously bother her.

But Georgia joined the other colonies in rebellion. She suffered through seven years of war. Savannah was occupied by the British, besieged and partly destroyed. When the British force left on July 12, 1782, the American troops under General James Jackson found the city in miserable condition.

British cannon balls lay imbedded in cracked, crumbling house walls. Churches and public buildings had been used as hospitals. They were filthy, and had a charnel smell. Weeds grew tangled in some of the streets. Watering troughs were dry, and fountains littered with broken masonry. The slaves were disaffected, felt no compulsion to work.

The city cleaned itself, and rebuilt. Help came from the owners of the large plantations eager to sell their crops. There were ships in the harbor waiting for cargo. Flatboats and rafts loaded with tobacco, lumber, beef, corn and wheat moved down to Savannah from the inland farms of the Piedmont region.

Trade was so brisk that in 1785 the city could afford a theater. A Charleston troupe put on performances of *Cato*, and *Catherine and Petruccio*. The theater was run by a pair of men named Godwin and Kidd, and Godwin also conducted a dancing school. He advertised that "young ladies and gentlemen might receive expert tuition in the polite and necessary accomplishments of dancing."

A Jockey Club was formed. The city was incorporated in

Tobacco became a large cash crop in Georgia. Growing was on a wide scale after the Revolution. The leaf was picked by hand, then hung to cure. The drying sheds were open to sunlight and air. It was sorted by women skilled at the work. Packed in hogsheads, it was kept under shelter. Then it was taken to state warehouses at Augusta. Inspectors graded the tobacco and the packing. They marked the hogsheads, gave origin and weight. The last operation was the river ride to Savannah.

SAVANNAH

1789. There was not very much, the young men who spent their evenings at Tondee's said, that separated Charleston from Savannah any more—except a lot of false Carolinian pride.

But most of the young men gave their concentrated interest to the tobacco business. It had been very important as a means of recovery from the depression which followed the Revolution. Huge hogsheads were dragged laboriously along the back roads to Augusta, or rafted down the tributaries of the Savannah.

The state maintained fourteen inspection points, but the largest part of the work was done at Augusta. Three warehouses known as Call's, Richmond and Augusta handled it. The inspectors graded the tobacco and checked the packing, then stamped the hogsheads "Georgia" and marked also the name of the warehouse, the quality of the leaf, the net weight and the tare. The inspectors were civil servants, and greatly respected; there was never any question of their integrity.

Augusta had begun to lose its reputation as a tough, sometimes violent frontier town. During the early years of the colony, the Indian traders, the pack-train men, the raft crews, and the renegades and runaways had gath-

ered there. The appearance of Jean Couture was still remembered.

He smelled of buffalo fat, and wore buckskins made in the style of some tribe that lived far beyond the mountains. His English was broken, filled with French and Shawnee and Cherokee. He admitted that he was French, and that he had come from the Mississippi by way of the headwaters of the Tennessee, then down the divide.

293

PORTS OF CALL

Couture caused a great stir in the town for a few days. Men who were on the Indian Board confused him with another Frenchman, Baron de St. Castin, who came from up in Maine and was famous along the border. The Indian Board thought that maybe the French were about to lead the tribes in a mass attack against the colony. But all Couture was doing was looking around; he was just another forest wanderer. He went off to visit in Carolina and see that part of the country.

The men who worked the Petersburg boats also belonged to the wandering kind. But they came back to Augusta after each trip, because it was the head of navigation for them, and they spent their money in the town. They were very proud of their trade. A lot of the fights they started in the taverns were because they insisted they were better than a man who worked in a sawmill, or handled an axe or a plow.

The Petersburg boats carried the bulk of the tobacco from Augusta to Savannah. Those varied in size from thirty-five to eighty-five feet, with a six- or seven-foot beam and a draft between ten to twenty feet. They were built from inch-and-a-half planking taken from long-leaf pine, and each end decked over, with a plank around the gunwale that served as a walk for the polemen. The polemen walked slowly from bow to stern to push a boat upstream.

SAVANNAH

Bound downstream, the pilot stood at the bow. He conned the steersman, who used a pole or a sweep. When the pilot wanted the course changed to starboard, he shouted, "Georgia!" That state was on the starboard side, and South Carolina on the port. He called, "South Carolina!" for a course change towards it.

The average crew aboard a boat was seven or eight men, both white and Negro. They cooked on a fire set over a thick layer of earth in a caboose at the after end. The boats were owned by people living in the river towns, and they took pride in the runs made by their crews.

For about twenty miles below Augusta, the river was smooth. It swept even-flowing between rows of maples and elms, and hickories, walnuts, ash, pine, magnolia and mimosa. Plowed fields and neat farms lay past the river banks. Then the river changed.

The trees were much bigger, somber, giant cedars, and cypresses. Their roots hunched stark and white in marsh water, and behind them were canebrakes and thick jungle vegetation. Snakes were here, and alligators, and big turtles.

But wharves that lay at the ends of country roads were along the bank. They bore the names the rivermen had given them: Blue House, Robinson Round, Poor Robin, Hog's Nose Round, Cut Finger Cut, Saucy Boy and Ring Jaw. The boats picked up more  cargo, swung back out into the current and kept on to Savannah. That was the last of the haul for some crews; the others went along to Brunswick and Fernandino.

When the cotton trade expanded after 1800, the Petersburg boats were used less on the river. Their place was taken by flat-

295

boats, or rafts that were called "cotton boxes." Savannah shipped 27,600 bales to Liverpool in 1805, and that was a quarter of the entire American crop.

The Jefferson embargo hurt the port. But after the War of 1812, Savannah took back her trade, and got more. She was in the front rank of Southern ports for twenty years afterward. Her cotton shipment in 1826 was 190,000 bales.

Then Savannah lost interest in the sea. Her ambitious young men turned their backs on it. They moved inland, along with the rest of the new plantation aristocracy. Growing cotton was their major concern, and they severed their connections with the English shippers, never regained them. Augusta became the center of their lives, and they called that "the city."

CHAPTER 11

≈ *New Orleans*

THE SPANISH CAME FIRST to the Mississippi, upstream from the Gulf of Mexico. They were small and very strong men, burnt almost black by years in the tropical sun. Beneath the slant of the helmet brims, the eyes stared distended in the narrow faces, strained by the effects of fever, the sun and the ceaseless dream that somewhere here on this immense continent gold would be found.

But the Spanish did not stay. Alvarez Pineda, the leader of the original expedition in 1519, was intent upon the exploration of the gulf coastline from Florida westward. He did not go more than a couple of miles up one of the Mississippi passes. Then he kept on towards Texas, and with the trend of the land, south to the Panuco River and the settlement called Vera Cruz.

Hernando de Soto was one of the most determined and ambitious of the Spanish explorers. He reached the Mississippi in overland marches, crossed it in 1541 south of Memphis, then in   *297*

PORTS OF CALL

1542 returned to it from a trip that took him into present-day Oklahoma. The fever caught him when he came back to the river, and he died of it.

The survivors of his expedition under the command of Luis de Moscosco de Alvarado went on downstream in Indian dugout canoes. They did not halt anywhere, though, except to camp overnight or to hunt for game. Their objective was Vera Cruz, and all they sought was survival. They had long since relinquished the dream about gold.

It was the French who opened the Mississippi, from the tightly winding bends of the Chicago River and Lake Michigan to the four great passes that spread through the delta country to the gulf. They had more persistence than the Spanish, and a keener, more subtle imagination. They were able to dismiss the mirage of cities paved, walled, roofed with gold. The French thought about the slow but certain wealth to be made from the trade in furs and the cultivation of crops, a port city that would be the heart of their colonial empire here.

De Soto was a brave and intelligent man. But he lacked the foresight of René Robert Cavelier, Sieur de la Salle. The Frenchman had come down the fast-water rivers from Quebec, paddled in a birchbark craft among waves as high as his shoulders and past boulders and fouled tree limbs that would tear the canoe apart at the slightest impact. He knew the almost unbelievably savage, hate-crazed tribes of the Five Nations of the Great Lakes region, and the Shawnees, the Creeks, the Sioux who came from the forest or to the edges of the Mississippi prairie bluffs to stare in silent distrust at the white men. He knew the Choctaws, and a dozen other tribes of the lower river, most of them to him nameless.

298   La Salle had no accurate idea of the magnitude of the region he explored and on April 9, 1682, claimed for his king, Louis XV.

NEW ORLEANS

There was no way for him to calculate it. Still, he comprehended the vastness, the potential wealth and the importance of its possession by France. He stopped on his way to the gulf at the site where New Orleans was to be built, camped alongside the river near the rolling, pine-covered hills.

It was 110 miles from the New Orleans camp site to the coast through the enormous, alluvial marshes. The river water was greasy, streaked brown with clay and sediment. Big, submerged balls of mud rose towards the surface, bumped against the canoe hulls and exploded with a sharp hiss of pent gas. The paddlers cursed. They were glad to be out of the river, although the gulf rollers pitched the canoes widely yawing from the steersmen's courses.

A tough professional soldier, Pierre le Moyne, Sieur d'Iberville, was sent out from France in 1697 to colonize the region. It had been given the name of Louisiana, and Iberville was conscious of the tremendous responsibility assigned to him. The French, already well established in Canada, believed that with the creation of various strategically placed forts along the Mississippi they could hold the river forever. Their new empire would be one of the wealthiest in the world, make France a supremely powerful nation.

But it was difficult to find a suitable site for the fort at the lower end of the river. Belize, and Dauphin Island on the gulf were not satisfactory, and served only as an anchorage for ships while they discharged or loaded cargo. Iberville went upstream from Belize in one of the tricky Indian pirogues, a Choctaw brave hired as his guide.

They found high land only when they reached the present-day location of Baton Rouge. That was almost 200 miles from the mouth of the river, though. Iberville went back, downriver. The fort must be closer to the sea.

Southern Indians shown while fishing a river. The sixteenth-century study is quite accurate. The craft marked "Cannow" is a typical dugout. The two warriors cook fish over a fire amidships. It has a stone and sand base to protect the hull. The fish weirs in the background were common. Fish that swam into the rectangle were trapped. The spear-handlers wade in the shallows. They are after big fish pursued close inshore. A porpoise in the foreground moves near a shark.

His Indian paddlers worked the pirogue slowly along the stretch of water on the eastern bank where, the guide said, a portage started. Iberville studied the bank. He saw Choctaws who hid among the canebrakes. Buzzards sat on the knobby elbows of mangrove roots and pecked at lice. Otter slid happily in the mud.

300

NEW ORLEANS

Turkeys gobbled at each other in the underbrush. A water moccasin swam against the current within triangular ripples. Iberville gestured at the guide; he wanted to be put ashore for a look at the portage.

He wrote about it in his journal on January 18, 1700:

> I have been to the portage. I found it to be about half a league long; half the way being woods and water reaching well up on the leg, and the other half good enough, a country of cane-brakes and woods. . . . I have had a small desert made, where I planted sugar-canes brought by me from Martinique; I do not know if they will take, for the exhalations are strong.

Iberville died two years later, and it was his brother, Jean Baptiste le Moyne, Sieur de Bienville, who built the settlement. But that was in 1718, and first the French colonists went through extreme suffering. Bienville took his brother's place and moved the base of the colony to Mobile. There were repeated Indian attacks against the settlements, and a number of casualties, and desertions aboard homeward-bound ships.

A census taken in 1712 showed that the entire population, scattered inland from Mobile to the New Orleans portage and up the river as far as present-day Natchez, was only 324 men. But in 1717 a crafty and wholly unscrupulous Scot, John Law, decided that he would exploit the region.

Law was a highly accomplished promoter of risky enterprises, among them the Scottish colonization venture at Darien. He had lost no money there, though, and in fact made a large amount. He was able to form in France an organization he called "The Company of the West." His new scheme was to send thousands of emigrants to Louisiana, at a price. He had just completed work on the establishment of the first national French bank, and enjoyed the confidence of the Regent, the Duke of Orleans.

He easily found in Paris a number of associates who were willing, for a share in the profits, to help develop the monumental fraud that was known finally as "The Mississippi Bubble." Law sold land at very small prices. He had the illimitable Louisiana wilderness at his disposal, and there was nobody in France to restrain or correct his absolutely false statements about conditions in the colony.

He put his first shipload of men and provisions ashore at Dauphin Island in February, 1718, and Bienville as govenor-general took immediate advantage of the fact. Bienville had been waiting for years to start construction of a settlement at the site chosen by his brother near the Indian portage.

Work gangs cleared away the brush between Bayou St. John and the Mississippi. Streets were laid out, and Bienville insisted that ground for a church be broken, with the fitting ceremony performed. A levee made of loose earth was put in place along the river bank to check the annual floods. The huts were small, built of cypress or palmetto logs with palm-thatch roofs. The church was a shallow, half-finished excavation. The levee would very probably collapse with the next rise of high water. But this was New Orleans, named after the Regent, and in time the place must grow, thrive and become a great city and port.

John Law's corps of land agents were loud with optimism about the future of the colony as they went through the Parisian cafés. The ship that had carried the first load of settlers was back. The colony was an almost incredible success. New Orleans was already a splendid, well-built city, the agents said. People should
hurry up and buy land while the low prices lasted.

NEW ORLEANS

The agents put up placards that gave details of the delights of life in Louisiana. Gold and silver and precious gems were all around, could be taken in barter from the Indians for a cheap knife, some glass beads or a piece of imitation lace. Frenchmen who went to the colony, even the simplest of men, would live like kings.

The placards were illustrated. Frenchmen in attitudes of languorous pleasure were surrounded by bronze-skinned and splendid women who treated them with outright ardor. Naked Nubian slaves stood ready to serve their French masters. The scene was set in moonlight, with palm trees in the background.

Frenchmen by the hundreds and then thousands sold everything they owned and bought land in Louisiana. They were sent to Dauphin Island and put on the beach there just as fast as the ships' crews could unload them. But nobody was on the island to meet the new colonists; it was deserted. The men who had gone before them had left no food, no water. Shelter was insufficient. Boats could not be found to make the passage to the mainland.

The boats that had put the settlers ashore were hauled back aboard the ship. The ship sailed. It did no good to shout at her, the settlers understood. Her crew was paid by John Law.

The men trapped on Dauphin Island died from exposure, fever, sunstroke, hunger or suicide. Some of them went insane, and walked out into the azure reach of Biloxi Bay where the shark and the barracuda waited. Others, more resolute, made rafts, gathered turtle eggs, speared fish and caught the water from rain squalls with banana leaves and conch shells. They got across to the mainland and went up the river to New Orleans, or overland through the swamps.

The bodies of those who remained were left unburied on   *303* the beach. Gulls picked at them, and the carrion crows. New arrivals from the next ship asked questions when they landed. Several shiploads were criminals from French jails; Law had arranged their release so they might be used in the colony as cheap labor. But most of them stayed on the island and died, and with them a shipload of Negroes, collected to serve as slaves for the colonists.

Then Law's glittering, lie-tangled bubble broke. The fraud was exposed in Paris. Creditors and purchasers of land asked for their money. The Company of the West was a total failure.

A ship from France brought the news to Louisiana. People went over to Dauphin Island to see what had happened to the stranded men. There were some skeletons on the beach above high-tide mark. That was all.

New Orleans persisted, though, and gradually the rough little settlement became a city. Bienville appointed the Chevalier Le Blond de la Tour engineer for the colony. It was de la Tour who made the survey, and laid out the streets.

The central square was the Place d'Armes. This faced the river, and on the opposite side, also facing the river, the first log-walled church was built. Levee Street, as the name indicated, led along the river bank at the top of the small embankment which was supposed to contain the river's floodwaters.

The river was almost a mile wide here, and during the cool hours of late afternoon and evening the colonists met beneath the trees on the Place d'Armes. They stared forth across the immense brown curve of the river at the forest that stood massive on the western bank. Then, while the moon rose, they talked inevitably of France. Everything, even the street names, reminded them of their homeland.

The next street parallel to the river was called Chartres. The 304 merchants kept their shops on Royal Street, the one next to that.

NEW ORLEANS

Then there were Bourbon Street, and Dauphine, and Burgundy, and Conti. The main cross-street, named after the Duke of Orleans, began in back of the Place d'Armes.

A man taking his time could walk through every street in about two hours. The squares were small, and the streets narrow. The population in 1726, eight years after the colony was started, was only 880 people, with 65 servants and 129 slaves. There were, according to this census, no more than ten horses in the settlement. Newcomers complained about the flat and swampy ground chosen for the location.

New Orleans lies behind her levee at the big bend of the Mississippi, the current against her. When the river rose, water moccasins came out of the sewers, sandbags slipped, the levee was treacherous. People stood in the streets and looked up at the shipping, could recognize various vessels and the crews.

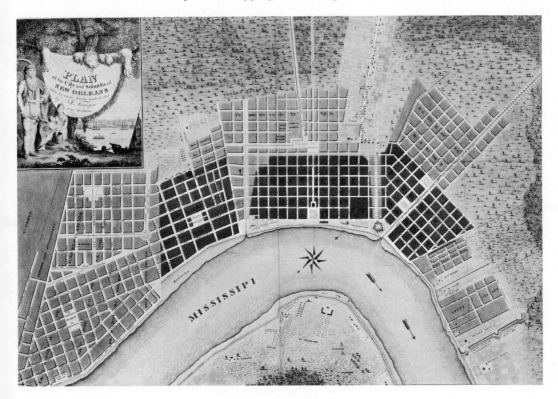

River water filtered through under the soil. Crayfish abounded, and tobacco and vegetables were hard to raise. Rice was the single crop that could be cultivated with success. Fogs were frequent, and the air was fever-charged. The mosquitoes in summertime were a terrible menace, clustered in black clouds on the settlers' sleeping nets at night.

But Bienville had no intention of relinquishing the site. He wrote in his journal on June 10, 1718, when the wilderness had still not been cleared, "I am grieved to see so few people engaged in a task which requires at least a hundred times the number. All of the ground of the site, except the borders which are drowned by floods, is very good, and everything will grow there."

He planned to construct a canal about three miles in length from the Mississippi to Lake Pontchartrain along the route of the old Indian portage. The St. John's River flowed into the lake, and could be used to reach the sea less than forty miles from Mobile.

This was much better than the passage through the mouth of the river. The delta country where the Mississippi flowed into the gulf had been described as "very difficult," and "often flooded and filled with alligators, serpents, and other venomous beasts."

Aligator

NEW ORLEANS

There were forty plantations established early in the immediate vicinity of New Orleans. One of these was owned by Bienville. His work force was made up of twenty slaves, some Negroes, and some Indians from the broken and debased local tribes. He had six head of "horned cattle," and sowed half a cask of rice for his first crop. Mulberry trees were planted, and there was talk of extensive silk culture. But Bienville continued to grow rice and sell it at a good price in France.

The next major undertaking for Bienville was to marry off some of the young women who had arrived in the colony in March, 1721, in the care of a group of nuns. Eighty-eight of them were sent out aboard a ship named *La Baleine*. They had been taken from various houses of correction in Paris, and not all of them were immediately acceptable as brides. Quite a few of the younger settlers said that they were happy in their relationships with young Choctaw squaws, maintained in cabins outside the city limits.

But Bienville was able to report to his superiors in France:

> Thirty-one girls have been married off between the 24th of April and the 25th of June. All were from those sent from *La Baleine*. Several were given to sailors who asked insistently for them. These could scarcely have been married off to good residents. Nevertheless they were granted to the sailors only on the express condition that they should settle in the Colony, to which they have agreed. These sailors will supply practical navigators to the special conditions of the region, and this was much needed.

A young woman who settled in New Orleans during the first years of the colony did not suffer many of the usual discomforts of frontier living. The houses were built with cypress logs, *307* and the spaces between the logs chinked with a mixture of mud and Spanish moss. Whitewash was used inside and outside the houses. Each house was set in a garden where orange trees grew. A high picket fence surrounded the garden, and the fence was whitewashed.

There was no glass for the windows in the early houses. But heavy batten doors kept out wind and rain. Four houses were customarily built on a city square. Orange trees planted as hedges inside the picket fences kept the houses separate and made an almost impenetrable barrier. So it was possible to leave all doors and windows open during hot nights, and there was no fear of intruders.

Each square was surrounded by a deep ditch. The ditches were lined with cypress, and garbage and ordure were tossed into them. These were cleaned daily by gangs of slaves, most of whom were prisoners from the city jail and wore iron collars, dragged chains.

The sidewalks were called *banquettes,* and paved with brick imported from France at first, and afterwards of local manufacture. Housewives or servants swept the *banquettes* with twig brooms early in the morning. Water was sold from carts that brought it from the river. It was put in huge earthenware jars, and filtered or cleared with alum or charcoal.

Some of the prosperous houses gleamed at night with the light of scores of candles held in crystal chandeliers. The ceiling beams were still rough, and the floor planks. But the floors were covered with pelts that formed a fur carpet from wall to wall. Hostesses appeared to greet their guests dressed in the style of the court at Versailles. Conversation might be about local conditions and scandal, then shift to news of Quebec and Montreal. Many of the officers in the Louisiana colony had served in Canada, considered themselves Canadians. But the talk always turned in the end to Paris. There was a street song that said New Orleans was a little Paris. The Negro slaves often sang it.

Plantation life was a good deal different from that in the city. The plantations, because of their isolation, were self-contained units, with the planter in possession of enormous power. The original land grants were given for tracts along the river. These, because of the river curves and bends, were on strips only an *arpent* wide. An *arpent* was slightly less than an American acre, and as a consequence the grants stretched back from the river for several miles. Some were forty *arpents* deep, and planters owned several grants, occasionally scattered, and under separate cultivation.

The plantation houses were at first low, cypress-built structures of the same sort of simple architecture used in the city. Then broad porches were added, and upper storys, and galleries. The rooms were high-ceilinged for coolness, and the windows and doorways and halls were tall and broad. Furniture was imported from France whenever possible, and brought ashore right at the plantation wharf from bateaux which had hauled it upriver from the Dauphin Island anchorage or Mobile.

The slave quarters were in roughly built huts or cabins in back of the main house. The infirmary was near them, and the stables, and the almost innumerable out-houses that held tools or other farm equipment or were used for cooking, the smoking of meat and the storage of vegetables.

Huge cypresses hung with moss, and catalpas, magnolias, acacias and chinaberry trees grew around the plantation houses. The buzzards, called *carancros,* were unsightly and noisy, but they were needed to keep other birds from the fields under cultivation. There was a five-*piastre* fine for anybody in the colony who killed a buzzard.

PORTS OF CALL

Planters hunted deer and woodcock at night by the light of pine torches that slaves carried in long-handled iron sconces. They inspected their levees for holes started by crayfish or muskrats. With their overseers riding the correct three paces behind them, they checked fields, the growth of crops, and the handling of the irrigation ditches, the cutting of timber, the building of fences and the care of the tick-plagued cattle. Then they sat on their porches with their boots off and listened to the complaints made by the Choctaws.

The Choctaws presented a problem to the colony. They were aware that they had been grievously cheated, and robbed of their land. Isolated settlers had been scalped, and killed. Some of the warriors had gone over to the eastern tribes or joined the war-eager Seminoles in Florida. Most of them who stayed in Louisiana were victims of alcohol.

They were worthless as servants or field-hands. When they needed money for rum, they disappeared into the forest and returned with pelts ready for barter. Both warriors and squaws wore cheap trade blankets. Blue, sinuous tattoos stretched on the warriors' cheeks to their mouths, and the corners of their jaws. The warriors had a liking for felt hats, and hung pieces of tin on the bands.

The tin pieces gave a slight, musical jingle when the warriors, drunk, lurched from side to side, stumbling through the New Orleans streets. The Negroes kept apart from the Choctaws. They did not show contempt, only a silent unwillingness to be involved with a people who so readily accepted self-destruction.

The colony grew slowly for some years, at times almost forgotten by Paris, and suffering from the effects of European politics. France ceded Louisiana in 1762 to Spain, and there was a great deal of hard feeling. The newly installed Spanish officials resented the supercilious, antagonistic attitude of the French residents, and there were street fights after dark near the Place d'Armes, the city jail now called the *calabozo* was full and a number of challenges for duels were passed and accepted.

But in 1760 the arrival of French Acadians from Nova Scotia had begun, and this was not stopped by the Spanish tenure of the colony. The Acadians were being expelled systematically by the British. Ships continued to bring them in large groups until 1790, when approximately 4,000 of the hardy, penniless people were in Louisiana. They settled on farm land in the Bayou Teche region outside New Orleans, soon acclimatized.

Other French settlers, a number of them Royalists who fled the Revolution, entered between 1789 and 1792, and were well received. Spanish officials and the officers and soldiers of the garrison force in New Orleans had married French girls. A new social class was being formed. It was called *criolla,* or *creole,* and meant "native-born." New Orleans was a placid backwater of cosmopolitan culture, and much more European than American. The few English-speaking North Americans who ventured there to enter trade or escape debts or the law were sharply reminded of that.

Then, by a secret treaty, the colony was returned in 1800 to France. The transfer was made at the request of Napoleon, who wanted the revival of a French empire in North America. It was a cause of great concern to President Jefferson, who saw it as a threat to national security. Jefferson realized that Napoleon might close the Mississippi to western commerce. He wrote on April 18, 1802, to Robert R. Livingston, the American minister at Paris, "The day that France takes New Orleans . . . we must marry ourselves to the British fleet and nation."

The President instructed Livingston to negotiate for a tract   *311* of land on the lower Mississippi for use as a port. If he failed to get that, he should obtain an irrevocable guarantee of free navigation and the right of deposit. James Monroe was sent to Paris to handle the negotiations with Livingston's assistance.

They found Napoleon ready to make the sale for a surprisingly low figure. The French troops in Hispaniola had been unable to put down the Haitian slave revolt. War was about to break out again with Great Britain, and Napoleon needed them on the Continent. He had given up the idea of a French empire overseas. He sold Louisiana for sixty-million francs, approximately $15 million.

The acquisition doubled the area of the United States. It added a tract of some 828,000 square miles between the Mississippi and the Rocky Mountains. And the American negotiators admitted that they were not clear whether the purchase included West Florida and Texas.

But the Senate approved the purchase treaty, and on December 20, 1804, the United States took formal possession of Louisiana. A Virginian, William C. C. Claiborne, was installed at New Orleans as territorial governor.

Many American merchants established along the eastern seaboard had agents and factors in New Orleans before Claiborne took office. The population of the city was only 8,000 in 1803, but it was the terminus, the clearing-house for all of the enormous and swiftly expanding river traffic. New Orleans would soon become under the American flag a world-known port of call.

Merchants, shipowners, traders and adventurers of all sorts came to Louisiana from the United States and from Europe. Planters moved from the seaboard states with their slaves. They crossed the river and in the region above New Orleans bought land. Both French and Spanish planters were already there. Sugar,

indigo, cotton and fruit were being cultivated in the fertile alluvial soil, and fortunes were being made. This part of the Louisiana Purchase was known as the Territory of Orleans. The population of the settlements in 1810 was more than 76,000, and two
years later Louisiana became a state.

Vigorous protests were made first, though, by the New Englanders in the Senate. Their constituents feared the increase of
trade in the South, and the growth of western power. The men
who recently started business in New Orleans agreed. More wealth
flowed down the Mississippi than could be found in Massachusetts Bay.

The really great era for New Orleans came after the War of
1812, when General Andrew Jackson had brilliantly defended the
city against British attack. Back in 1795, a local planter, Etienne
de Boré, discovered a practical method to granulate cane sugar
syrup. Then steam was used to operate the crushing mills on the
sugar plantations, drastically reduced cost. Sugar brought a better price than indigo or rice, was almost as valuable as cotton.

Schooners and brigs tied up at plantation wharves along the
river and loaded direct for the northern market. The port tonnage at New Orleans had by 1803 increased thirty-seven percent.
The products exported from the province in the same year were
worth two million dollars, and the imports cleared through the
Custom House were two-and-a-half million dollars. Ships took
aboard 34,000 bales of cotton, 4,500 hogsheads of sugar and 2,000
barrels of molasses. There were in addition 50,000 barrels of
flour, 3,000 barrels of beef and pork, large shipments of furs, lumber products, and corn, butter, hams and hides.

The Northern merchants who put their names on the sign-
boards in front of their New Orleans offices carefully checked
these figures, and watched them increase each year. They were   *313*

not at all popular with their Creole neighbors, and treated as foreigners and interlopers in the affairs of the city. But they stayed and gradually improved their contacts, took Creoles into business with them whenever possible and patiently pursued local girls until it was safe to talk about marriage.

During 1811, the first steamboat on what was known as the "western waters" came down the Ohio and the Mississippi. She was built at Pittsburgh by Nicholas Roosevelt under Fulton-Livingston patents. She was a 116-foot vessel of sidewheel design, and named *New Orleans*. Her crew took her without damage through the difficult stretch of water at the falls of the Ohio, then handled her successfully in the New Madrid earthquake. She reached New Orleans on January 10, 1812, and went alongside the levee, was uproariously welcomed.

The vessel was put into service between New Orleans and Natchez. The ungainly, tall-stacked steamboat with her long and resinous clouds of smoke trailing after her became a familiar sight on the river. She joined the myriad kinds of craft that jammed the New Orleans waterfront and floated, sailed, were pushed or poled from the headwaters of the Ohio, the Missouri, the Red River of the North and their tributaries. Among that fleet were Mackinaw boats, flatboats, keelboats, rafts, barges and bateaux.

Deepwater ships lay alongside each other four and five together at the levee. They carried passengers, the mail and premium cotton. A special type of full-rigged ship, her hull almost as sharp as that of a clipper, had been designed for the New York-New Orleans cotton trade. Although her bottom curves were flattened to allow her to cross the sandbars at the mouth of the Mississippi, still she was very fast.

The Collins Line of New York operated the best of these *314* ships and gave them the classification of packets. Captain Na-

The keelboat was the hardest-working craft on the Mississippi, and this is a fine example of her kind. Her cargo house runs almost her full length, and she carries a smartly cut jib, mainsail and topsail.

thaniel Brown Palmer, born in Stonington, Connecticut, and seagoing since he was able to haul and steer, was in command of the finest ship owned by the line. She was *Huntsville,* and he drove her for all that she would take without dismasting.

The reputation he gained for the ship and for the Collins Line was worth it. The company received forty percent more for passenger fare than the unscheduled ships, and thirty-three-and-a-third percent more for freight. Captain Palmer took *Huntsville* out of Belize, the pilot station for New Orleans, around the Florida capes and into New York in ten days on a run filled with favorable wind conditions. That broke the record, and his usual time   *315* was fifteen days. But for the rest of the cotton fleet it was nineteen or twenty.

Captain Palmer had a great liking for New Orleans. One of his brothers had been in business there for some years. When the tensions of driving a packet ship became too severe, the captain went ashore for a few weeks. He and his wife, Eliza, stayed with his brother, and Palmer read, dozed, completely relaxed.

When he needed sailors for his *Huntsville* crew he took them from the flatboat men he had seen around the waterfront. He had stood unobtrusively aside while they fought drunk or sober Texans, Mexicans, trappers, fur-traders, soldiers, the police, any citizens handy and each other. They were conspicuous because of their blue-flannel shirts and their extraordinary ability in a fight.

Captain Palmer recognized them as splendid material for deepwater-ship sailors. With a couple of weeks offshore and some suggestions from himself, the mate and the bosun, they would serve *Huntsville* very well. These were homeless men, wanderers without wives or families, misfits even along the frontier. Money had little value to them. They spent their pay in the space of hours. Now, with it gone, they would start to walk back to the far reaches of the Ohio and to the Kentucky mountain valleys unless he hired them.

Captain Palmer recruited a number of *Huntsville* crews on the New Orleans waterfront. He completely ignored the requests for jobs that came from veteran sailors off the slave ships at anchor in the river. Those men were almost useless in his estimation, and he would first make sailors out of the flatboat men.

Other shipmasters followed Palmer's example. Packet ships on the New Orleans run gathered a large percentage of fo'c'sle *316* hands who less than a year before had never been aboard a full-rigged vessel. Some of them still loved the land, though, and they sang about it in the chanteys they left behind them when they drifted off in the ports, were incapacitated by disease and drink or finally killed in a fight.

They created "Shenandore," the most beautiful of all chanteys. It was sung at dusk at sea when the ship rode under easy sail. There was just the rustle of the royals and topgallants, the faint chirping of the gear and the retreat of the sea along the shipside. The man who took the solo part was rough-voiced. But when the sailor at the helm put the wheel over a spoke, the sound seemed very loud. All hands joined in the chorus, and without shame some men wept.

The soloist, head back, eyes half-shut, sang then, of Shenandore's daughter, and how he loved her. It was "seven long years since last I see'd you." The chorus came in, gentle, soft and deep, "Away, you rollin' waters! I've gone away, across the wide Missouri!"

The longing was too poignant. The chantey was not repeated. The men sang instead, "Oh, Looie Was the King of France!" Then the chantey-master went on to "Rio Grande." He leaned against the locust wood of the capstan, his sun-faded hair stirred by the breeze, his foot tapping the deck for rhythm:

Now you Bowery ladies, list and you'll know,
Way, you Rio!
We're bound to the south'ard, so let her go!
For we're bound for the Rio Grande!
Oh, hey, you Rio! Way, you Rio!
Sing fare you well, saucy young maids,
For we're bound for the Rio Grande!

PORTS OF CALL

The words didn't make much sense, the chantey-master knew. The ship was bound for New Orleans, and nowhere near the Rio Grande. But it was a right nice tune. The men liked it, and that was enough.

Sailors were strictly treated in New Orleans during the 1820s and 1830s as more ships entered the port. A cannon was fired at eight o'clock on winter nights and nine o'clock in summer to warn all sailors, soldiers and Negroes to get off the streets. They needed a special pass signed by their masters or superiors, and if they failed to have it they were taken to the *calabozo.*

Large oil lanterns in wrought iron frames were hung on ropes across the streets in the Vieux Carré, or on hooks set in the walls of houses. No streets were marked; they usually took the names of the big family houses on the corners. A stranger who had stayed in a tavern until closing time could easily be confused, and the police waited in unlighted alleys to step forth and arrest the late and unwary.

Citizens who used the streets at night generally had a slave with a lantern to find the way for them. Water moccasins slid out of sewers during the rainy season. Some of the older streets over towards the ramparts became gumbo mud morasses. Carriages broke axles and wheels in them, and wide detours were often necessary.

Most of the houses were of brick, and some of the bigger residences were built of dressed stone. The roofs were of slate, or tile. Long *porte-cocheres* which were really passages led from the street into the house courtyards. These were cobbled, and echoed to any heavy footsteps and the turn of a carriage wheel. The house balconies and galleries were decorated with delicate iron-work made by Spanish blacksmiths. Every window that faced the street had a small balcony with an iron railing.

318

NEW ORLEANS

Crape myrtle, oak, pecan and orange trees grew in the courtyards of the houses owned by the wealthy. Etienne de Boré, who had invested his wife's money in seed cane and made a fortune, kept his town house at Chartres and Conti Streets. It was an old Spanish building with broad doorways, fine ironwork and a roof terrace filled with flowers and shrubs, figs, pomegranates and oleanders.

Street vendors began their calls at dawn. They were Negro women known as *marchandes,* and carried wicker trays on their heads. The musical, slowly repeated calls they gave advertised vegetables, and fruit, and sweets: *"Belles de figues! Bons petits calas!"* They wanted the prospective customers to know the freshness of the merchandise, and that it had just arrived from downriver and the gulf. "Barataria! *Confitures coco! Pralines, pistaches, pacanes!"*

The wealthy families had their own *marchandes.* These women brought meat, seafood, vegetables and the news heard at the market. They put down their baskets and squatted wide-kneed while the family ate breakfast on the balcony. Their traditional costume was a bright head-kerchief, gold hook earrings, a white fichu and a white or flower-designed cotton dress. The *gardienne* who helped the butler with the breakfast dishes was dressed in the same way, but wore shoes and stockings.

The men of the family went to work after they had drunk several small cups of bitter French coffee, lit a cheroot. The Creoles were careful to keep to the south side of Charles Street, in the middle of the city. The Americans kept to the north side. They met at the Bourse during the day, or in each other's offices, and some were partners in the same firms. Both factions met, too, at the famous old restaurant called Le Veau Qui Tete. They had lunch there and went later to start the day's drinking at the St. Louis Hotel bar or the new St. Charles.

An 1803 view of New Orleans, looking north. Many houses are still wooden-built. Foot paths go across open land to the levee. Cows and horses graze on the open pasture. A single carriage uses the levee road. But the city gathers thickly beyond.

COURTESY CHICAGO HISTORICAL SOCIETY

PORTS OF CALL

The Haitian sugar planters who had been forced to leave Hispaniola in the 1791 slave revolt still gathered in the Café des Emigrés. It was on Chartres Street, between Dumaine and St. Phillip Streets, and the proprietor kept *le petit gouave,* their favorite liquor, in stock for them. That was compounded from rum and coffee as a base, with various herbs added.

When the Haitians had passed an afternoon in the café, they were able to forget that they would never get back their property or their fortunes. But they had been very generously received here in the United States; all told, a quarter of a million dollars had been raised for their support. Such aid, in a slave-owning country, might somehow be renewed.

Most of the Haitians, a number of the young Creoles from wealthy families and quite a few Americans went often to the *salles d'escrime.* These were maintained by a group of fencing masters in Exchange Alley, which ran from Canal Street to Conti Street. Duelling had been declared illegal in Great Britain and a large part of the United States. But it was still permitted in Louisiana, and considered to be essential as a means of defense for a man of honor.

That word—"honor"—held mystical meaning for the Louisianans who cherished the belief that their personal bravery should be given the same high regard as their position as gentlemen. They brandished it at each other during Quadroon Balls, or at the theater, or at the card table. They fought and died for it, and in Exchange Alley the duelling masters were well paid for instruction.

The duelling masters were a mixed lot. Some were former officers with records of service in European armies. Others were from the slums of French, Italian and Spanish cities, had learned to fight first with a stiletto or the jaggedly broken neck of a wine bottle. A few were Creoles who claimed connection with famous families. One, Bastile Croquere, was a mulatto, and supposed to be the most handsome man in New Orleans. He was a great dandy, wore a green broadcloth suit, a very wide black stock, cameo rings, a breast pin and a cameo bracelet. His home was an old house at the corner of Exchange Alley and Conti Street.

The usual instruction was in the sword, saber, epée and pistol. Fights were held on the levee, beyond the ramparts. But the formal duels, for complete satisfaction of honor, were always fought beneath the famous oaks on the Alland plantation. Here a duelling master named Marcel Dauphin killed another named Nora with a shotgun blast, and gained a lasting reputation. He became a specialist in the fine points of the *Code d'Honneur,* was frequently consulted by men who thought their honor had been put in doubt.

The Lafitte brothers, Jean and Pierre, were often in Exchange Place during the first years after the War of 1812. But, despite the fact that they were French-born and were considered to be men of high spirit, they never joined in the duelling practice. Their personal courage had been signally proven in the Battle of New Orleans, and they were known to be fierce fighters when aroused to anger. It was also known that they were smugglers, and very probably pirates. So plenty of opportunity was offered them to make practical use of weapons.

They did not need instruction. Their visits to the alley were only social. They came to see their friends.

Then, though, the brothers disappeared from New Orleans. It was claimed that they were back at their old trade of piracy, and that Jean Lafitte had gone to Galveston Island in the gulf to take command of a large outlaw force. Stories about Lafitte's raids on gulf shipping could no longer be disregarded.

PORTS OF CALL

Even the pair of American lawyers who had previously defended the Lafittes and won acquittal for them on several piracy charges were reluctant now to discuss their clients. They were both men of high intelligence and legal skill, and it was coffeehouse gossip that the Lafittes paid them exorbitantly for their services.

One of them was Edward Livingston, who had made a distinguished career as a lawyer and public official in the North before coming to Louisiana. He was born in 1764 at Livingston Manor, his family's estate on the Hudson River beyond New York City. His older brother was Robert Livingston, who served as American Minister at Paris during the negotiation of the Louisiana Purchase, and was Fulton's partner in the invention and then commercial use of the first successfully operated steamboat.

Edward Livingston was graduated from Princeton, studied law and began practice in New York City. He was elected to Congress in 1795, and afterward was appointed United States Attorney by President Jefferson. Then he was elected mayor of New York. But, through the dishonesty of a clerk, he found that he was in default for a large sum of money to the federal government. He resigned his office as mayor, sold all of his property and belongings to make good the shortage and in 1803 went to Louisiana to start a new career.

He soon became the most prominent American lawyer in New Orleans. The Code of Procedure for the Territory of Orleans was framed by him, and was incorporated into state law. He was the leading figure in a number of famous court cases, and was accepted socially by the Creoles and very popular among them. His connection with the Lafitte brothers was unbroken, and he employed great skill to maintain their innocence.

324 The attorney who worked with Livingston to defend the brothers was a young Virginian named John Randolph Grymes. He was almost as respected as the former New Yorker, and had served as District Attorney in New Orleans. He was just twenty-four and had been admitted to the bar in Virginia the year before, in 1808, when he came to New Orleans. His efforts to keep the Lafittes free from lengthy terms of imprisonment were considerable and untiring.

But a crew of pirates that took orders from Jean Lafitte was caught in early December, 1819, by the United States cutter *Alabama.* The pirates had gone to New Orleans to pick up a new schooner for Lafitte. They were led by two of his lieutenants, Robert Johnston and Jean Desfarges. When *Alabama* came over the horizon at the mouth of the Mississippi, the Lafitte crew was busy looting a ship they had just overhauled and seized.

Alabama challenged, and the pirates were told to surrender. Johnston and Desfarges chose to fight. They fired volleys at the cutter which wounded some of her crew and ripped her rigging. Then the *Alabama* people boarded the schooner and captured her after a cutlass scrimmage. The entire crew, wearing wrist-and-leg irons, was brought to New Orleans and held for trial.

Jean Lafitte came over from his headquarters at Campeachy on Galveston Island. He conferred with Livingston and Grymes and they planned a series of defense measures for the accused. Money was spent by Lafitte, and old memories recalled. A number of half-regenerate pirates who had served under him in the Battle of New Orleans and before that, during his earlier period as a freebooter, were summoned. They entered the city and spoke out in favor of the prisoners.

They said that as men from the Barataria district, whose bravery in battle had been publicly praised by Andrew Jackson, they had every right to believe that the accused should not be   *325* convicted. The federal government was described as a pack of lousy northerners, and the crew of *Alabama* severely criticized for gross discrimination against local people. Innocent fishermen, out to make a few dollars by taking a bit of cargo from an abandoned vessel, had been falsely arrested.

Passionate speeches were delivered along with free rum in the Place d'Armes, and in Congo Square, outside the ramparts, where steamboat roustabouts, flatboatmen, unemployed sailors and Negro slaves gathered. A mob was organized. The *calabozo,* a rather frail old building, was surrounded. Then a threat was made to tear it down.

The governor ordered militia companies mustered. The National Lancers were called out, and Hind's Dragoons, and Beale's Rifles, and the Bataillon d'Orleans. The militiamen took fixed posts around the *calabozo* for a couple of weeks. The mob was awed by the helmets with the horsetail plumes and the tall shakos, but more by the show of weapons.

Their leaders concentrated on attempts to burn the city. The state armory and several buildings near the jail were set afire and destroyed. But the pirates were tried in United States District Court, and convicted. The sentence was death by hanging.

Nothing more could be done to save them. Both Livingston and Grymes recognized that the case was hopeless. Jean Lafitte went to Washington, though, carrying letters and recommendations for clemency from influential merchants and politicians. He saw President Monroe, and the men were reprieved for sixty days, and one of them was freed.

Then Johnston and Desfarges were taken on May 25, 1820, from the *calabozo* to a United States Navy ship berthed at the foot of St. Ann Street. They were marched aboard, and exactly at noon were hanged from the main yardarm.

326

NEW ORLEANS

Jean Lafitte left the city right after the execution. He and his brother never returned. They had lost the final remnants of their power. New Orleans had become too wealthy to have dealings with them. It was the second largest port of call in the country, and intensely proud of the fact.

Illustration Credits

GRATEFUL ACKNOWLEDGMENT is made for pictures used from the following sources:

THE CHARLESTON LIBRARY SOCIETY, p. 248

THE CHASE MANHATTAN BANK MUSEUM, N.Y., pp. 88, 158, 190

CHICAGO MUSEUM OF SCIENCE AND INDUSTRY, Dunbar Collection, pp. 5, 63, 85

CITY ART MUSEUM OF ST. LOUIS, pp. 98–99

CLEMENTS LIBRARY, University of Michigan, Ann Arbor, Michigan, p. 300

EWING GALLOWAY, p. 118

LIBRARY OF CONGRESS, pp. 53, 268

THE MARINERS MUSEUM, Newport News, Va., pp. 25, 48 (Photograph from Ralamb, *Skeps*)

COLLECTIONS OF THE MARYLAND HISTORICAL SOCIETY, p. 223

THE METROPOLITAN MUSEUM OF ART, pp. 120 (Purchase, 1940, Joseph Pulitzer Bequest); 126 (Bequest of Benjamin Altman, 1913); 163 (Collection of H. Dunscombe Colt); 288 (Gift of Edgar William and Bernice Chrysler Garbich, 1963)

MUSEUM OF THE CITY OF NEW YORK, p. 327

THE NEW-YORK HISTORICAL SOCIETY, New York City, Bella C. Landauer Collection, p. 88

THE NEW YORK PUBLIC LIBRARY, p. 36, Wheeler, G. A., *A History of Castine*, 1923; 77, Duhamel du Monceau, *Traité générale des pesches*, 1769–77; 138–39, Manuscript Division, Emmett Collection; 262, Map Division; 267, Picture Collection; 96 (Facsimile); 198–99, Prints Division; 169, 176, Prints Division, Eno Collection; 69, 93, 102, 142, 161, 172, 175, 188, 203, 212, 215, 230, 236–37, 251 (Detail), 278, 305, Prints Division, Phelps Stokes Collection. P. 6, De Bry,

ILLUSTRATION CREDITS

America; 7 (Detail), Le Moyne, J., *Narrative,* 1591; 18, Bacqueville, *Histoire de l'Amerique,* 1722; 55, Anburey, *Travels through the Interior,* 1789; 75, Smith, *Generall Historie,* 1624; 148, Irving, W., *Knickerbocker History of New York,* 1804; 240, 241, 272, 293, 306, Breckell, *Natural History of North Carolina,* 1737; 282, 292, 293, 294, 296, Tatham, *An Historical and Practical Essay,* etc., 1800 (Rare Books Division)

COURTESY OF THE PEABODY MUSEUM OF SALEM, pp. 106, 112, 123

PRATT'S PHOTO SERVICE, Castine, Maine, p. 33

THE PRESERVATION SOCIETY OF NEWPORT COUNTY, Newport, R.I., p. 130

RHODE ISLAND DEVELOPMENT COUNCIL, p. 131

Reproduced with the permission of CHARLES SCRIBNER'S SONS from *Atlas of American History,* plate 29, edited by James Truslow Adams. Copyright 1943 Charles Scribner's Sons: p. 14

THE SMITHSONIAN INSTITUTION, p. 234

STRAWBERRY BANKE, INC., p. 40

Selected Bibliography

ADAMS, JAMES TRUSLOW. *THE EPIC OF AMERICA,* Boston: Little, Brown & Co., 1931.

ANDREWS, CHARLES M. *THE FATHERS OF NEW ENGLAND,* New Haven: Yale University Press, 1919.

———. *COLONIAL FOLKWAYS,* New Haven: Yale University Press, 1919.

ANDREWS, MATTHEW PAGE. *VIRGINIA, THE OLD DOMINION,* New York City: Doubleday, Doran & Co., 1937.

BOWES, FREDERICK P. *THE CULTURE OF EARLY CHARLESTON,* Chapel Hill: University of North Carolina Press, 1942.

COFFIN, ROBERT P. TRISTRAM. *KENNEBEC—CRADLE OF AMERICANS,* New York: Farrar & Rinehart, 1937.

COULTER, E. MERTON. *GEORGIA: A SHORT HISTORY,* Chapel Hill: University of North Carolina Press, 1947.

CUNEO, JOHN R. *ROBERT ROGERS OF THE RANGERS,* New York: Oxford University Press, 1959.

HANDLIN, OSCAR; SCHLESINGER, ARTHUR MEIER; MORISON, SAMUEL ELIOT; MERK, FREDERICK; SCHLESINGER, A. M., JR., editors. *HARVARD GUIDE TO AMERICAN HISTORY,* Cambridge: The Belknap Press of Harvard University Press, 1963.

HOWE, HENRY F. *PROLOGUE TO NEW ENGLAND,* New York: Farrar & Rinehart, 1943.

INNIS, HAROLD A. *THE COD FISHERIES,* New Haven: Yale University Press, 1940.

MAYO, LAWRENCE SHAW. *JOHN ENDECOTT,* Cambridge: Harvard University Press, 1936.

MOLLOY, ROBERT. *CHARLESTON: A GRACIOUS HERITAGE,* New York: D. Appleton-Century Co., 1947.

MORISON, SAMUEL ELIOT. *THE OXFORD HISTORY OF THE AMERICAN PEOPLE,* New York: Oxford University Press, 1965.

SELECTED BIBLIOGRAPHY

MORRIS, RICHARD B., editor. *ENCYCLOPEDIA OF AMERICAN HISTORY,* New York: Harper & Bros., 1961.

PEABODY, ROBERT E. *MERCHANT VENTURERS OF OLD SALEM,* Boston: Houghton, Mifflin Co., 1912.

PHILLIPS, JAMES DUNCAN. *SALEM AND THE INDIES,* Boston: Houghton Mifflin Co., 1947.

———. *SALEM IN THE SEVENTEENTH CENTURY,* Boston: Houghton Mifflin Co., 1933.

PHILLIPS, PAUL CHRISLER. *THE FUR TRADE,* 2 vols., Norman: University of Oklahoma Press, 1961.

ROWE, WILLIAM HUTCHINSON. *THE MARITIME HISTORY OF MAINE,* New York: W. W. Norton & Co., Inc., 1948.

SCHARF, THOMAS J. *BALTIMORE CITY AND COUNTRY,* 2 vols., Philadelphia: Louis H. Everts, 1881.

SEMMES, RAPHAEL. *CAPTAINS AND MARINERS OF EARLY MARYLAND,* Baltimore: Johns Hopkins Press, 1937.

TROUP, FRANCIS ROSE. *JOHN WHITE, THE FOUNDER OF MASSACHUSETTS,* New York: G. P. Putnam's Sons, 1930.

WILKINSON, GEORGE F. *SAINTS AND STRANGERS,* New York: Reynal & Hitchcock, 1945.

WRONG, GEORGE M. *THE CONQUEST OF NEW FRANCE,* New Haven: Yale University Press, 1918.

Note: This list does not include all of the excellent The Rivers of America *series, published by Farrar & Rinehart, New York.*

Index

333

INDEX

INDEX

INDEX

INDEX

INDEX

INDEX

INDEX

INDEX

INDEX

INDEX

INDEX

973

Carse, Robert, 19
    Ports of call
    ML '67 18906